Postfeminist Whiteness

Dedicated to the memory of my nana Shirley Marston
1925–2015

I will always remember our UKTV, gin and chips evenings in Capalaba

Postfeminist Whiteness

Problematising Melancholic Burden in Contemporary Hollywood

Kendra Marston

EDINBURGH
University Press

Edinburgh University Press is one of the leading university presses in the UK. We publish academic books and journals in our selected subject areas across the humanities and social sciences, combining cutting-edge scholarship with high editorial and production values to produce academic works of lasting importance. For more information visit our website: edinburghuniversitypress.com

Edinburgh University Press Ltd
The Tun – Holyrood Road
12 (2f) Jackson's Entry
Edinburgh EH8 8PJ

First published in hardback by Edinburgh University Press 2018

Typeset in 11/13 Monotype Ehrhardt by
Servis Filmsetting Ltd, Stockport, Cheshire

A CIP record for this book is available from the British Library

ISBN 978 1 4744 3029 6 (hardback)
ISBN 978 1 4744 3030 2 (paperback)
ISBN 978 1 4744 3031 9 (webready PDF)
ISBN 978 1 4744 3032 6 (epub)

Contents

Figures

Acknowledgements

First, I wish to acknowledge my gratitude to the School of Communication and Arts at the University of Queensland for their faith in this project and financial support in the form of an Australian Postgraduate Award (funded by the Australian Federal Government). I must also extend my deepest gratitude to my PhD advisors Associate Professor Jane Stadler and Associate Professor Fiona Nicoll for their unwavering encouragement and always thorough and thought-provoking feedback on this book. Their broad knowledge base, passion for their subjects, and always considered and caring approach to supervision were assets on my research journey. A big thank you is also due to Professor Diane Negra and Professor Yvonne Tasker for taking the time out of their undoubtedly busy schedules to read this work and provide invaluable insights on the project. Gillian Leslie, Richard Strachan and Rebecca Mackenzie at Edinburgh University Press ensured that the book publication process ran smoothly and were always prompt and friendly in their communications.

Relocating to Brisbane from my hometown in Wellington, New Zealand, to research this project was a bit of a daunting endeavour. I therefore wish to acknowledge those friends and colleagues who welcomed me to the city and helped make my time there an enjoyable experience. Special thanks must go to Jessica Rothwell, Jessica Hughes, Prateek, Lauren Clayton, David Baker, Wilson Koh and Emily Zong for accompanying me on various outings and helping me to explore Brisbane's highlights. Lastly, I want to thank my family – Mum, Dad, Juliet, Claude, and Gus for their support, encouragement and willingness to let me live at home in times of post-PhD financial hardship.

Chapter 1 of this book was first published as the article 'The world is her oyster: negotiating contemporary white womanhood in Hollywood's tourist spaces' by Kendra Marston from *Cinema Journal, Volume 55, No. 4, Fall 2016*, pp. 3–27 (Copyright © 2016 by the University of Texas Press). Part of Chapter 5 was previously published in 2015 as 'The tragic ballerina's shadow self: troubling the political economy of melancholy in *Black Swan*' in *Quarterly Review of Film and Video* 32:8, 695–711. Portions of Chapter 2 first appeared in the article 'English ladies to liberators? How *Pirates of the Caribbean* and *Alice in Wonderland* mobilise aristocratic white femininity', published in *Jump Cut* 54 (2012) <https://www.ejumpcut.org/archive/jc54.2012/MarstonWhWomenRace/index.html> I am grateful to be granted the right to reproduce this material here.

Introduction

In 2011, the second film in Lars von Trier's 'depression trilogy', *Melancholia*, was released to critical acclaim at the Cannes Film Festival in France. Exhibiting a romantic aesthetic notably distinct from the Danish director's previous foray into the world of existential trauma and isolation – the dark and bleakly violent *Antichrist* (2009) – *Melancholia* paints a sublimely poetic image of the earth's destruction. Set to the operatic strains of Richard Wagner's *Tristan und Isolde*, the film's prelude evokes the world's demise through a series of tableaux capturing irregularities in the normative human experience of space–time as well as the destruction of gravity's laws. Majestic views of the cosmos illustrating the planet Melancholia's impending encroachment upon the earth's atmosphere are interspersed with images documenting the effects of this celestial event on earthly life. A dark horse collapses in a moonlit field, birds die and drift downward from the sky, and a lone bridal figure struggles to move through the atmospheric density as gnarled tree roots rise from the soil and impede her journey forward. This bride, the film's melancholic protagonist Justine (Kirsten Dunst), literally experiences the weight of the world against her and yet her calm acquiescence to the earth's annihilation is subsequently illuminated by the film as a resultant feature of her existential crisis. Justine's belief that the world is 'evil' and that 'no one will miss it' operates as a counterpoint to that of her sister Claire (Charlotte Gainsbourg), who exhibits increasing levels of anxiety and distress at the imminent cessation of her earthly existence.

Justine's prophetic awareness as to Melancholia's ultimate path also contrasts with her brother-in-law John's steadfast investment in humanity's ability to chart nature's course. John (Kiefer Sutherland), unable to cope with the false conclusions of a scientific inquiry which has determined that Melancholia will bypass Earth as it has done Venus and Mercury, chooses to commit suicide in the stables rather than confront the ultimate powerlessness

Figure I.1 Kirsten Dunst as Ophelia in *Melancholia*.

of humanity. Human powerlessness is encapsulated in the promotional poster for the film, in which Justine is imagined in a pose that evokes painter John Everett Millais' depiction of William Shakespeare's tragic heroine Ophelia. Wearing her bridal gown and clutching a bouquet of flowers, Justine appears as a figure caught between life and death, her body half-submerged amongst the foliage of a lily pond as her veil forms a ghostly halo trailing in the watery depths.

The loss of world that the audience witnesses in this film is, however, the loss of a particular *type* of world built upon wealth, privilege and social prestige. Justine's melancholia becomes most evident throughout the proceedings of her lavish wedding, during which she expresses irritation at her mother's hostility towards the occasion and with her boss's repeated insistence that she come up with a tagline for his company's new advertising campaign. Justine has promised Claire that she will endeavour to be happy throughout the event, yet she appears to hold little regard for wedding ritual as she arrives two hours late to the reception and has to be coaxed from her room prior to the cake-cutting ceremony. Justine's depression eventually deepens to the point where she can no longer sustain the social performances required of her, culminating in her erratic decision to flee the reception in a golf cart, have outdoor sex with a young male guest and urinate on the lawn. Justine's rejection of the codes of bourgeois whiteness is reflected through what Marta Figlerowicz refers to as the film's 'tragi-comic' treatment of the interactions amongst the wedding guests, noting that 'the more operatically characters express frustration at Justine's inappropriateness, the more wanton a figure each of the bride's detractors cuts against their always grander setting' (2012: 23). Referring to the curious actions of Justine's French wedding planner (Udo Kier), who emphatically declares his refusal to look at the woman who ruined his wedding and covers his face upon passing her, Figlerowicz hypothesises that the insignificance of the party's quarrels correlates to 'the insignificance of the cultural models it tries to follow' (23). Robert Sinnerbrink, too, points to the emptiness of the wedding guests' pursuits in noting that the image of splayed models that Justine is obliged to create a tagline for bears a striking resemblance to Renaissance artist Pieter Bruegel's 1567 work 'The Land of Cockaigne', 'an allegory of moral vacuity in a land of plenty' (2014: 115). Sinnerbrink argues that while Justine has a 'refined aesthetic sensibility', she is unable to cope with the destructive world of commerce that her boss Jack (Stellan Skarsgård) personifies, and reads the strained interactions between the pair as a sign that 'commerce really owns and controls art' (117).

A treatise on the moral decay of the Western world is thus narrated through a melancholic white female's depressive episode – her disillusionment with marriage, consumer capitalism and familial ties permeates the mood of a film hailed by some film reviewers as an artistic masterpiece of contemporary cinema.[1] Thomas Elsaesser notes that von Trier, like David Lynch and Michelangelo Antonioni, is a director who utilises the cultural association between femininity and heightened empathy in order to stage 'acts of protest and refusal' in his heroines. The protagonist's experience of depression or melancholia may indicate her refusal to abandon a lost object or the desire to return to an imaginary sense of plenitude, but also a reluctance to adhere to social norms such as marriage, with Elsaesser stating that such films can be psychoanalytically or politically interpreted (2015). *Melancholia* may impress critics for its experimental formalism that is able to capture Justine's experience of the interminability of time, or for its intertextual artistic literacy, or for the startling lead performance of Hollywood actress Kirsten Dunst. But the film is also, I argue, part of a broader cultural moment in popular cinematic representation where young women of melancholic disposition are utilised as vehicles through which to explore the excesses of late capitalism and the failures of neoliberal postfeminism. These failures are framed in several films through narratives of 'white burden', in which white women are situated as victims of governmental forms and associated corporate structures that have promised members of socially empowered groups happiness and fulfilment yet have inevitably failed to deliver. Whiteness may be critiqued in relation to patriarchal power structures, but what is markedly less common in these films is a critique of how such power structures disadvantage those who are neither white or of a privileged socio-economic class.

In the films to be analysed within this book, which encompass such diverse fare as travel romance *Eat Pray Love* (Ryan Murphy, 2010), fantasy film *Alice in Wonderland* (Tim Burton, 2010) and the psychological thriller *Black Swan* (Darren Aronofsky, 2010), women who are both white and of a privileged class status are very much centralised within their fictional onscreen worlds. The continued privileging of white characters and performers within Hollywood cinema is, of course, nothing new and was the subject of virulent media debate in relation to the lack of diversity amongst the nominees at the eighty-eighth Academy Awards.[2] Yet in utilising melancholia as a tool through which to distance female protagonists from white patriarchal power structures, these films are able to engage in commentaries that position the heroines' race privilege and affluence as disabling sicknesses of the contemporary political and cultural moment. A primary concern of these texts centres upon the female protagonist's feelings of disempowerment and her ultimate search for alternative forms of agency, and so the types of commentary that these films engage in could be construed as feminist and certainly as at least critical of postfeminist and neoliberal discourses. Whiteness is framed as a 'burden', yet it is primarily a burden that forms a barrier to female emancipation as opposed to a hierarchical, hegemonic system that works on a political, economic and social level to hierarchise and oppress. To be free of this burden and associative melancholia, the heroine desires to detach herself from the social obligation to invest in popular postfeminist and neoliberal philosophies, which Yvonne Tasker and Diane Negra state are 'white and middle-class by default' in their elision of socio-economic inequalities that may impact on a woman's freedom to choose (2007: 2). The necessity of relinquishing this attachment may come with the heroine's corresponding endeavour to renegotiate her relationship to her own privileged race and class identity, with many of these films ultimately participating in forms of what Sarah Projansky and Kent A. Ono term 'strategic whiteness' (1999: 153).

Whiteness, the authors argue, has had to undergo various modifications in response to social movements and social change throughout US history to renegotiate its centrality, power and authority (152). Such modifications can occur in these texts through narratives in which the rediscovery of feminism occurs because of the adjustment to the heroine's raced and classed ideological beliefs in ways that are certainly not radical, yet speak to social dissatisfaction with facets of late capitalism and neoliberal rhetoric. Yet these modifications also occur in texts where the heroine finds that she is *unable* to renegotiate her relationship with white privilege, such as in *Black Swan* or the films of Sofia Coppola, and thus becomes a tragic victim of the contemporary political moment and of her social circumstances. These texts thus inscribe the declining mental health or even deaths of white women with artistic weight and cultural gravitas.

While the heroine's experience of melancholia differs amongst the films to be analysed throughout this book, her characterisation and the rationale behind her precarious mental state bears marked similarities across these disparate generic forms. The white woman within these texts is typically idealised and the object of the crowd's fascination within the film. She lives her life under an intensified social gaze, yet feels unfulfilled within her social milieu.

Justine's despondency despite her wealth and successful advertising career in *Melancholia* is thus comparable to Elizabeth Gilbert's unhappiness despite her elevated position in elite literary circles and affluent New York lifestyle in *Eat Pray Love* (2006), or Lux Lisbon's existential despair regardless of the admiration she receives at school and within her suburban community in Sofia Coppola's *The Virgin Suicides* (1999). In keeping with Angela McRobbie's formulation that postfeminist philosophy requires adherence to stringent standards of heteronormative femininity in exchange for cultural visibility and upward mobility (2009: 57), the heroines abide by normative standards of white, feminine beauty and idealised cultural notions of romantic love, yet find themselves suffocated by these societal obligations. It is not insignificant that Justine's Ophelia appears as a drowning bride, or that her melancholia reaches its apotheosis during her wedding reception. For Elizabeth Swann (Keira Knightley) and Alice Kingsleigh (Mia Wasikowska), the female protagonists in fantasy films *Pirates of the Caribbean: Curse of the Black Pearl* (Gore Verbinski, 2003) and *Alice in Wonderland* respectively, this moment comes during their engagement ceremonies. For Elizabeth Gilbert and Francis Mayes (Diane Lane) in *Under the Tuscan Sun* (Audrey Wells, 2003), the epiphany occurs at book launches held to celebrate their achievements, where they also come to realise they are stuck in loveless marriages. Furthermore, these protagonists are burdened by a materialistic culture that demands women spend excessively to maintain an appealing, fashionable appearance while also creating commercialised, disposable objects of the women themselves. As Tasker and Negra observe, 'the construction of women as both subjects and consumers or perhaps as subjects only to the extent that we are willing and able to consume is one of the contradictions at the core of postfeminist culture' (2007: 8). The heroines in the tourist romances experience a sense of newfound freedom in travel zones where conspicuous consumption and bodily discipline do not appear to be a priority for the local inhabitants. Marie Antoinette in Sofia Coppola's 2006 reimagining of the historical figure spends excessively in reaction to her realisation that she is merely a pawn in the political agenda of others, and in fact holds no real power herself – an aspect of her rule that ultimately leads to her execution in the French Revolution.

The majority of these filmic heroines are notably of artistic or creative temperament, in keeping with melancholia's longstanding historical association with those exhibiting a 'creative energy' (Radden 2000: 4). If these protagonists are not involved in the artistic industries in some way, then they are characterised as dreamers or fantasists longing to escape from their mundane bourgeois existence. Liz and Francis in the travel romances are creative writers, Nina in *Black Swan* is a dancer, Elizabeth and Alice in the fantasy films are precocious dreamers, while Charlotte in *Lost in Translation* (Sofia Coppola, 2003) is a philosopher and would-be photographer and the teenage girls in *The Virgin Suicides* like to write poetry. Melancholic experiences within these films are not necessarily comparable to Justine's severe state of depression and catatonia, and in fact can encapsulate more mild forms of malaise and dissatisfaction with the status quo, to be overcome throughout the course of the narrative. This variant of melancholic white femininity is more likely to be observed in films belonging to genres that contain a utopian drive, such as the tourist romances and fantasy films analysed in Chapters 1 and 2. In these films, melancholia contains an affective potentiality that allows the heroine to rediscover lost or repressed elements of the self and simultaneously reconstruct her relationship to social systems in a manner that will ultimately advantage her. In *Affective Mapping: Melancholia and the Politics of Modernism*, Jonathan Flatley observes that there is a fundamental difference between a 'depressing, depoliticised melancholia' and a 'non-depressing, politicising melancholia' (2008: 8), a division that finds its parallel here in the disjuncture between the melancholic experience of heroines in popular, blockbuster fare and those in films aiming toward prestige or auteur status.

In the more popular texts, peripheral characters to the melancholic white woman exist as teachers aiding her on her journey toward self-discovery. Such peripheral characters importantly do not inhabit the same socio-economic position as the protagonist, and her relationship with them ultimately serves the heroine's therapeutic interests as well as working to modify both her relationship to neoliberal postfeminism and the privileged race and class position that successful investment in such discourses typically requires. In the latter group of films, the question as to whether such co-dependent relationships can be mutually beneficial is often raised only to be discarded, with the individual ultimately encountering a sense of powerlessness as she attempts to renegotiate her relationship to systems that ultimately prove deterministic in sealing her tragic fate. If we take Woody Allen's 2013 film *Blue Jasmine* as an example, destitute New York socialite Jasmine French (Cate Blanchett) is given the opportunity to relinquish her attachments to materialism and hierarchical class stratification through relocating to her sister's San Francisco working-class milieu, yet she ultimately fails to seize the chance to alter her values and priorities. However, while Jasmine or indeed Justine's experience of melancholia may appear fundamentally disempowering at the level of diegetic narrative, this is less true when we consider the extra-textual circulation of these films as part of the Hollywood industrial machine. The packaging and selling of tragic white femininity and a melancholic cinematic 'mood' is integral to the continued success of auteur Sofia Coppola's brand, while Kirsten Dunst's critically acclaimed performance as Justine, which won her the Cannes Film Festival award for Best Actress, has helped reinvigorate her career and market her as an actress equipped for 'serious' dramatic roles. Cate Blanchett and Natalie Portman both won Academy Awards for their performances in *Blue*

Jasmine and *Black Swan* respectively, with Portman's self-reflexive turn as Nina aiding in shedding some of the more limiting aspects of her child star persona. These texts then, regardless of whether the heroine's melancholic experience is empowering at the level of narrative, are *always* politicised. This is not only because these films engage in a commentary on neoliberal postfeminist philosophies that are inevitably political, but because melancholia, which I will argue is a mood associated with social privilege, can be strategically deployed as a means of enhancing celebrity capital.

POSTFEMINISM: THEORETICAL EXCLUSIONS AND CULTURAL EVOLUTIONS

This book aims to draw attention to a body of films that comprise both an evolution and a fracturing within postfeminist popular culture in the Anglo-American context, and to ascertain how melancholic whiteness works to negotiate ambivalence over the term 'feminism' as well as the centrality of privilege to postfeminist discourse. The relationship these filmic heroines harbour towards neoliberal postfeminism can be described as a kind of 'cruel optimism', which Lauren Berlant defines as the discovery that 'something you desire is actually an obstacle to your flourishing' (2011: 1). The centre of this desire, Berlant explains, is 'that moral-intimate-economic thing called the good life', the attachment to which promises an enabling transformation of the self, and yet also works to inhibit the very same beneficial transformations for which people risk striving (2). This interrelationship can become sustaining and yet cruel in the sense that such optimism may also comprise less-than-positive feelings of anxiety or dread. Berlant notes that people remain invested in 'conventional good life fantasies' consisting of 'enduring reciprocity in couples, families, political institutions, markets and at work' despite evidence of their fragility, instability and significant personal costs (2). Fantasies that Berlant perceives as being in a process of decay include political equality, durable intimacy and upward mobility (3) – fantasies that postfeminist discourse, in its interrelationship with neoliberal governmentality, typically seeks to promote. While investments in postfeminism may always have been beset by accompanying anxiety and indeed melancholia as one gives up various attachments in striving to become the ideal neoliberal female subject, such investments have undergone a more intense fracturing over the last decade. This has occurred not only due to a resurgence in interest in feminist politics (evident within the celebrity sphere) or conflicts in US race relations, but also because of the shifting international image of the US due to unpopular interventions in the Middle East and the role of Wall Street financial institutions in the global economic downturn. Such events inevitably impact on the perceived viability and security of the American dream and the power of the individual to attain it. In *Blue Jasmine* after all, it is Jasmine's husband's fraudulent investment scheme, reminiscent of similarly unscrupulous dealings leading to the financial crisis of 2007–8, that forces the heroine to renegotiate her optimistic relationship to neoliberal postfeminism, and leads to a misplaced melancholia for an elite lifestyle that is no longer viable. The Hollywood celebrity – who has supposedly achieved wealth and success based on individual talent and specialness, and who therefore is the ultimate embodiment of the American dream – becomes a mediated vehicle through which such cultural anxieties are negotiated. These anxieties are not only narrated through the celebrity's film roles, but also through mediated constructions of the star's private life and perceptions of her choices in relation to labour and leisure.

Any study of postfeminism must acknowledge the methodological debates that have taken place over a term that has had a wide and varied application. Academic commentators have sought to utilise 'postfeminism' as both a theoretical position signifying an epistemological break with dominant patterns of second-wave feminist thought and as an object of study in media analysis. Critics aiming to provide an overview of how the term has been theorised and debated have noted its association with Girl Power popular philosophy, the conservative backlash thesis first offered by Susan Faludi in 1991, third-wave feminist thought that seeks to distance itself from 'apolitical' populist postfeminism and feminist theory influenced by poststructuralism.[3] My study is best situated in the tradition of academic work that aims to describe postfeminism as a cultural philosophy and object of enquiry identifiable through a range of popular consumable media forms including film, television, advertising and the novel. Initially most often analysed in relation to Anglo American 'chick culture', including the romantic comedy, chick-lit novel and female-centred television drama, the term postfeminism has been used to describe a dominant 'cultural sensibility' (Gill 2007), which champions conspicuous consumption, corporeal discipline and self-management, heteronormative romance and the illusion of 'free choice'. Arguing for a more nuanced account of the relationship between feminism and postfeminism than Faludi's backlash thesis allows, McRobbie hypothesises that postfeminist culture 'draws on and invokes feminism as that which can be taken into account, to suggest that equality is achieved, in order to install a whole repertoire of new meanings which emphasise that it is no longer needed' (2009: 12). She utilises quintessential postfeminist texts such as *Sex and the City* (HBO: 1998–2004), *Ally McBeal* (Fox: 1997–2002) and especially *Bridget Jones's Diary* (Sharon Maguire, 2001) to illustrate what she calls this 'new gender regime' (21). Self-discipline, Rosalind Gill elaborates, is an important hallmark of the postfeminist sensibility with 'femininity defined as a bodily property rather than a social, structural or psychological one' (2007: 149). This shift posits the female body as a primary source of power and yet as always unruly and in need of constant management, remodelling and consumer spending in order to meet narrowly defined standards of feminine beauty (Gill 2007: 149) – a cultural preoccupation that Gill sees as at work in the proliferation of makeover television and women's magazines dedicated to the scrutiny of celebrity bodies (150). This pervasive aspect of postfeminist culture is critiqued in contemporary Hollywood narratives featuring melancholic white femininity in a number of ways, from Nina's mental breakdown as resulting in part from an obsessive preoccupation with bodily discipline in *Black Swan*, to fantasy films in which heroines can shed restrictive costuming and run, play and fight in magical lands far from home.

Postfeminism, in its emphasis on free choice, competitive individualism and consumer citizenship, exhibits a prominent interrelationship with key features of neoliberal governmentality. Like postfeminism, neoliberalism is a term that has also been broadly utilised to various intents and purposes across academia, with Terry Flew in his article 'Six theories of neoliberalism' warning against an intellectually unsustainable use of the term as 'an all-purpose denunciatory category or where it is simply invoked as the way things are' (2014: 51). Flew, however, points out that certain definitions of neoliberalism are more well-defined than others, in particular that of neoliberalism as a post-Keynesian political ideology that gained ascendency in the US and UK through the governments of Ronald Reagan and Margaret Thatcher respectively, and is associated with the rise of financial capitalism and economic globalisation (56). As David Harvey describes it, neoliberalism is best explained as a theory of political economy which proposes that human wellbeing is best advanced through championing individual entrepreneurial freedoms within a framework characterised by free markets, trade, and private property rights (2005: 11). Individual freedoms are assumed to be guaranteed by the freedom of the market, yet Harvey notes that these freedoms inevitably 'reflect the interests of private property owners, businesses, multinational corporations and financial capital' (16) and as a result have been remarkably effective in restoring or creating 'the power of an economic elite' (28). Neoliberalism, however, is also assumed by many commentators to operate as a form of hegemony that affects citizens at the level of individual subjectivity and daily choice.

Wendy Brown, utilising Michel Foucault's influential theories on governmentality and biopower as articulated in his 1978–9 *Collège de France* lectures, argues that 'neoliberal political rationality' has emerged as a mode of governance that 'produces subjects, forms of citizenship and behaviour, and a new organisation of the social' (2005: 37). Meanwhile, Rosalind Gill and Christina Scharff point out that the neoliberal subject is always gendered, drawing a strong parallel between 'the autonomous, calculating, self-regulating subject of neoliberalism' and the 'active, freely choosing, self-reinventing subject of postfeminism' (2011: 7). Such observations do not suggest that neoliberal techniques of government work in a totalising, unified manner or that there can be no forms of agency or resistance within the confines of such an influential ideology. As previously articulated, several of the Hollywood texts that I will go on to discuss are critical of these power structures, with some even attempting to propose renegotiated (albeit utopian) value systems that will be of benefit to the gendered neoliberal subject. What the observations of scholars such as Brown, Gill and McRobbie do suggest however, is that the pervasiveness and influence of neoliberal postfeminist ideologies at the level of government, corporate organisation and indeed within consumer culture inevitably place constraints upon identity formation and associated notions of choice. While the civil rights and second-wave feminist movements prioritised collective action as a key site of social evolution and political empowerment, neoliberal and postfeminist ideologies promote a competitive individualism.

Neoliberal postfeminism's disavowal of feminist politics and the meaning of female empowerment has not gone unchallenged in recent years, and has frequently been the subject of intense debate within the heavily mediated celebrity sphere. While the Hollywood films analysed within this book were all released before this recent resurgence of interest in feminist politics, they do demonstrate a more latent variety of cultural discontent that may have prefigured the emergence of celebrity feminism. Furthermore, what a brief discussion of the circulation of celebrity feminism demonstrates is not only the means by which a selectively defined feminist politics can be promoted and disseminated through popular culture, but also the need to consider 'how the popular operates as a site of struggle over the meanings of feminism' (Hollows and Moseley 2006: 8). In recent years, stars including Reese Witherspoon, Emma Watson and Jennifer Lawrence have professed an interest in feminism and gender equality, while others such as Lena Dunham and Lorde have a feminist agenda firmly incorporated into their celebrity branding that differs markedly from sexualised girl power formulations. In 2014 for instance, Watson gave a highly publicised address to the United Nations as part of the #HeForShe initiative about the need for men to get involved in the fight for gender equality, while Witherspoon's 2015 Academy Awards #AskHerMore campaign called for red carpet journalists to ask female nominees questions beyond which designer dress they chose to wear for the evening. Following a Sony email leak which revealed that both Jennifer Lawrence and Amy Adams received less money than Bradley Cooper and Jeremy Renner for their roles in *American Hustle* (David O. Russell, 2013), Lawrence wrote a much-applauded essay on Dunham's feminist website *Lenny* entitled 'Why do I make less than my male co-stars?' (2016). Patricia Arquette, meanwhile, utilised the platform afforded by her Academy Award win for Best Supporting Actress in *Boyhood* (Richard Linklater, 2014) to campaign for gender wage equality. These feminist pronouncements, while raising important issues in relation to the overvaluation of female appearance and parity in remuneration, have been greeted with exasperation by some media outlets and with caution by cultural commentators. As Hannah Hamad and Anthea Taylor note, the term 'feminism' was considered so over-utilised in 2014 that *Time* magazine even sought to include it in their annual 'word banishment poll' (2015: 124).

A professed point of concern with any celebrity's endorsement of feminism is the inevitable association between the commercialised celebrity brand and a politics of gender equality. Roxane Gay, in her column for *The Guardian* entitled 'Emma Watson? Jennifer Lawrence? These aren't the feminists you're looking for', expresses her annoyance that feminist messages appear palatable only when sold through a youthful, beautiful and famous celebrity brand ambassador (2014). Anita Brady, meanwhile, notes that the feminism these celebrities promote tends to reinforce their broader signifying systems, pointing out that the 'fierce and independent' Beyoncé joined Sheryl Sandberg's 'Ban Bossy' campaign, while the hypersexualised Miley Cyrus sought to Free the Nipple in protest against the double standards inherent in Instagram's nudity policy (2016: 434). Additionally, as Nathalie Weidhase in her discussion of Annie Lennox's denunciation of Beyoncé as 'feminist lite' contends, celebrity feminist discourses have overwhelmingly been shaped by white women (2015: 130). Beyoncé has indeed recently been a disruptive figure in this regard, combining her feminist politics with calls for racial equality through her 2016 anthem 'Formation' and its accompanying music video, which references both police brutality toward black youth and the destructive aftermath of Hurricane Katrina. While the existence of non-white celebrities is necessary to neoliberalism's advocating of a 'post-racial' society where anyone can succeed regardless of skin colour, commentary by high-profile stars drawing attention to racial injustice and abuse has been more common in recent years. The release of 'Formation' was followed up by a controversial Super Bowl performance, in which Beyoncé's dancers dressed in outfits reminiscent of those worn by the Black Panthers, the black nationalist organisation active in the US from 1966–82 that advocated the militant self-defence of black communities. What these examples demonstrate is not an inherent lack of validity in any individual Hollywood celebrity's claim to feminism, but the broadly complex power dynamics in any cultural discussion of a politics that has been conceived of markedly differently amongst various social groups. This is evident too in the recent circulation of the suffragette figure within the pop-cultural sphere, with the tagline for Sarah Gavron's 2015 film *Suffragette*, 'the time is now', drawing a direct correlation between the battles of white first-wave feminists and current fights for gender equality. As Rebecca Carroll for *The Guardian* points out (2015), the film's marketing campaign featuring four of the lead actresses posing for *Time Out* in t-shirts bearing the Emmeline Pankhurst quote 'I'd rather be a rebel than a slave' operates as a stark reminder of the erasure of black women from the feminist history and conversation.[4] There is an important parallel to be drawn here between the politics of celebrity feminism – which have been shaped predominantly by white women – and the whiteness of the melancholic white woman narrative. Not only does dissatisfaction with the limitations of postfeminism commonly express itself in relation to a select group of women who were supposed to feel empowered by its terms, but the female actress or auteur in enacting or depicting such forms of burden may find such performances of value when incorporating a feminist agenda into her celebrity brand.

An important feature of the interrelationship between postfeminism and neoliberalism is therefore not only the emphasis upon individual responsibility and its implications for a feminist politics, but also the ramifications this emphasis has for cultural understandings of systemic race and class inequalities. These films, while indulging in narratives of white disenfranchisement that prefigure inaugurated President Donald Trump's oft-repeated lament that the United States and its people have fallen from greatness, nevertheless signify prominently in relation to the 'post-racial' politics of the Bush and Obama eras. Postfeminist philosophy shares some ideological common ground with what has become known as 'colour-blind racism', with Eduardo Bonilla-Silva explaining that it has become commonplace for white people in the US to insist on the irrelevance of skin colour in determining one's life chances (2006: 13). Despite ongoing discrimination and inequality in relation to income, employment opportunities and property valuation, Bonilla-Silva claims that many whites are likely to blame these issues on the bad habits of dark-skinned minorities rather than on a systemic racial prejudice that remains nationally pervasive (13). Seeking alignment between the 'post' discourses of postfeminism and postracialism, Tanya Ann Kennedy observes that postfeminist ideology is involved in forms of racial 'policing', whereby women of colour are included on the provision that they meet dominant market demands and adhere to heteronormative lifestyles (2017: 6). The whiteness of postfeminist discourse, she elaborates, obscures postfeminism's origins in ideologies of anti-blackness and economic individualism (7). As Brown explains of neoliberalism, this form of governmentality 'carries responsibility for the self to new heights: the rationally calculating individual bears full responsibility for the consequences of his or her action no matter how severe the constraints on this action', which may include a lack of education, access to child care, high unemployment rates (2005: 42), or prejudice based on race or gender. As a result, a life is considered 'mismanaged' when one fails to navigate such impediments to economic stability and personal happiness, with the ideal neoliberal citizen being one who strategically chooses amongst various economic, political and social options, yet does not seek to alter the options on offer (43). Kennedy points to the political rhetoric around the so-called poor choices made by black women in relation to family and children, arguing that bad decision-making is invoked as a rationale for the imagined crisis state of these institutions. Kennedy notes that successful women (both white and black) are called upon to act as role models for others, chastised when they fail to act accordingly, and are held additionally responsibility for complex social failings (10).

While the ideal of an individualist, 'post-racial' society still holds weight, there has been mounting opposition to this attitude and to the continuing injustices faced by black people, most notably through the Black Lives Matter campaign, which was organised in response to several shootings of unarmed black men by police officers. Furthermore, the resurgence of white nationalism fuelled by Trump's bid for the presidency, and his racist rhetoric on the campaign trail that called for a ban on Muslims entering the country and infamously referred to Mexican migrants as rapists, has sparked much-publicised mass protests around the world.[5] The films under discussion in this book indeed centralise, and sometimes romanticise, white melancholia, yet do so in a manner that seemingly reflects a 'desire' on the part of the industry to associate burden with privilege, visibility and/or beauty. As such, they participate in a forgetting not only of the non-white subject, but also of the white 'underclass' – with the perceived political and indeed mediatised elision of the white poor additionally serving as fuel for the Trump campaign. As Angus Deaton explains in his study of material wellbeing in the United States, 'inequality is often a *consequence* of progress' (2013: 1). Using the 1963 John Sturges film *The Great Escape* as an analogy for arguing that we must consider the non-heroic individuals who are left behind rather than the few who manage to 'escape', Deaton states that the rise in economic growth from the mid-1970s has not made a substantial difference to the poverty rate (180). He argues that researching inequality matters, not only because it impacts upon the measurement of improvement, but because inequality itself produces a range of effects (168). Films that purport to represent the cost of poverty in the United States, however – *Winter's Bone* (Debra Granik, 2010) or *Wendy and Lucy* (Kelly Reichardt, 2008) for instance – tend to belong to the low-budget independent scene and are likely to be subject to limited release unless they exhibit a strong showing on the festival circuit.

While the Hollywood texts studied within this book critique forms of neoliberal governance and recognisable postfeminist tropes, they do so in a way that prioritises the female character's investment in the postfeminist sensibility and the psychological distress that this investment causes her. Characters signifying as 'Other' or 'not quite white', for instance the pirates in *Pirates of the Caribbean*, the Italian citizens of *Under the Tuscan Sun* or the exotic Lily (Mila Kunis) in *Black Swan*, often appear carefree and liberated in comparison to the heroine, as it is anglicised, white femininity that constitutes the ultimate social burden. It is telling that even when a film does attempt to explore the class inequalities produced by neoliberal governance, as occurs in *Blue Jasmine* through the lead character's ill treatment of her working-class sister, the film places a disproportionate degree of blame on Jasmine herself as opposed to the dominant societal value systems that have produced her as a subject. Because Jasmine's melancholia is misplaced, because she *refuses* to relinquish her unhealthy investment in neoliberal discourse and uses this investment to oppress others, she is a markedly less sympathetic figure than the female protagonists in other films. Upwardly mobile young women, like the heroines of these texts, have been used as metaphors for social change, as McRobbie argues is evidenced by the figure of the 'A1 girl', who is usually a 'glamorous, high achiever destined for Oxford or Cambridge' pictured 'clutching an A-level examination certificate' (2009: 15). Yet such governmental expectations, she argues, also work to displace an autonomous feminist politics and feminism as a political movement (15). The melancholic white women within these Hollywood films come to an awareness that their idealised subject position is but a ruse, or a social performance that does not really benefit them. Yet their wish to discover alternative variants of female agency becomes problematic when one considers the race and class exclusions at the heart of neoliberal postfeminism.

Neoliberal postfeminism is a limiting cultural philosophy in the sense that it assumes the availability of unconstrained choice in relation to parenting and domesticity, professional labour and consumer citizenship, and as such centralises an affluent elite (Tasker and Negra, 2007: 2). Because the figure of the A1 girl, or Anita Harris' younger variant the 'can-do girl' (2004), are highly visible symbols of neoliberalism in good health, they are also in their melancholic and burdened incarnations important sites of resistance and of cultural shifts taking place within these same discourses. Strategies of resistance within these films are therefore defined in relation to these same limitations, yet lines of dialogue do open up between neoliberal postfeminism's privileged subjects and those it typically seeks to exclude. Issues of race are uncommonly confronted directly in these films, and rarely in a manner that considers the systemic inequalities of neoliberal ideology and its impacts. Rather, race operates as a concept and a potent question as to whether exploration beyond the parameters of the upper-class, white milieu could potentially be curative to the melancholic state. Such narratives, while not particularly progressive, operate in a manner that comprises a shift in observable racial dynamics within postfeminist popular culture. McRobbie has argued that along with a disarticulation of feminist politics, postfeminist culture has additionally exhibited nostalgia for whiteness in its prioritisation of Western glamour and favouring of fair-skinned models and celebrities (2009: 69–71). Sarah Projansky similarly claims that postfeminist culture constructs middle-class, white women as its ideal subjects through its denial of the ongoing socio-economic barriers facing minority groups (2001: 87). This is not to suggest that non-white people never appear in mainstream popular culture texts, but rather that they typically appear as equally successful beneficiaries of the gains afforded to white people (Projansky 2001: 87) and in less centralised roles. Theoretical observations of this kind have not gone unchallenged within academic analysis. As Kimberly Springer points out, the studious notation of the whiteness of postfeminism's icons often fails to subsequently deliver a deeper analysis of this pervasive cultural sensibility's racial politics (2007: 249).

Jess Butler similarly argues that women of colour regularly 'embody and enact' postfeminism, particularly in the domains of reality television and the popular music industry, so claims that non-white, working-class or non-heterosexual women are excluded from, or unaffected by, postfeminist popular philosophy seem inadequate (2013: 48). Furthermore, I would add that the media landscape described by McRobbie and Projansky remains more persistently evident in Hollywood film than popular television, despite a degree of intertextuality between the two mediums. Television comedy, as well as the conflation of comedy and drama, has recently provided a key site of intervention into the cultural fetishism of the thin, white female body and the 'can-do' discourses of neoliberal postfeminism. Writing on Lena Dunham's *Girls* (HBO: 2012–), Sean Fuller and Catherine Driscoll note that the central female characters come from a background of privilege and yet find themselves aimless and without purpose – rather than 'can-do girls', they are 'girls who should-be-able-to-but-don't' (2015: 257). Tisha Dejmanee, discussing the emphasis on food and corporeality in *Girls* and *The Mindy Project* (Fox/Hulu: 2012–), notes that both Dunham and Mindy Kaling have been labelled as brave and courageous for baring their 'unconventional' bodies on screen (2016: 128). While *Girls* utilises food to 'speak to the primal drives of necessity and lack' in the insecure post-recessionary context (127), Dejmanee argues that *The Mindy Project* frequently exaggerates the corporeal difference of its lead protagonist not only because she is larger than her fellow cast members and the only female gynaecologist in her male-dominated practice, but also because she is not white (128). Comedic tropes are additionally employed in *Jane the Virgin* (The CW: 2014–), which uses strategies associated with the *telenovela* to tell a tale about a young, religious Venezuelan-American woman living in Miami who, despite wishing to save her virginity for marriage, is accidentally artificially inseminated by her doctor at a routine check-up. Comedy is thus employed in television to satirise dominant discourses of postfeminist culture, and the constitution of the idealised postfeminist subject, in a manner that not only explores the gendered dimensions of an investment in such a sensibility, but the complications of having to navigate one's race and class identity in relation to these discourses as well.

This is not to suggest that the melancholic white woman never makes an appearance on television. The recent HBO miniseries *Big Little Lies* (2017), which chronicles the lives of a group of melancholic mothers in the lead-up to a murder in the affluent, seaside town of Monterey, exhibits some shared traits with the films under discussion here. Yet the deployment of drama alongside comedic technique on television, the greater presence of the female comic auteur, as well as the serial nature of the form and new means of producing and screening content may allow for a more nuanced treatment of the subject matter than does popular Hollywood cinema. Kathleen A. McHugh argues that Jenji Kohan's *Orange is the New Black* (Netflix: 2013–) offers key interventions in postfeminist representational strategies at the level of production through the feminist auteur, the social and political context of the US prison system, and the distinctive generic and aesthetic attributes of the show (2015). *Orange is the New Black* is particularly interesting as it bears some of the hallmarks of the melancholic white woman text in centring upon an affluent New York PR executive, Piper Chapman (Taylor Schilling), who learns to alter her priorities and value systems upon encountering those who do not share her privileges. However, this text segregates these incarcerated women from neoliberal postfeminist culture in representing the constraints placed upon their individual freedoms and their lack of access to commodities such as fashion and make-up. More importantly though, the show undercuts Piper's narrative centrality in having each episode focus on the distinctive backstory of individual inmates and by emphasising how Piper's self-perceived propriety 'utterly depends upon the civil, racial, and economic privileges and protections that exist "outside" of that self' (McHugh). While neoliberal ideology celebrates the individual who succeeds despite race and/or class disadvantage, *Orange is the New Black* illuminates the extent to which liberal values of freedom are not only racialised in the US, but are in part maintained through coercive and carceral forms of governmentality that are not easily reconcilable with neoliberal dreams of formal equality. In a season two episode in which the inmates are required to take part in a mock jobs fair, for example, the representative of the organisation Dress for Success informs the inmates that they must not 'think small' and that they will have a much better chance of obtaining the career they desire if they put their wishes out 'into the universe' and dress professionally in their job interviews. As Amy Walker points out, the character Flaca (Jackie Cruz) demonstrates awareness as to the limitations facing the inmates in relation to paid employment when she asks if they should then be dressing in McDonalds or maids' uniforms. This in turn highlights the naivety of the Dress for Success representative's world view, informed as it is by her privileged race and class position (Walker, 2015: 22). The Hollywood films to be analysed throughout this book are part of a cultural turn to which *Orange is the New Black* belongs, in that they are texts in which investments in neoliberal postfeminist discourses are explored and the importance of privilege to these investments is highlighted. Yet the heroine's melancholic state within these films works to bestow her sense of burden with a heightened social significance, so much so that her feelings of missed opportunity can only be alleviated through a fall from the subject position of white, socio-economic privilege. In addition, whether she succeeds in this endeavour is often of prime importance to the social milieu to which she belongs. The protagonist's degree of success in renegotiating her relationship with neoliberal postfeminism varies amongst the texts under discussion. Yet what is important for theorists interested in charting the ruptures and evolutions of postfeminist culture is not only to consider how non-white women 'do' postfeminism, but also to consider how white hegemonic power structures fluctuate in relation to the political and cultural shifts within these same discourses. As Richard Dyer puts it, such academic analysis should endeavour to 'make whiteness strange' (1997: 4).

RACE PRIVILEGE IN CINEMA AND THE AMBIVALENT RELATIONSHIP OF WHITE WOMEN TO HEGEMONIC WHITENESS

Because my analysis aims to explore how gendered and racial identities intersect and shift through the corporeality and narrative trajectory of the melancholic white heroine, I situate my study within the interdisciplinary field of whiteness studies, which is closely related with earlier and continuing research known as 'critical race studies'. Whiteness studies aims to challenge the idea of whiteness as a social category unmarked by race, examining the social, political and cultural advantages of those who are socially interpellated as white, as well as exploring whiteness as a constructed ideology. Rather than simply noting the systematic exclusion of African-American, Asian or Hispanic performers within classic Hollywood or contemporary popular cinema, whiteness studies seeks to disrupt the invisibility of white, hegemonic power structures by exploring how these structures are not only maintained through popular forms such as the blockbuster, science fiction and horror genres, but also through the star texts of powerful industry players. There have, of course, been several highly influential, landmark texts aiming to chart the appearance and distorted representations of various racial groups within mass-produced Hollywood product. Originally published in 1973, Donald Bogle's *Toms, Coons, Mulattoes, Mammies, and Bucks*, for instance, is a seminal text in the field in its analysis of the stereotyping of black American characters. Ed Guerrero's *Framing Blackness: The African-American Image in Film*, published in 1993, explored the shifts of such characterisations in relation to historical and political context as well as how race could function as metaphor and allegory within science fiction and horror texts – key insights integral to my discussion of race in the fantasy film genre in Chapter 2. Gina Marchetti's *Romance and the 'Yellow*

Peril': Romance, Sex, and Discursive Strategies in Hollywood Fiction (1993), meanwhile, is an influential text analysing the prohibitions surrounding the representation of interracial love in the context of fear that Eastern influence could endanger Western values. Canonical in the field of whiteness studies in relation to cinema, however, is Richard Dyer's *White* (1997), which aims to examine the idealisation of white people in the mediums of photography, art and film. In exploring the relationship between racial privilege and lighting codes, the colonial discourses of 'aid and antagonism' in narratives featuring muscular white men, as well as manifestations of the anxiety that whiteness may constitute a type of corporeal absence or death in horror and zombie fare, Dyer succeeded in theorising ways in which whiteness could be analysed within the popular culture text. *White* was followed by Gwendolyn Audrey Foster's *Performing Whiteness: Postmodern Re/Constructions in the Cinema* (2003), which utilises a postmodern approach to explore 'the cracks and fissures' inherent within white performativity (2003: 2–3), including forms of white minstrelsy and instances where whiteness could become its own bad Other. Daniel Bernardi's three edited collections – *The Birth of Whiteness: Race and the Emergence of US Cinema* (1996), *Classic Hollywood, Classic Whiteness* (2001) and *The Persistence of Whiteness: Race and Contemporary Hollywood Cinema* (2007) – also comprised formative interventions in the field, in bringing together scholarly analysis of the maintenance of white hegemony from the very beginnings of Hollywood, to the classic years of studio dominance, through to the present day.

To analyse images of white femininity, however, is perhaps particularly challenging in that women, despite occupying a privileged position in enjoying the benefits of whiteness, have never had full access to the political, economic and social power that white patriarchy confers upon middle and upper-class males. To analyse variants of female oppression and feminism *within* the popular as opposed to 'testing' popular images for the degree to which they adhere to an authentic feminism is therefore especially important given the numerous challenges posed to a feminist political agenda that historically has privileged issues facing white, middle-class people. As such, my analysis of recent popular Hollywood films will aim to explore how such texts make sense of the always interlocking systems of white privilege and cultural definitions of female agency – in this instance, in relation to a set of pervasive ideals promoted by neoliberal postfeminism. As Ruth Frankenberg argues, female lives are not only shaped by gender but are also racially structured, with whiteness acting as a location of structural advantage that informs the standpoint from which white women look at themselves, at others and at their society (1993: 1). White cultural practices, which Frankenberg notes are usually unmarked and unnamed (1), have worked to frame feminism through a tendency to treat variants of oppression in a monolithic manner or through a utopian drive to assimilate voices of difference.

Chandra Talpade Mohanty has written of a colonial tendency within feminist writing to construct an ahistorical notion of the 'third world woman', a problem that she sees as occurring because of both white privilege and the tendency to bind women together through a logic of shared oppression that elides the division between '"women" as a discursively constructed group and "women" as material subjects of their own history' (1988: 65). Ien Ang, in turn, has called for feminism to be recognised as 'a limited political home' that cannot absorb difference through appeals to community or commonality and must leave room for ambivalence and ambiguity (1995: 57–8).

There have, also, been studies exploring the ambivalent relationship of white women to patriarchal power structures. Anne McClintock's *Imperial Leather: Race, Gender and Sexuality in the Colonial Contest*, for example, explores the ambivalent relationship of colonial women to Western imperialism in noting that while women rarely made economic or military decisions relative to the expansion of empire, they still held power over colonised members of both sexes (1995: 6). White women were 'not the hapless onlookers of empire but were ambiguously complicit both as colonisers and colonised, privileged and restricted, acted upon and acting' (6). Both the exclusionary practices of feminism and the historical relationship of white women to patriarchal power structures are important to consider given that postfeminist culture can provide contemporary and culturally specific 'updates', though not necessarily subversions, of such influential modes of thought and social organisation. Popular culture forms, such as the fantasy genre, can become sites where the mixing and inversion of the ordinary performances that sustain racial privilege regularly occur, but may undergo a process of displacement and resignification. In *Alice in Wonderland*, for instance, Alice's interventions in Wonderland may not necessarily be read as colonial given that her journey invites a dominant reading as a feminist coming-of-age story. Yet the feminism the film promotes is built upon the ideal of shared oppression, and thus signifies in relation to the exclusionary nature of much white, Western feminist thought. The ambivalent relationship of white women with white patriarchy, therefore, exhibits itself within cinematic texts in narratives that feature female protagonists and appear critical of the patriarchal standards that oppress women, yet ultimately may invite analysis for their gender politics as opposed to a politics of race or class.

An idea evident within contemporary texts featuring melancholic white femininity, that empowerment may lie outside the parameters of white identity formation, does in fact have cinematic precursors that relate to potent issues facing white women at given historical periods. As Pat Macpherson explains in her 1997 chapter 'The revolution of little girls', 1960s' suburban narratives including *Splendour in the Grass* (Elia Kazan, 1961) and *Bye Bye Birdie* (George Sidney, 1963) explore the heroine's flight from the oppressive 'white picket fence' milieu, with such stories signifying in relation to second-wave feminism, the civil rights movement and the sexual revolution. Macpherson's analysis of *Bye Bye Birdie* is particularly interesting for its exploration of how the female protagonist's transformation is facilitated through an engagement with rock 'n' roll, a musical genre dependent on the appropriation of black music and culture (1997: 291). In relation to the female star image, Foster has analysed the bawdy and irreverent persona of popular 1930s actress Mae West, who she argues enacted simultaneously a drag performance of male sexuality, black women and gay men in her musicality, body language and manner of speaking (2003: 36). Foster questions whether West's drag performances allow her to challenge stereotypes of not only heteronormative femininity but of blackness as well, yet ultimately concludes that her transgressions are not necessarily racially subversive and compares West's problematic appropriation of blackness to that of Madonna. As bell hooks argues, it is white privilege that allows stars like Madonna to 'imitate the joy of living which they see as the "essence" of soul and blackness' without understanding the complexities of racial oppression (1992: 158). Sean Redmond, meanwhile, argues that stars like Kate Winslet are 'made up' to wrestle with the contradictions of white feminine identity, which plays a crucial role in the appeal of their star persona (2007: 263). The texts analysed in this book create meaning in a 'postfeminist' and 'post-civil rights' context, and are cognisant of certain limitations in relation to challenges posed to white patriarchal power structures by activists over the decades. It is therefore important to note that whiteness is not a transhistorical construct. Rather, as Frankenberg explains, 'the range of possible ways of living whiteness, for an individual white woman in a particular time and place, is delimited by the relations of racism at that moment and in that place' (1993: 236). This is perhaps one reason why a number of these films prefer to relegate a more explicit commentary on race to the sidelines, or to explore these issues through the types of racial allegory and metaphor that Guerrero identifies. Additionally, the politically contextualised emotional and affective state of melancholia is used as a tool through which to distance the protagonist from white patriarchal power structures. Therefore, an exploration of melancholia's historical association with privilege as well as its creative capacity – which in this case can have the effect of altering the white woman's relationship to her social environment – is imperative.

MELANCHOLIA AS PRIVILEGED AFFECT WITH GENDERED RESTRICTIONS

To explain what characterises a melancholic state is a somewhat difficult task given its ambivalent construction throughout history, and the oscillation in defining the condition as negative or desirable as well as fluctuations between scientific/psychological definitions of melancholia and a more romantic notion of it as a poetic ideal (Bowring 2008: 15). Yet it is precisely melancholia's ambivalent cultural life that lends itself to an analysis of the female character's narrative trajectory. Her emotional state simultaneously signifies malaise and dissatisfaction with the status quo while also endowing her with the affective tools for remodelling her relationship with the world, if she is able to. If this desire to remodel her relationship with the codes of privilege remains within the realms of fantasy, her tragic downfall may be inscribed with a poetic weight less afforded to those who are neither white nor feminine. In his now classic treatise on the distinction between mourning and melancholia, Sigmund Freud argues that the mourner is eventually able to overcome his or her grief through a withdrawal of the ego from an object perceived as lost. The melancholic, however, will continue to identify with this lost object, despite not necessarily being aware of its significance, which then equates to a loss in the patient's sense of self (Freud [1917] 2000: 285–6). While Freud's psychoanalytic theories may be deemed by some critics to be incompatible with cultural studies frameworks, the article has nevertheless been influential to developments in the historical conceptualisation of melancholia and thus has been integral to contemporary understandings of the term. Furthermore, the ambiguity inherent within Freud's definition and his attribution of the melancholic state to a conscious rather than an unconscious loss means that his formulation avoids some of the methodological pitfalls associated with the psychoanalytic emphasis on the formation of sexuality, and is compatible with sociocultural understandings of melancholia. The female heroines' various states of mental malaise are indeed emblematic of tensions and contradictions relating to the meaning of empowerment for girls and women in the contemporary cultural moment. Arguing for an investigation into the cultural, as opposed to biochemical, causes of depression and associated illnesses, Ann Cvetkovich argues that depression can be utilised as a means of describing the impact of the neoliberal political economy in affective terms (2012: 11).

Taking a similar approach in her discussion of contemporary gendered illnesses, McRobbie has argued for the existence of a specifically postfeminist melancholia, hypothesising that idealised contemporary femininity requires the repudiation of feminist ideals, with feminist politics becoming an 'object of loss and melancholia' for those girls and women forced to give it up (2009: 94). Partially as a result, she argues, certain pathologies disproportionately associated with women, such as eating disorders, are becoming increasingly normalised in contemporary Western societies (95). The female characters within these popular texts are afflicted with a culturally induced melancholia that appears analogous to the social phenomenon that McRobbie describes, and come to realise that their adherence to the codes of bourgeois, white femininity constitutes a series of performative acts designed to serve gendered social regulation. My use of the term 'performance' here is influenced by Judith Butler's theories of gender performativity, and her hypothesis that 'one is not simply a body, but in some very key sense, one does one's body and indeed, one does one's body differently from one's contemporaries and from one's embodied predecessors and successors as well' (1997: 404). As Butler explains, however, sexual difference does not precede that of race or class in the constitution of the subject, with 'the symbolic also and at once a racialising set of norms' (1993: 130).The female heroine, as such, comes to the realisation or the suspicion that her adherence to a neoliberal postfeminist sensibility is but a series of acts required for gendered legitimacy and intelligibility, while her enactment not only of femininity, but whiteness as well, comes to seem imitative, unreal and self-limiting.

Important to my analysis is not only a consideration as to how popular Hollywood texts utilise the melancholic state to provide a cultural 'working through' of neoliberal postfeminism's limitations, but also how the representation of melancholia within these films both relates with and differs from its historical functioning as a form of cultural capital bestowed upon gifted white males. In ancient Greek medicine, an individual's characteristics could be measured in relation to their physiological makeup and their constitution of four governing types of bile – phlegm, blood, yellow bile and black bile – each of which was attributed to the influence of various seasons and elements and was said to culminate in the dominance of specific temperaments (Bowring 2008: 16). Melancholia, an excess of black bile, was associated with the twilight, autumn, coldness and the influence of the planet Saturn – elements which, as Bowring notes, have reappeared throughout melancholia's history in the disparate discourses of medicine, mythology, astrology, art and literature (17). Yet melancholia was also considered to be a state of contradiction, in that the experience of it comprised both positive and negative aspects of experience as well as both positive and negative potentialities for the afflicted individual. In particular, melancholia was associated with creative capacity, artistry and even genius. As Sander Gilman points out, the Greek philosopher Aristotle saw most poets as being of a melancholic constitution, with an excess of black bile held to be a simultaneous source of mental despair and a key feature of the creative mind (1985: 219). While humoral medicine may no longer harbour the claims to scientific validity that it once did, Gilman rightly asserts that the association between creative uniqueness and melancholy has remained remarkably persistent in Western thought (219).

To describe female characters as melancholic, however, may be controversial given that patriarchal culture has historically ascribed less cultural significance to female grief than to male, and has traditionally excluded women from the historical canon of melancholia (Schiesari 1992: 3–4). Representations of male melancholia certainly have a rich lineage within Hollywood cinema, with Mark Nicholls pointing out that the emotional state is central to genres such as the melodramas of the 1940s and 1950s that 'depict male characters in the context of emasculation, masochism, repression and containment' (2004: xii). According to Nicholls, the melancholic aesthetic within Hollywood cinema typically functions to reinstate and romanticise male characters who admit to weakness or defeat, and who are then 'able to adopt an emotional stance historically seen as feminine yet retain a privileged position of power and authority' (xv). Hannah Hamad, meanwhile, points to the recuperation of masculinity through the ubiquitous trope of 'paternal postfeminist melancholia' in contemporary Hollywood cinema, which she argues 'engenders audience investment in melancholic fathers and their emotional trajectories, as they transcend grief and/or cement bonds with their children' (2014: 24). Writing on the Renaissance period that saw the 1621 publication of Robert Burton's *Anatomy of Melancholy*, the artwork of Albrecht Dürer and the poetry of Torquato Tasso, Juliana Schiesari claims that 'depression became translated into a virtue for the atrabilious man of letters', with melancholia becoming an 'elite illness that afflicted men precisely as the sign of their exceptionality, as the inscription of genius within them' (1992: 7). The world of the melancholic, Schiesari argues, was a realm of hyper-exclusivity in which the afflicted individual became 'a self split against itself, fleeing the social into a perpetual dialogue with its own imaginary' (8). This is not to suggest that women are *always* excluded from the canon of melancholia, but rather that throughout melancholia's historical cultural discourse this has more often systematically been the case. The 1800s and 1900s, for example, gave rise to such female artists and writers as Emily Dickinson, Sylvia Plath, Virginia Woolf and Frida Kahlo, who in their combination of mental dis-ease, creative capacity and frustration with daily social life could easily be characterised as melancholic. Not dissimilarly, it is the lived experience of social burden coupled with an artistic temperament and a desire for alternate forms of empowerment that characterises the filmic heroine within these texts as afflicted by melancholia. While most of these protagonists are creatives, they certainly do not exhibit the genius of a Vincent van Gogh or Fyodor Dostoyevsky, and it cannot be over-emphasised that the dramatisation of melancholia within these films is thoroughly gendered and politicised in relation to how 'well' the heroine navigates the melancholic state. Melancholia in this book is therefore a structuring term characterised by a degree of elasticity. This not only reflects the ambiguities in understanding as to what constitutes this mental state, but also the fact that these female characters' lives are represented as operating along a continuum in relation to the melancholic, always at the risk of succumbing to a less agential mental illness.

To fail to recognise the investment in neoliberal postfeminism as a faltering one and to then commit acts of physical or verbal violence in the hope of successfully retaining this investment, as do Jasmine French and Nina's mother in *Black Swan* for instance, is to risk a characterisation more in accordance with the gendered history of psychopathology and neuroses. As Elaine Showalter explains, Western dualistic thought has historically aligned men with rationality and women with madness (1987: 3), culminating in diagnoses such as hysteria, which implicated the female reproductive system in the patient's disturbed mental state. The heroine's ability to work through her feelings of burden, therefore, is entirely conditional. It is also the case that some of these texts self-reflexively comment on the gendered history of mental distress in relation to the cultural appeal and elevation of melancholia, and the role of the melancholic woman in art. *Black Swan*, for instance, explores the relationship between melancholia and mental illness in chronicling the psychological decline of a prima ballerina as she over-invests in the melancholic art form of the ballet. *The Virgin Suicides* similarly explores the relationship between the experience of female melancholia and the tragic white woman as a commodified cultural symbol. The inclusion of *Blue Jasmine* within this book is perhaps especially important in that this film dramatises the social exile of a woman who refuses to alter her investment in neoliberal postfeminism and subsequently fails to realise her creative and intellectual potential – she is melancholy for all the wrong reasons and as such is socially exiled for her 'madness'. Yet despite the political precariousness of female melancholia within these texts, the idea of melancholia as a form of cultural capital still holds relevance when considering the race and class privilege of the suffering heroine, and how her burden is not only framed through her gendered disadvantage but by her whiteness as well. The degree to which the filmic heroine experiences mental despair is less important to my arguments than the political dimensions of mental illness – or, who gets to have their feelings of burden dramatised within media culture, to what purposes and why? It is for this reason that my analysis does not situate itself in relation to debates as to how specific mental illnesses are represented on screen or attempt to engage in diagnostic critique.[6]

The diagnosis of mental affliction is informed not only at times by gender bias, but by race and class bias also. After all, the very fact that it is even hypothetically *possible* within these texts for the white woman to alleviate her melancholia by renegotiating her relationship with her own privileged race and class identity speaks to a certain performative power that white people enjoy at the expense of non-white and/or working-class people. While Cvetkovich argues that depression and melancholia may be traced back to the histories of genocide, slavery, colonialism, segregation and exclusion, she points out that the medical and historical literature tends to privilege a white middle-class subject 'for whom feeling bad is frequently a mystery because it doesn't fit a life in which privilege and comfort make things seem fine on the surface' (2012: 115). There have indeed been philosophical accounts of melancholic experience as arising from the pain and injustice of racial oppression – Frantz Fanon's *Black Skin, White Masks* (first published in English in 1967) is a canonical text from the Afro-Caribbean perspective. More recently, Joseph R. Winters argues in *Hope Draped in Black: Race, Melancholy, and the Agony of Progress* that the rhetoric of progress in the United States has been used to 'downplay tensions, conflicts and contradictions in the present for the sake of a more unified, harmonious vision of the future' (2016: 6). Utilising the work of black writers such as W. E. B. du Bois, Ralph Ellison and Toni Morrison, Winters points to a literary tradition 'that often underscores themes like melancholy, remembrance, loss, and tragedy in ways which gesture towards a different kind of hope' (16). Yet it is certainly uncommon to see such forms and experiences of politicised melancholia represented within popular Hollywood cinema, which has largely participated in exclusionary practices when framing the representation of melancholia and mental illness. Melancholia within these films is very much defined in relation to the socially constituted white psyche, with some texts demonstrating ambivalence as to whether the heroine's encounters with spaces of alterity are even 'real' encounters at all, or merely manifestations of her own sense of loss.

A challenge of this book, therefore, is to explore how gendered forms of melancholia operate in accordance with the particular power dynamics faced by middle- and upper-class white women, and to analyse how their navigation of the melancholic state is framed in terms of the degree of allegiance they exhibit in relation to ideologically questionable political discourses. The experience of melancholia segregates the heroine from her initial social environment, with negative facets of neoliberal postfeminism assumed within these texts to affect white women especially strongly. These protagonists may be idealised, scapegoated or rendered tragic in relation to how they work through their experiences of social burden, with melancholia containing an affective drive that shapes the way many of the heroines learn to relate to people of differing socio-economic status. But what is consistent throughout these films is that the purpose of such characters is to highlight the white woman's alienation and frequently also to serve her goal of melancholic alleviation, not to exist as fully rounded characters within their own right, or as citizens that may be affected in different ways by aspects of neoliberal governmentality. While the melancholic state typically speaks to problems inherent within neoliberal postfeminist paradigms, the films ultimately struggle to find tenable forms of empowerment that lie beyond the confines of these same ideologies or the race and class hierarchies that they depend upon.

RATIONALE FOR FILM CHOICES AND LIMITATIONS OF THE STUDY

The films that I have selected are comprised of Hollywood output produced from approximately the turn of the millennium – the earliest case study being 1999's *The Virgin Suicides* – to more recent fare released at the time of writing, with the latest inclusion being 2016's *The Girl on the Train* (Tate Taylor). Because the scholarly identification of postfeminism as a popular philosophy emerged in the early 1990s, and gained traction in the late 1990s and the first decade of the millennium, the chosen timeframe is ideal to chart the cultural lineage of the postfeminist sensibility and recurrent dissatisfaction with some of its key messages. Most of the films analysed are 'popular' in the sense that they enjoyed a wide release and made money on their initial budget allocation, with the majority proving to be significant financial successes. Popular cinema, as Mike Chopra-Gant argues, constitutes an important site for analysis in that it can be said to reflect and shape audience tastes, albeit those comprising of specific demographics, over a given time period (2006: 12). For example, *Alice in Wonderland*, on a budget of $150m, grossed over a billion dollars at the box office, while *Black Swan*, with a budget of $13m, made $329.4m. Sofia Coppola's *Lost in Translation*, which cost only $4m to make, earned $119.7m at the box office. While *The Virgin Suicides* and *Marie Antoinette* did not enjoy the commercial success of *Lost in Translation*, recouping $10.4m from a $6.1m budget and $60.9m from $40m respectively, they do comprise integral films in Coppola's female alienation trilogy, of which *Lost in Translation is* a part. These films also influenced the aesthetics of Coppola's lucrative fashion collaborations, most notably the top-selling Marc Jacobs perfume *Daisy* – thus justifying their inclusion here. My study examines Hollywood product due to its continued status as the dominant cinema for Western audiences in both production and distribution, especially within English-speaking countries. While there is a strong emphasis on the US political and cultural context within this book, the country's international political, economic and cultural influence ensures that these texts signify well beyond the level of the national. The interrelationship between neoliberal and postfeminist discourses is not, of course, a specifically US phenomenon, which in part accounts for the broad appeal of these films in international markets.

The films selected as case studies are diverse in genre, yet bear marked similarities in the parallels drawn between the heroine's melancholic state and her investment in both idealised whiteness and neoliberal postfeminism. While there may be several films featuring melancholic heroines produced each year, not all of these characterise the female protagonist as burdened due to the false promises of upward mobility, the requirement to participate in consumer capitalism, the cultural obsession with competition and bodily discipline and/or the necessity to perform as an idealised object of the crowd's gaze. While, for example, Jane Campion's cinema frequently features female protagonists of a melancholic disposition, these characters are less obviously melancholic in relation to the limitations of neoliberal postfeminism than Sofia Coppola's. My selection of films offers a broader analysis as to how postfeminist tropes are deployed in relation to popular cinema than most studies in the field, which as earlier stated have largely tended to focus on texts with a specifically feminine address, such as romantic comedies, television dramas with female-led casts and chick-lit novels. This book is an attempt not only to illustrate the existence of postfeminist discourses in alternate genre forms, but also to explore how these discourses manifest themselves in ways that are not always consistent with their representation in 'girl culture'.

Chapter 1 analyses the travel romances *Eat Pray Love* and *Under the Tuscan Sun* – films that feature middle-aged white women who, having recently gone through painful divorces, attempt to alleviate their melancholia by travelling abroad. Both film heroines are creative writers who feel stifled by their urban environments, and discover that the value systems they encounter outside the US allow them to feel creatively reinvigorated as well as liberated from the societal dictates that declare true happiness to reside in long-term marriage, upward mobility and bodily discipline. In these films, the tourist zone must appear to exist independently of the globalising forces of neoliberal capitalism, with the inhabitants of foreign locations only able to signify in relation to the white woman's drive for fulfilment. These gendered narratives, I argue, must be read for their racial implications given that they present affluent white women as the ultimate bearers of burden in contemporary US society, and must also be analysed as offering a commentary on the extra-diegetic global image of the United States in the wake of the global financial crisis and unpopular invasions in the Middle East.

Chapter 2 explores the manifestation of melancholic white femininity in fantasy films featuring proto-feminist heroines. The protagonists of *The Pirates of the Caribbean* franchise and *Alice in Wonderland* experience feelings of burden due to the expectations placed upon aristocratic white women with regards to appropriate decorum, restrictive dress standards and the selection of suitable marriage partners. The heroines dream of alternate magical lands that will allow them their freedom, and are rewarded by a series of events that allow them to enter these magical spaces and transgress idealised standards of white upper-class femininity. The protagonists form bonds with victims of oppression in these fantastical spaces, and ultimately come to realise that their freedom from gender norms will occur upon realising their long dormant leadership potential and liberating the inhabitants of the magical zone. Feminism here is recognised as a type of social charisma with white hegemonic power structures not deposed but rather reframed through the coming-of-age journey and the benevolent intentions of a melancholic white heroine. As with the travel romances, I will argue that these texts speak to discomfort with the nationalism of certain Western powers and their associated agendas on the international stage.

Chapter 3 analyses *Blue Jasmine* as an instance where the protagonist's melancholia appears misplaced and is thus unable to be alleviated by a journey away from home. Rather than desiring to relinquish her attachment to neoliberal postfeminism, Jasmine French maintains her steadfast belief in social competition, class stratification and the power conferred by a designer wardrobe, despite having lost her luxurious lifestyle as a result of her husband's fraudulent investment scheme. *Blue Jasmine* takes a more nuanced approach in its exploration of the painful social inequalities that neoliberal rhetoric perpetuates, with Jasmine's working-class adoptive sister Ginger (Sally Hawkins) frequently expressing her feelings of failure in relation to her older sibling. However, this text also demonstrates the precarious nature of gendered, politicised melancholia in that Jasmine's failure to navigate the melancholic state allows her to become a social and political scapegoat. A Woody Allen comedy of manners that references the global financial crisis and associated unethical business dealings becomes a story about a woman's tragic over-adherence to the 'wrong' kinds of femininity.

Chapter 4 studies the recent psychological thrillers *Gone Girl* (David Fincher, 2014) and *The Girl on the Train*, arguing that the suspense of these texts lies in their ambiguity as to whether the female protagonists are capable of inflicting not only psychological harm, but also physical violence, in the name of adherence to neoliberal postfeminist discourses. Melancholic attachments to 'suburban dreams' are represented as concealing an inner capacity for pathological behaviour. Both films play on tropes associated with gothic fiction, questioning whether the heroines have been the victims or aggressors within their suburban marriages, and engage in commentary on the instability of the white, nuclear family in the wake of the recession.

Chapter 5 argues that *Black Swan* provides a pertinent social commentary on the culture of competitive individualism and bodily discipline. The film achieves this through its referencing of Hollywood's historical treatment of the classical ballet, the play with genre tropes as related to the protagonist's experience of her own corporeality, and the way in which the text works to collapse the boundaries between what constitutes melancholia and what constitutes mental illness. The film's politics, however, are frustrated not only by the insistence on framing gendered pathologies in terms of white burden – with the *Swan Lake* ballet telling the tale of a dark, exotic threat to the aristocratic way of life – but by its own strategic self-reflexivity in relation to Hollywood image construction. This chapter therefore contains the most sustained analysis as to how melancholic variants of method acting comprise a key strategy in redefining the terms of female stardom, given that female actors face greater challenges in relation to wage disparity, ageism and typecasting than do male actors. The chapter also examines how such capabilities are informed by social privileges as related to class and race.

Chapter 6 offers a close reading of Sofia Coppola's first three feature films – *The Virgin Suicides*, *Lost in Translation* and *Marie Antoinette* – arguing that these texts provide critiques of neoliberal postfeminist culture through the heroines' experience of a melancholic existential inertia. While these films provide scope for a feminist reading given that they explore the role of young white women within a neoliberal economy and an intensified commodity culture, they also fetishise ethereal whiteness through the character's narrative trajectory and the films' aesthetic mood. This chapter will explore how Coppola has managed to capitalise on a cultural mood of postfeminist melancholia to sell stories of white female burden through not only her cinematic endeavours, but also her fashionable collaborations. Like the actresses in *Black Swan*, Coppola can utilise melancholia as a tool for surviving in a tough commercial environment.

Through these case studies, I emphasise the importance of analysing postfeminist popular discourse in relation to neoliberalism as an ongoing ideological project. Using the melancholic white woman as a figure through which to chart the ruptures and fissures inherent within this project, I explore how the race and class status of the idealised postfeminist subject is debated within the popular in a manner that speaks to a current fracturing in facets of the American image.

NOTES

1. Lisa Schwarzbaum, for instance, in her 2011 review of the film for Entertainment Weekly describes *Melancholia* as 'the work of a man whose slow emergence from personal crisis has resulted in a moving masterpiece, marked by an astonishing profundity of vision'. Meanwhile, Sukhdev Sandhu in *The Telegraph* claims that 'Von Trier takes a B-movie storyline and from it creates an utterly singular work of art that leaves you stunned and winded' (2011).
2. Throughout media coverage of this controversy, which resulted in a boycott of the ceremony by African-American director Spike Lee and actors Will and Jada Pinkett-Smith, various outlets requested soundbites on the issue from nominated actors as well as other powerful industry players. Attitudes towards the outcry were many and varied, from actress Charlotte Rampling's comment that to boycott the Oscars would be to tantamount to a form of 'anti-white racism' – a comment that she later claimed to CBS News was misinterpreted (Steinberg 2016) – to those of stars such as Viola Davis who in a red-carpet interview with *Entertainment Tonight* correspondent Nischelle Turner drew attention to broader problems within the film industry in terms of casting and the greenlighting of productions (Boone 2016).

3. See Stéphanie Genz and Benjamin A. Brabon's *Postfeminism: Cultural Texts and Theories* (2009) for a comprehensive overview on the varied theoretical manifestations of postfeminism.
4. The highly anticipated Christmas episode of BBC's *Sherlock*, 'The Abominable Bride', also used the character of an avenging suffragette figure to draw parallels between past and contemporary battles for gender equality and to engage in a meta-textual commentary on the gender politics of Arthur Conan Doyle's original series. The theme of the show also signified in relation to star Benedict Cumberbatch's celebrity feminism, with Shelley Cobb stating that the value of such an identity for male stars is often 'the way it creates a personal identity of a male celebrity who "loves" and respects women, even as his on-screen roles may contribute to mediated hegemonic masculinity' (2015: 137).
5. *Newsday* web staff outline Donald Trump's most controversial quotes from the campaign trail in 'Donald Trump speech, debates and campaign quotes', accessible at <www.newsday.com/news/nation/donald-trump-speech-debates-and-campaign-quotes-1.11206532>.
6. Much of the literature in the field discussing representations of mental illness on screen focuses on verisimilitude and seeks to assess the accuracy and representativeness of depictions of psychological disorders in film and television. Examples include David J. Robinson's 2003 book *Reel Psychiatry: Movie Portrayals of Psychiatric Conditions*; Danny Wedding and Ryan M. Niemiec's 2014 edition of *Movies and Mental Illness: Using Films to Understand Psychopathology*, and Steven E. Hyler, Glen O. Gabbard and Irving Schneider's article "Homicidal maniacs and narcissistic parasites: stigmatisation of mentally ill persons in the movies," published in *Hospital and Community Psychiatry* in 1991.

CHAPTER I

The World Is Her Oyster: Negotiating Contemporary White Womanhood in Hollywood's Tourist Spaces

The contemporary Hollywood travel romance offers a number of pleasures for those cinemagoers looking to indulge in a bit of armchair travel at the multiplex. Frequently boasting a fair-skinned star with a warm, infectious giggle, a combination that has proven valuable at the box office, these films allow their female protagonists the opportunity to marvel at historical Parisian architecture, navigate a crowded New Delhi marketplace, enjoy panoramic views of the Mediterranean seascape from a Santorini villa or salivate over fresh plates of pasta and bottles of red wine while seated at a Roman sidewalk café. The appeal of these films, however, lies not merely in the postcard-perfect images of carefully selected international locations and artfully constructed sets designed to evoke romance and excitement, mystery and glamour, but rather in the transformative potential they offer their white, middle-class tourists who frequently initiate their journeys while suffering forms of urban bourgeois malaise. It is my hypothesis that the middle-aged protagonists of recent popular Hollywood fare like *Eat Pray Love* and *Under the Tuscan Sun* need to be read as cinematic manifestations of cultural discomfort with the heightened focus on female aspiration and achievement under neoliberal governance. However, these characters played by bankable stars such as Julia Roberts and Diane Lane, respectively, also serve as fantasy ambassadors sent beyond US borders to be schooled in appropriate forms of international relations in an age of imperial politics, advanced consumer capitalism and immigration anxiety. These journeys abroad are invested with a sense of higher purpose, with the filmic heroines represented as having been 'chosen' to take part in the excursion following prayers to God or the Virgin Mary requesting spiritual clarity. The protagonists are seemingly embraced and protected by specific icons of religious worship in the foreign countries they visit, which works to designate as exceptional both the white female individual and her country of origin. Encountered opportunities for healing, growth and salvation are therefore understood as the result of divine intervention and constitute a shift away from prior life trajectories associated with the secular ideologies of neoliberal postfeminism.

While these films provide solutions to individual crises in keeping with romance genre formulae, the usage of the tourist trope results in an ideological signification that extends beyond the personal problems of the protagonist. When travelling, one is typically found to represent or is asked to speak for his or her country of origin in various ways. In the travel romance it is these encounters with other cultures and subsequent reflections on the differences from the US lifestyle that facilitates the protagonist's changing sense of self. This transformation results in a renewed understanding of the restrictions placed upon white, middle-class femininity in the US context and a changing relationship with feminism in a 'postfeminist' era, in which the meaning of the word is fraught with ambivalence and contradictions. And yet these tourist films create cosmopolitan citizens through the mobilisation of idealised women, played by Hollywood stars, whose renegotiated understanding of feminism is made possible by a renegotiation of white hegemony. There is a disavowal of the importance of racial hierarchy to these narratives of gendered liberation. The films seek to segregate the female protagonist from the influence of neoliberalism, yet engage in a white fantasy of self-perceived racelessness that David Theo Goldberg argues is typical of a neoliberal climate that seeks to disavow the persistence of racial inequality.[1] Racial difference functions within the films in the form of the heroine's exotic perception of her encounters with foreign cultures. Yet while alterity can operate as muse to the female creative, thus contributing to her emancipation from previous performances of femininity, *racism* ceases to exist. Forms of oppression beyond those concerning the white heroine become suppressed in favour of exploring the social tensions and contradictions experienced by the white postfeminist subject of neoliberalism. The travel romance film, I suggest, engages in strategies in which white dominance and privilege undergoes subtle discursive adjustments made possible by the question these films posit – what does female empowerment mean today? White hegemony is never deposed but rather re-centred via the mobilisation of a conflicted female character.

This ideological trope, while typical of most contemporary Hollywood travel romances, is most pronounced when featuring a middle-aged as opposed to a younger protagonist.[2] In films such as *Eat Pray Love* and *Under the Tuscan Sun*, travel becomes beset with heightened emotional urgency as a result of the female protagonist's increasingly melancholic disposition in the urban space of home. These films adopt a sombre and reflective tone, with more depicted to be at stake should the female character fail in her quest for self-discovery. Although the rationale behind the decision to travel demonstrates marked similarities in films featuring younger protagonists – for instance in *When in*

Rome (Mark Steven Johnson, 2010) and *Letters to Juliet* (Gary Winick, 2010) – the configuration of mental distress as brought on by decades of urban female masquerade is absent, even though the promise of its eventual manifestation is strong. Both *Eat Pray Love* and *Under the Tuscan Sun* feature high achieving, white middle-class women who have reached a pinnacle in their careers and yet are in the midst of crumbling marriages. These women, despite their financial success, are also represented as being creatively inclined. The protagonist's melancholic projections in the tourist space thus operate simultaneously to enable liberation from gendered constraints while also providing an alternate realm of discovery for those of artistic temperament.

The representation of melancholia as female illness in *Eat Pray Love* and *Under the Tuscan Sun* has particularly powerful implications for a cinematic politics of gender and race because of its creative and affective potentials in the foreign countries the white woman visits. It is for this reason that the bulk of my analysis focuses on these films, albeit with reference to others in the subgenre. *Eat Pray Love*, while initially entirely consistent with the ideological drive of the typical European travel narrative, also has its protagonist visit India and Indonesia following the initial Italian sojourn. Italy, the most popular destination in contemporary variants of the travel romance, here operates as a training ground for this female tourist seeking her enlightenment. India and Indonesia provide her the opportunity to share her newfound knowledge, create affective bonds with local women, and ultimately engage in a more benevolent, but nonetheless imperialist, feminism within these tourist spaces. It is this additional element that aids in greatly illuminating the questionable politics of the contemporary travel romance, thus making the text particularly worthy of analysis. *Eat Pray Love* participates in a fantasy of universal sisterhood, which Mohanty argues allows for a visibility of gender at the expense of categories of race and class, ignoring the particularities of localised lived existence (2003: 107).

In *Eat Pray Love*, Liz Gilbert is a successful New York novelist about to launch the release of her new book, yet she experiences frustrations that her dreams of travel are not shared by her husband Stephen (Billy Crudup) and are not granted the same social validation as the desire to start a family. Stephen has been unable to match Liz's success and his frequent career changes become an additional source of dissatisfaction and one of her prime motivations for divorce. Following an ill-fated, post-separation fling after the divorce with young actor David (James Franco), Liz decides to set off on a year-long adventure during which she will spend time in Italy, India and Indonesia. In these countries, Liz gains a new sense of self through newfound friendships and through the consumption of the food and religions on offer in her chosen locations. Eventually she is rewarded through a romance with fellow divorcé and traveller Felipe (Javier Bardem), who similarly is trying to alleviate a sense of loss and disconnectedness through travel and as a result has acquired forty-six stamps on his passport.

Like Liz Gilbert, Frances Mayes in *Under the Tuscan Sun* is a successful and influential novelist struggling to make sense of her life following a divorce. Also like Liz, Frances' husband, Tom, has failed to reach the levels of success that she has while working to support him, and is unfaithful to her with a younger woman. Worried about the state of Frances' mental health, her friend Patti (Sandra Oh) decides to send her on a trip to Tuscany in the hope that a change of scene will set her on the path to happiness. While there, Frances decides on a whim to buy a Tuscan villa, finds a surrogate family in the local inhabitants, and achieves a newfound spirituality and sense of guidance through her discovery of Roman Catholicism. Like Liz, Frances also glimpses the possibility of true love in the form of a fellow traveller and writer at the close of the film.

THE BURDEN OF HEIGHTENED VISIBILITY

The protagonists of both films first feel the stirrings of loss and alienation in their urban milieu during events at which they are the objects of admiring gazes due to their professional successes. Liz is the guest of honour at a literary *soirée* to promote her new novel held by her agent Delia Shiraz (Viola Davis) and she spends the evening meeting influential members of her chosen field who wish to congratulate her on her work. It is at this party, however, that she realises her lack of fulfilment despite achieving the ambitions she held in her twenties. Upstairs, Liz confides to Delia that she harbours a stash of *National Geographic*s and travel magazines full of places she wishes to see before she dies, and that for her these dreams eclipse that of the desire to be a mother. It is following this promotional *soirée* that Liz discovers that her love for Stephen has faded. When he confesses that he does not wish to go to Aruba with her, Liz replies that she no longer wants to be married. A similar opening scene in *Under the Tuscan Sun* provides the catalyst for the female protagonist's deepening sense of loss and disconnectedness with her life in the US. In this film, Frances, a professor of Creative Writing, attends a literary launch held for one of her young protégés, a writer who declares his gratitude to her during a celebratory monologue. Like Liz, Frances is clearly an influential figure in her professional sphere – the person at the party that everybody wants to meet. It is also noted by a colleague that Frances is a particularly successful example of modern femininity, able to balance the demands of career with traditional modes of feminine work. 'Tom is a lucky bastard,' this event attendee assures her, 'a literary wife who makes brownies'. At the event, she happens to meet a male writer whose book she has reviewed as reminiscent of 'a middle-aged man living out his horny teenaged fantasies'. The author takes the opportunity to respond that Frances' poor review is ironic given her husband's infidelities, and her world begins to unravel.

Both Frances and Liz, however, are examples of successful neoliberal femininities, maintaining restrictive standards of female attractiveness while striving towards upward mobility in their professional lives. *Eat Pray Love* and *Under the Tuscan Sun* feature women who have abided by the rules of neoliberal feminism, engaging in a rigorous monitoring of the self and conforming to heteronormative gender standards while aspiring to career success. Despite this dutiful adherence however, they have failed to achieve the feelings of empowerment and fulfilment promised to their younger selves through this ethos. Because of Liz's investment in this gendered neoliberal ideology in her younger years, her dreams of self-fulfilment through travel have been suspended, thus contributing to her current midlife crisis. Frances learns that her investment in career aspiration has only sustained her romantic partnership in the economic sense, and has not given her enough leisure time to indulge in life's pleasures. Both women harbour a sense of loss, felt most keenly during a particular moment when they should be feeling proud of their achievements. The gaze of the crowd upon the bourgeois white woman suddenly begins to feel heavy and burdensome despite her previously held ambitions to reach the current state of success. Liz and Frances exemplify what Negra has described as the postfeminist time crisis, where female lives are defined as lived in a perpetual state of temporal anxiety in relation to the achievement of marriage and motherhood as well as the maintenance of an ideally youthful appearance (2009: 48). The sense of being 'out of time' and the subsequent melancholic state is here presented as resolvable by adjustments to the relationship between neoliberal and feminist ideologies that occur as a result of a literal and metaphoric journey of discovery. It is by venturing into the tourist space that the protagonist comes to read her previous model of femininity as a social performance resulting in mental stasis. This occurs not only through a rediscovery of sensuous pleasures and the capabilities of the female body in the tourist space, but also through a problematic formation of empathetic bonds with peoples who are victims of social inequalities in their countries of birth. As such the fantasies of resolution these texts offer, while indicating an important shift in how Hollywood texts present neoliberal femininities, signify on multivalent levels with regard to gender and nationality, and how we make sense of the national through the mobilisation of gender.

There is an indication in these films that the focus on female mobility in the professional sphere has come at the expense of male achievement and that this is not conducive to the formation of the nuclear family, with Tom dependent on his wife's income and Stephen unable to commit to a single career path. Writing on trends in contemporary romantic comedy, Negra has pointed to the prevalence of the 'miswanting' narrative, in which the female protagonist comes to realise that her life as an urban career woman is deficient, leading her to re-prioritise romance and family through a change in location from the city space to a regional idyll (2001: 18). While this trope is evident to a degree in the travel romance, Liz and Frances notably differ in that they remain sympathetic figures despite achieving their career ambitions. By contrast, the female protagonist in romantic comedies including *13 Going on 30* (Gary Winick, 2004) and *The Proposal* (Anne Fletcher, 2009) tends to find that her career success has resulted in an unfavourable alteration of personal disposition, leaving her narcissistic, selfish and unable to appreciate either homespun, traditional values or the love of a good man. It is up to this good man to teach her the correct personal values so that she can be transformed as worthy of true love and deeper human connection. Liz and Frances, however, remain likeable characters throughout the films and it is never indicated that career achievement has hindered their sexual desirability or capacity to form close friendships built on respect and trust. Frances, for instance, is shown to have a loyal and loving friendship with Patti and while at the literary launch has to laughingly remind young novelist William that she is married after he requests a kiss. Husband Tom remains a faceless villain throughout the piece, his lack of appearance in the film ensuring our sympathies reside with Frances. He is the man who does not appreciate his luck at having the 'literary wife who makes brownies'. While Stephen in *Eat Pray Love* is a more sympathetic figure than Tom, shedding tears throughout the divorce proceedings, Liz's frustrations at not being understood by her New York City peers are vindicated through discussions she has with others outside the US, who agree it is more difficult for women to feel that they can make their own choices. Furthermore, the decision to travel abroad operates to reinvigorate both protagonists creatively, which in turn benefits them professionally given that their chosen career paths as novelists depends on the ability to convey real or imagined experience compellingly through the written word. While *Eat Pray Love* and *Under the Tuscan Sun* do remove their female protagonists from a masculinised professional environment, it is important to note that both films were based on best-selling autobiographical novels. This suggests a certain cultural capital inherent in translating the personal experiences of urban neoliberal femininity and a capitalisation on stories of transcending an associated melancholic state through fantasies of escaping the US. For in these tourist films, blame for personal dissatisfaction does not lie with any one individual but rather within the individual's environment.

THE PERIL AND PRESTIGE OF URBAN MELANCHOLY

The protagonists' state of melancholy in both films manifests itself in feelings of physical inertia and lack of direction despite cultural emphases on increased socio-economic mobility for women. 'I don't know how to be here', Liz complains to David, who angrily retorts that she should 'stop waiting for something'. Frances, following her divorce in *Under the Tuscan Sun*, moves into a halfway house which she soon learns is full of divorced men and women who, despite initial intent for a temporary stay, have failed to move on from their derelict accommodation and thus have failed to transcend their state of existential crisis. The landlord informs Frances that, as a writer, she may wish to help her co-inhabitants with their suicide notes, pointing out that the resident doctor hands out the sleeping pills and the attorney provides free legal advice. In referring to the depressive residents of the halfway house by their middle-class professions, the landlord suggests that a life lived in pursuit of bourgeois professional respectability is doomed to failure. This scene may also serve as a commentary on the declining value of middle-class professions in a neoliberal 'risk society' that glorifies celebrity and successful entrepreneurs. While whiteness in the US has historically operated as a form of insurance against poverty and literal homelessness (Cheryl Harris 1993: 1713), and continues to confer benefits on the labour market, here it becomes associated with a creative and spiritual 'excess' that prevents the white woman from finding fulfilment within everyday middle-class routine. As the Hollywood travel romance features female protagonists and appeals largely to a female audience, the state of melancholy depicted in these films, along with the eventual transcendence of this state, is of course thoroughly gendered – yet it is also raced and classed. Although McRobbie's analysis of postfeminist melancholia indicates that it may transgress class boundaries, the ideal neoliberal female subject is, or aspires to, middle-class status, and claims to cultural intelligibility and respectability for working-class women have always been compromised by ideological prejudice. Furthermore, McRobbie explains that female melancholia is given 'dramatic form' through the high-fashion image, which provides 'an oscillation between possibilities of freedom from the constraints of gender subordination and the reestablishment of order and control' (2009: 100).[3] This suggests not only a reflection of feminine cultural malaise but also an economic interest in reproducing the melancholic state – and the fantasised escape from it – within a photographic showcase for luxury couture and, I argue, through popular cinema.

The visibility of female melancholia in commodity form in the contemporary moment is dependent for its ideological signification on restrictions placed upon women in patriarchal culture, and there may be an exploitative element inherent in the fact that fantasies of escape are being sold to women through various media forms. Nevertheless, female melancholia is not invisible and there is a certain 'cultural prestige', to use Schiesari's terminology, for white middle-class women in having their burden represented and recognised. Both Elizabeth Gilbert and Frances Mayes, though not associated with genius, are certainly creatively gifted. It is these creative abilities that allow them to give their sadness a voice and speak the tourist space into being in a way that serves their therapeutic interests. Both films privilege the female narrative voiceover, allowing the characters to continually relate the tourist experience back to their changing mental state while paying homage to the literary source material behind both films. In fact, the association between female protagonists and the creative arts operates as a trend in the Hollywood travel romance. Beth in *When in Rome* is an art curator, Sophie (Amanda Seyfried) in *Letters to Juliet* is a journalist whose perceptions of Florence are shaped by Shakespeare's play *Romeo and Juliet*, while the protagonists Amanda (Cameron Diaz) and Iris (Kate Winslet) in Nancy Meyers' *The Holiday* (2006) work in the film and book industries respectively. While the power associated with creative capacity in the tourist space may not be consistent with the feminine position, it is certainly dependent on the capital afforded these protagonists by their class and race.

NURTURING BURDENED WHITENESS

If it is white middle-class women who are the ideal representatives of a successful neoliberal society, then it is also white middle-class women who are represented as feeling its burdens most strongly. This is how female melancholia comes to be associated with relative privilege in the Hollywood travel romance. Both Frances and Liz have non-white friends whose primary role is to act as a counsellor or therapist to the burdened white woman in her time of need. It is Delia Shiraz, an African-American literary agent, in whom Liz confides that she 'wants to go someplace where I can marvel at something ... language, gelato, spaghetti, something!' while pointing out that she has not been given 'two weeks of a breather, to just deal with myself'. The views of Shiraz and those Liz encounters in Italy, India and Indonesia are offered as philosophies to be consumed on the journey toward inner peace. Part of this journey includes partaking in the national cuisine as a form of therapy. The gustatory pleasures involved in sharing food and wine with newfound friends allow the melancholy white woman to shed the corporeal restrictions placed upon her in the US environment as well as to overcome neoliberalism's emphasis on competitive individualism. Those who do not bear the apparent burden of white privilege exist to offer advice to the female melancholic, their wisdom imbibed as of nutritious value to the woman in need. Delia's last name, Shiraz, prefigures a joke made by Liz in Rome regarding the consumption of red wine as ideal therapy. Despite her role as counsellor and confidante, Delia, as an inhabitant of New York, is less able to understand her friend than are those Liz encounters on her travels due to her belief in the city's values of upward mobility

Figure 1.1 The role of Delia Shiraz is to provide advice to Liz in *Eat Pray Love*.

and ambition. Yet her appearance in the film works to prefigure the nature of the division between anglicised whiteness and non-whiteness that this tourist film creates. The close friendships that Liz and Frances harbour with Delia and Patti, an Asian-American lesbian in *Under the Tuscan Sun*, distance the protagonists from the values of the upwardly mobile bourgeoisie in that they serve to provide a therapeutic outlet for the white female melancholic. This lays the narrative groundwork for the semiotic function of the tourist space, in which the land, building structures and inhabitants must all relate to the white female protagonist's goal of alleviating personal crises. Liz later encounters an Italian barber named Luca Spaghetti (Giuseppe Gandini), whose knowledge regarding the differences in American and Italian lifestyles is consumed with as much relish as the famous pasta his last name invokes. While Delia and Patti are portrayed as of similar social standing to the lead female characters, there is little indication of the ongoing socio-economic inequalities and prejudice encountered by racial minorities in a neoliberal America that has insisted on the irrelevance of race. The Hollywood tourist romance therefore engages in a powerful ideology of 'colour-blind racism' (Bonilla-Silva 2006: 2) to construct a gendered narrative predicated on burdened whiteness.

Eat Pray Love and *Under the Tuscan Sun* champion what bell hooks has termed 'eating the Other' as a fantasy liberation strategy for those white middle-class women who have failed to achieve the fulfilment promised to them in the American urban environment. The protagonists rediscover an authentic self that was presumed lost to the requirements of neoliberal femininity in the US ultimately through an engagement with the inhabitants of the tourist space, who by necessity are reduced to a racial cliché in their role as cultural rehabilitators. The search for the authentic self is thus reliant on a validation of one's fantasies of cultural difference, which serves to reinforce the centrality and power enjoyed by anglicised white femininity in the tourist space. As hooks points out, the commodification of race serves to provide an 'alternative playground' for white hegemony looking to affirm its dominance (1992: 23). It is Patti in *Under the Tuscan Sun* who realises the therapeutic benefits that Italy will offer Frances, warning her friend that she is 'in danger of never recovering' and becoming an 'empty shell' of a person who did not take an opportunity to move forward when it was presented to her. When Patti informs Frances that her reluctance to travel is just 'depression talking', Frances replies that her 'depression doesn't speak Italian, only a little high school French'. Of course, Frances eventually learns that the Italian environment is indeed capable of alleviating her depressive state as her newfound milieu unlocks her writer's block, which had been leading her into 'abject self-loathing'. While on a sojourn to Cortona, Frances offers to assist a young male traveller who is struggling to describe his experiences of Italy in a postcard home to his mother. Explaining to this fellow tourist that she 'used to be' a good writer, Frances soon succumbs to the pleasures of her surroundings as she observes that Italians seem to know more than Americans about having fun, while noting amusedly the accuracy of cultural stereotyping in writing that 'clichés converge at this navel of the world'. Frances here takes pleasure in the apparent validity of the Italian stereotype, the semiotic shorthand for the country as sold to travellers through the tourist brochure now known to have an authentic base.

The commodification of race, hooks suggests, typically promises a conversion experience to the white individual that depends upon an eradication of the history of the racial Other, while utilising cultural difference as a resource for pleasure (1992: 31). In this scenario, hooks hypothesises, the desire to model the Other into a reflection of oneself is exchanged with the desire to become more like the Other (25). As Negra has noted of this subgenre, ethnicity operates as a trope of *empowerment* (2001: 82). The white woman can incorporate elements of ethnic identity at will in order to make necessary lifestyle adjustments, as for her, ethnicity operates as a floating signifier, even though the locals in the tourist space remain racially fixed. While this trope operates throughout *Eat Pray Love*, the film emphasises Liz's association with a variety of Italian people through her engagement in urban *flânerie*, while segregating her from the majority of the populace in India and Indonesia through her choice to stay at retreats. The religious retreat in India is predominantly frequented by devotees of international origin, whereas the retreat in Bali offers affluent tourists a temporary reprieve from the stresses of everyday living. Liz only ever gazes at Indian urban life from behind the window of a taxi stuck in traffic, pausing only briefly at the sight of a child sifting through a rubbish pile at the side of the road, as rapid editing highlights the fast-paced, frenetic energy of her surroundings and the transient role the scene will play in the overall narrative. Liz's association with Indian and Indonesian peoples is largely confined to those whom she perceives as spiritually enlightened, such as the Balinese medicine man Ketut Liyer (Hadi Subiyanto), in order to facilitate her own transcendence above personal pain. In India, Liz's engagement with Hinduism is predominantly filtered through her relationship with fellow American tourist Richard (Richard Jenkins), as the guru she travelled to see has ironically departed to visit New York. The emphasis on meditation and silence in these sections of the film operate to further remove Liz from her environment, ensuring that the relationship between person and place is solely a spiritual one and allowing the film to disengage from a potential exploration of the political, social and economic inequalities that separate Liz from her environment in both countries.

REDISCOVERING FEMINISM IN THE APOLITICAL ZONE

The Hollywood travel romance illustrates an important relationship between white hegemony and postfeminist ideological formations, mobilising feminist discourses in its presentation of narratives about US women who regain control of their lives through a literal and metaphorical change of direction. 'Feminism' is a battleground, with conflicting representations in contemporary popular culture sold to us as feminist with or without recourse to the discourses of the second wave. This is perhaps most evidently true of the romance and romantic comedy genres, as these films often deal with the role of middle-class women in the home and workplace, issues of concern for many feminists in the 1960s and 1970s. In *Eat Pray Love* and *Under the Tuscan Sun*, feminism is filtered through fantasies relating to the perceived healing power of travel. This form of feminist empowerment, however, is reliant on a phenomenological reawakening of the female body that is simultaneously empowered in its belonging to the white race and disempowered as a result of gendered social positioning. In *Under the Tuscan Sun*, as Frances writes her postcard, she becomes newly aware of the pleasures gained through a sensory engagement with the world, musing upon 'the velvet sweetness' of a hot grape that 'even smells like purple'. The tourist locale therefore becomes an idealised space in which the white female can thrive in her newfound mobility and rediscovered capacity for corporeal enjoyment, while the urbanised US environment becomes re-signified as a site of feminine restriction. This transformation narrative is dependent on racial ideologies privileging whiteness to explore the contemporary meanings of female empowerment for middle-class white women.

For the female character to reap the therapeutic benefits of her chosen destinations, these countries must be reimagined as completely separate from the influence of global capitalism, politics, trade and immigration. In particular, the ideological success of the films depends on the apparent immunity of the tourist space to any form of American imperialism, whether this be through foreign policy, value systems or product importation. In presenting travel as an idealised revitalisation method for its female protagonists, who can thus escape the perils of the postfeminist time crisis, the Hollywood travel romance gives rise to an interesting inversion in its representation of the changing relationship between the individual and her inhabited space. The female protagonist must learn to read her initial environment, with its socio-economic emphases on upward mobility and career advancement, as contributing to her sense of self limitation.

This realisation, however, is possible only in the tourist zone, where these factors are completely absent from daily social life. Negra, discussing the 1990s tourist romance as a burgeoning type of woman's film, hypothesises that the narratives address a lack of connection between American whiteness and 'heritage homelands' (2001: 82) through a polarisation of contemporary US society and nostalgic fantasies of Europe. European tourism therefore works to reconnect the protagonist with lost ideologies, values and lifestyles (89), while restoring the character to 'a simplified, purified economic realm' (82). Writing on the promoted ideologies of the tourism industry, Urry and Larsen point out that the mobility of the tourist is dependent on the immobility of those in the chosen locale whose bodies exist to be displayed and gazed at by the traveller (2011: 29). These tourist films operate first to connect the female protagonist, representing America, to the past through its representation of a pure and uncorrupted Italy whose inhabitants would never dream of migrating elsewhere due to their superior leisure lifestyle. As Thomas J. Ferraro points out in his study of Italian pop-cultural images in the American context, it is these ideals of 'solidarity and cultural retention' that not only prove attractive fantasies to the people of the United States, but also allow them to negotiate national identity and progress, including 'what they have never been' and what 'they would still like to be' (2005: 202). While Frances in *Under the Tuscan Sun* marvels at the ability of Italians to relax and have fun, barber Luca Spaghetti informs Liz in *Eat Pray Love* that American behaviour is dictated by over-investment in work and the commercial imperatives of capitalism. 'You don't know pleasure', he says, 'you need to be told you've earned it. You see a commercial that says it's Miller time and you say that's right and buy a six pack. An Italian doesn't need to be told.' In *Letters to Juliet*, protagonist Sophie is chastised for her refusal to take part in a communal meal by the Italian cook who declares that this 'is the problem of the American, always running'. Neither labour nor consumerism, it would seem, exists in contemporary Italy where people are represented as living according to instinct and desire, their sense of subjectivity uncorrupted by state or business intervention. This depiction of the Italian people is reliant on their socio-historical designation in the United States as ambivalently white,[4] for as Alistair Bonnett suggests, to live on the edges of whiteness is also to operate 'outside the cold and instrumental realm of modernity' (2000: 78).

It is not only Italy that is removed from the global order of advanced capitalism in *Eat Pray Love*, however, but India and Indonesia also. The white woman, who is herself not a full participant in patriarchal bourgeois whiteness due to the association of her gender with emotional excess and bodily spectacle, is able to connect with those in the tourist space due to lack of satisfaction in her role within the US neoliberal system. For this feminist salvation to occur, the white woman must relocate both herself and her work as outside history, and extraneous to contemporary sociopolitical history in the making, and thus apparently outside of patriarchal intervention. As Valerie Amos and Pratibha Parmar have noted, identifying countries as backward and 'underdeveloped', as unable to emerge into advanced capitalist life, not only informs imperialist ideology but also commonly constitutes a problematic in leftist politics (1984: 10). In these films, the fantasised *resistance* to development within these countries allows the white woman to craft a new feminist value system, negating the role of the US as a major contemporary imperial power and the role of affluent white womanhood within this system. These countries become ideal venues aiding in the rediscovery of feminism based upon the unity of body and mind, free from commercial and governmental imperatives, resulting in the American woman's pleasure in acting upon her desire to eat, pray and love. The adoption of the tourist gaze, which can be read as a feminist act given cinema's preoccupation with women displayed as passive spectacles for the active male look (Mulvey 1975), works to disrupt the female protagonist's previous role as an ideal citizen of neoliberalism. Yet her newfound mobility through triumph over space and place is possible only because of the tourist zone's temporal suspension, in its representation as timelessly cultural. The usage of feminist discourse in conjunction with essentialist portrayals pertaining to both gender and racial characteristics operate to situate white women as ideal candidates through which to renegotiate American whiteness.

REIMAGINING THE UNITED STATES ABROAD

The Hollywood travel romance needs to be read in a cultural context marked by growing discomfort and disillusionment with America's global image in its production of filmic fantasies whereby female heroines are both retrained in appropriate lifestyle values and also working to modify foreign viewpoints of the US. While *Under the Tuscan Sun* is unique in introducing Frances as an inhabitant of San Francisco, the majority of travel romance protagonists hail from New York, an urban space commonly represented on film and television as a city where femininity is made and shaped. As Deborah Jermyn argues, there is an inextricable link throughout cinematic history between New York and the 'independent, desiring and desirable woman' (2009: 15), from the iconic image of a Givenchy-clad Audrey Hepburn eating breakfast outside Tiffany's to Diane Keaton's offbeat Annie Hall, right through to the frivolous, fashion loving women of *Sex and the City*. Jermyn suggests that the association between New York City and themes of hope and possibility in relation to the archetype of the urban female consumer and tropes of romantic love have their genesis in New York's history as an arrival port for new immigrants. The allure of the American dream, with its emphasis on values of 'egalitarianism, enterprise and ambition', Jermyn states, formulates a key component of how New York signifies in the cinematic context as a magical space where 'anything can happen' (16). When female protagonists such as Liz in *Eat Pray Love*, Beth in *When in Rome* and Sophie in *Letters to Juliet* experience themselves as unable to achieve their desires in New York, this urban space – no longer able to accommodate the hopes and dreams of its female inhabitants – undergoes a resignification in terms of its relationship to female mobility and success.

The feminist re-appropriation of the characters' life trajectory corresponds directly to a change in relationship with American whiteness through an engagement with cultures that are seemingly entirely segregated from its influence. American intention in the foreign space can thus also be reframed as 'benevolent and benign', to use US foreign policy critic Noam Chomsky's description of an ideally mediated US foreign policy that works to obscure both the problematic politics and true rationale behind foreign intervention (2005: 130). In these films, this occurs with recourse to essentialist views of an idealised nurturing femininity able to provide care and support for those encountered overseas. The shifting representation of New York in the travel romance is not due solely to contemporary cultural discomfort with female career aspiration, as it also signifies in regard to the powerful yet ambivalent role New York has played as both victim and aggressor on the world stage over the past decade. The al-Qaeda terrorist attacks of 9/11 led to an upsurge of patriotism in the United States, resulting in increased support for then president George Bush's proclaimed 'War on Terror' as well as religious intolerance and hate crimes against those believed to be of Middle Eastern descent. However, as Chomsky explains, the 2003 invasion of Iraq, justified by claims that the state harboured weapons of mass destruction, was unpopular with Western European electorates, including those of Spain, Italy, Germany and France, and was opposed by a substantial proportion of US citizens.[5] Those opposed to the invasion questioned the legality of the exercise in accordance with international law, the large number of casualties the war would probably result in and the rationale provided for the invasion, with some opponents believing the US was looking to control Iraq's natural resources. The invasion of Iraq and the ongoing resultant war thus provoked global dissatisfaction with US international relations that was to be exacerbated again during the global financial crisis of 2007–8, which began with a US housing market collapse resulting from risky lending practices by Wall Street financial institutions. This led to nations around the globe spiralling into recession.[6] While certainly not directly or explicitly referencing these concurrent issues, the contemporary Hollywood travel romance illustrates subtle shifts in the cinematic representation of the American dream through the mobilisation of a female protagonist uncomfortable with a US value system that she perceives disadvantages her. American exceptionalism, the notion that the United States is unlike other nations in its global purpose to deliver equality and freedom abroad (Chomsky 2010: 39), is here modified for a dual purpose. The female protagonist is immediately identified by those in the foreign space as unique in her ability to provide care but only after she is recognised as an ideal representative through which to modify a US value system that has lost its way.

DIVINELY UNIQUE: RELIGIOUS GUIDANCE IN THE FOREIGN LOCALE

With recourse to both religious and feminist discourse, these films are able to portray the global expansion of American whiteness as both therapeutic and empowering to the US female citizen while also working to alleviate guilt or discomfort with similar facets of the contemporary American image. For the female protagonist to be deemed worthy of an education in lifestyle choice, she must first be marked out as uniquely special upon her arrival in the tourist zone in a manner that alludes to financial capital only in subtext. This gives rise to an interesting theme that locates the heroine as in God's favour, both through her need for spiritual salvation and in her capacity to act as a force of redemption through acts of good will in her visited countries. This theme, prominent in both *Eat Pray Love* and *Under the Tuscan Sun*, bestows a higher worth on the heroine who finds herself both 'chosen' and guided by icons of religious worship in the tourist space. This trope propagates a form of American exceptionalism while working to assuage white guilt, and ensures that the female individual learns to make peace with her past while preparing for a different future. The process of divine intervention allows for the projection of the protagonist's melancholic state upon the tourist space, so that healing transpires from a symbiotic bond between person and place. 'Romance' in the Hollywood tourist film does not merely allude to the 'boy meets girl, boy loses girl, boy gets girl back' conventional battle of the sexes formula continually played out on cinema screens through the romantic comedy. Given that they tend to possess a comedic as opposed to melancholic tone, tourist films featuring younger protagonists largely conform to genre requirements. However, the romances under discussion here introduce the romantic partner toward the close of the narrative and as such do not factor a male co-protagonist in as a plot driver. In *Eat Pray Love* and *Under the Tuscan Sun*, the romance is primarily between the heroine and the tourist milieu itself. During a luncheon in Rome in *Eat Pray Love*, Liz and her newfound friends challenge themselves to encapsulate the character of their cities of origin with just one word. The words purporting to describe such cities as London, Stockholm and New York are articulations of aspects of urban living the travellers feel has worked to impose limitation and restriction upon the self, and as such are described as stuffy, conformist and overly ambitious respectively. The equation of Rome to sex, however, elicits a collective cheer from the group in its evocation of a pleasurable bonding of bodies and it is a euphemism that extends beyond sexual intercourse to the liberation of acting upon bodily desire. When Liz visits a famous eatery in Naples for instance, she describes herself as 'having a relationship' with her pizza.

The symbiosis between person and place, while pleasurable in its liberating capacity to indulge the female protagonist's narcissism, is also curative to the melancholy state due to the mobilisation of affect. Although Liz has always harboured the desire to travel, her decision to divorce her husband and tour Italy, India and Indonesia comes to her following a prayer to God for spiritual guidance. Liz therefore understands every occurring event within these countries as serving the divine purpose of healing the fractures in her life. A tourist venture to the Augusteum in Rome allows her to make a clean break from David, as she not only begins to see the ruins of her life as reflected in the ruins of the historical building structure, but also learns to understand the transient nature of her personal pain. 'The place has withstood so much chaos,' Liz writes in her email to David. 'Ruin is a gift. Ruin is the road to transformation. The world is so chaotic and maybe the real trap is getting too attached to any of it.' The Augusteum here assumes the form of Liz's melancholy, both operating as a projection of burdened whiteness and offering redemptive potential in the eyes of God. In *Eat Pray Love*, Italy becomes a spiritual primer for Liz, who eventually leaves the country to practice Hinduism at an Indian ashram. Following a period of self-enforced silence and meditation, Liz comes to learn that 'God is not interested in a performance of how a spiritual person looks and behaves. The quiet girl who glides silently through the place with a gentle ethereal smile. Who is that person? It's Ingrid Bergman in *The Bells of St Mary's*, not me. God dwells within me, as me.'

The deployment of divine intervention as a trope in the Hollywood travel romance operates to define the heroine's intentions in the tourist space as pure as opposed to being driven by an imperialist capitalist greed.[7] While mobility afforded by capitalist imperatives is disavowed, the elevation of the white female protagonist as 'chosen' through her embrace of the religions on offer to her in the tourist space is thoroughly dependent on ideologies of white exceptionalism. *Under the Tuscan Sun* similarly employs the divine to bestow a sense of manifest destiny upon the female protagonist's arrival in the tourist space. After deciding to purchase a Tuscan villa that has fallen into disrepair, Frances encounters financial opposition in the form of an Italian couple who angrily declare that her interest in the property is typical of 'greedy Americans' who have an overinflated sense of entitlement, to which Frances replies that 'a lot of us feel really badly about that'. Frances is ultimately deemed the interested party who will most benefit from the acquisition, and is sold the property by a *contessa*, whose family has owned the villa for generations and who Frances is told has more interest in signs from above than money. As Frances struggles to tame the unruly land, repair shredded wallpaper and encounter various household appliances in dire need of maintenance, there is the sense that her labour exists as a form of healing spiritual dialogue with the encountered space. Polishing a picture of the Virgin Mary on her bedpost, her voiceover commentary emphasises the importance of inter-familiarity with new places. 'Go slowly through the house', she counsels herself, 'be polite. Introduce yourself, so it can introduce itself to you.' Like Liz, Frances is endowed with special significance in the tourist space through a form of religious anointing. The Virgin Mary in this film is very much connected with the Italian milieu Frances inhabits, appearing on pendants around necks, on pictures at grocery stores and idolised in festivals. The image of the Virgin Mary literally watches over the female protagonist during her time at the villa, her presence contributing to an 'internal juggling' within Frances as she struggles to come to terms with the role of Roman Catholicism in her life, despite identifying as 'a fallen away Methodist'. 'To my surprise I have become friendly with Mary,' Frances muses. 'I think it started the night she stood by me through the storm knowing full well I'm not a Catholic. Yet somehow she seems more like Mary my favourite aunt than Santa Maria. Aunt Mary is everywhere, her calm presence assuring us that all things will go on as they have before.'

The acquisition of land and property in the visited countries occurs as a result of divine right and is portrayed as a necessary step in the heroine's transcendence of the melancholic state as the tourist space comes to operate as an extension of the self. The right to command authority in space is not typical of the female position, with feminist phenomenologists, including Vivian Sobchack (2004) and Iris Marion Young (2005), having pointed to the relationship between restricted feminine comportment and an inability to command mastery over space. This extension of white female melancholy however, in allowing for a certain porousness between female corporeality and

Figure 1.2 The Virgin Mary presides over Frances as she learns valuable life lessons in *Under the Tuscan Sun*.

the tourist zone, is entirely consistent with the privileges of a white phenomenology that organises the world in its own image. Sara Ahmed, in an article aiming to explore the relationship between corporeality and white hegemony, suggests that white bodies have an ability to extend into space that is not enjoyed by those marked as non-white. In inheriting whiteness, Ahmed suggests, one also inherits an orientation that puts 'styles, capacities, aspirations, techniques and habits' into reach (2007: 154). In noting that white bodies exhibit a peculiar comfort in space, Ahmed declares that 'to be comfortable is to be so at ease with one's environment that it is hard to distinguish where one's body ends and the world begins' (158). In *Eat Pray Love* and *Under the Tuscan Sun*, the white body's extension into space is portrayed as a feminist act. Frances' acquisition of the Tuscan villa after her husband Tom purchases her share of their San Francisco home goes far beyond a simple realignment of woman with the domestic. The remodelling of the house allows Frances to unleash her creative capacity and thus remodel her life, recalling Virginia Woolf's influential thesis articulating the need for both a literal and symbolic space for female creatives looking to distinguish themselves in patriarchal society. In a review of *Eat Pray Love* in fact, *The Sunday Times* declared the novel 'a modern day *Room of One's Own*'.[8]

REFIGURING CONSUMPTION AND TRANSFORMATION

The emphasised specialness of the heroine in these texts is additionally informed by the discourses circulating in and around products of the

Hollywood 'dream factory', given that the star system relies upon the notion that its key players are uniquely special. Julia Roberts and Diane Lane, both high-profile leading ladies who have made regular appearances in the romance genre, are here utilised to lend Hollywood weight to this gendered ideological critique of US value systems. Yet they also serve as softening forces due to the individualising nature of social commentary to be found in popular film. For instance, while the tourism trope allows for an elision between the self and the origin of the self, discontent with the US environment is to a degree filtered through the shifting prisms of the protagonist's melancholic state as she undertakes both her literal and metaphoric narrative journey. The use of the religious trope to mark out the protagonist's exceptionality is however granted certain credence if one considers Chris Rojek's thesis that stars have replaced religious figures as icons of worship in contemporary secular society. Rojek notes the similarities between religious and celebrity worship, pointing out that 'magic is often associated with celebrities, and powers of healing and second sight are frequently attributed to them' (2007: 172). In the Hollywood travel romance, the heroine occupies a dual role as both worshipper of religious iconography and a figure worthy of attraction and admiration in her own right because of the actress's star image. The celebrity individual is thus utilised in her capacity to reignite interest in religious values that are perceived as being in danger in the US and mobilised as an individual capable of espousing her newfound value systems on the global stage. These films demonstrate an ambiguity in their approach to the ideological role of both cinema and celebrity in sustaining the values of neoliberal femininity. This is especially evident in relation to the emphasis on consumer capitalism, which in these films is cast in opposition to 'authentic' religious values, and is fundamental to the appeal of a star as an icon of personal and financial success. The travel romance engages in both self-reflexivity as to the role of the star and cinematic vehicle as Hollywood product, and a disavowal of the text and star commodity as part of that same Hollywood machine. When Liz upon her sojourn to India declares that God dwells within her, she first distances herself from an inauthentic spectacle of religion as exemplified through Hollywood star performance, claiming that she is not like Ingrid Bergman in *The Bells of St Mary's* (Leo McCarey, 1945). Bergman as a nun, it is implied, is too glamorous, too perfect, and ultimately deemed too inauthentic to be believable as a 'spiritual person'. Bergman's performance is made possible by a costumed decoration of the self, the exterior, while Liz has learned, as a result of consuming the philosophies of her visited countries, that God dwells in the interior.

This is an important point as Roberts' star text is inextricably linked with contemporary popular culture's 'makeover paradigm', which requires its participants to address the flaws in their lives via the alteration of appearances through conspicuous consumption (Gill 2007: 156). The hugely popular Julia

Roberts vehicle *Pretty Woman* (Garry Marshall, 1990), the story of a prostitute whose inner worth and capacity for romantic love is recognised after a wealthy client provides her with first-class accommodation and a designer wardrobe, provides an ideal model of neoliberal femininity through its protagonist Vivian. As Hilary Radner explains, Vivian's 'capital' resides primarily in the festishisation of her body and her ability to look good in designer clothing (1993: 67). The Hollywood travel romance does of course provide a makeover narrative of sorts, but requires forms of consumption that incorporate elements of the tourist space into the self to create the fantasy of the liberating, symbiotic bond between person and place. The makeover process works from the inside out rather than the outside in, and in doing so must distance itself from the type of makeover that promises empowerment as resultant from developing the body as spectacle. *Eat Pray Love*, like *Pretty Woman*, contains a Julia Roberts shopping scene. This scene, however, does not take place amongst the designer boutiques of Rodeo Drive, and Richard Gere is not on hand with his credit card to survey any glamorous transformation. Instead, Roberts' expedition to buy new jeans in Naples lies in both diegetic and extra-diegetic defiance of her previous role as both object of desire for the male gaze and the gaze of the crowd. Negra argues of the tourist film that it often explores the female protagonist's problematic relationship to her corporeality, with the texts establishing a 'contrast between the US as a site of body dysfunction and Europe as a place in which women enjoy an easy, settled relationship to food' (2001: 95). Declaring that she is 'tired of counting every calorie' so she knows 'exactly how much self-loathing to take into the shower', Roberts' character, Liz, takes her new friend Sofi (Tuva Novotny) to buy bigger jeans. This is to celebrate their newfound liberation, made possible by the conquering of an existential inertia through their status as mobile tourists who have subsequently adopted Italian philosophies through the consumption of national cuisine. In this segment, a long struggle with a zipper is cross-cut with images of pubgoers watching an Italian soccer game in which a skilled player is approaching the goal line. Corporeal expansion here, then, is associated with deft mobility through space; something normally reserved for masculine bodies and made possible for Liz only by playing the Italian game.

Both the patriarchal association of women with the corporeal and irrational, and the focus on bodily maintenance and discipline required of neoliberal femininities, seem to be disregarded in travel romances featuring middle-aged protagonists. The body does not constitute an obstacle, as coming to grant the body its wants and needs allows for a romanticised disentanglement of the corporeal from the nexus of power relations in which it has previously been caught up. Furthermore, this understanding of the body allows for the successful union of body with spirit, and the subsequent understanding of the body and mind as always interconnected with others, albeit on fantasised terms of equality. The travel romance thus engages in a utopian form of corporeal feminism, which Elizabeth Grosz articulates must reject the mind/body binary opposition, while developing both a phenomenological understanding of the corporeal and the lived body as cultural product (1994: 20–3). In these films however, this understanding must remain focused on the white American female of privileged economic status. The feminist reclamation of the body in *Eat Pray Love* allows for a renegotiation of the Julia Roberts star image from a glamorous consumer to an everyday woman who sometimes needs to shop for bigger jeans. This self-reflexive deviation from her Hollywood image as a young and beautiful ingénue has subsequently allowed Roberts to renegotiate her star persona in middle age and take on more 'serious', less glamorous roles designed to showcase her capabilities as an actress. Roberts was nominated for an Academy Award for her turn as Barbara Fordham, a woman struggling to keep her chaotic family together in *August: Osage County* (John Wells, 2013), and appeared as doctor and HIV researcher Dr Emma Brookner in the highly acclaimed television drama *The Normal Heart* (2014), helmed by *Eat Pray Love* director Ryan Murphy. The 'authenticity' of the Italian setting allows for a glimpse into the 'authentic' Roberts,[9] her role as Vivian the upwardly mobile prostitute recast as a performance not unlike Ingrid Bergman's as a nun.

Unlike Roberts, Diane Lane's performance in *Under the Tuscan Sun* does not allude to her past cinematic appearances and in fact two more roles followed as a melancholy divorcée in *Must Love Dogs* (Gary David Goldberg, 2005) and *Nights in Rodanthe* (George C. Wolfe, 2008). Like *Eat Pray Love*, however, *Under the Tuscan Sun* chooses to distance itself from promises of fulfilment as arising from conspicuous consumption facilitating the decoration of the self. After Frances is swept off her feet in Positano by a charming Italian named Marcello (Raoul Bova), she undergoes a physical transformation in opting for a voluminous blow-dry and white dress with a cinched waist for their next meeting. Unlike the makeover narratives seen in films of a similar genre – for instance *Maid in Manhattan* (Wayne Wang, 2002) or the aforementioned *Pretty Woman* – Frances' makeover concludes with romantic disappointment. Marcello, instead of learning to see Frances as the object of his romantic destiny upon witnessing her transformation, has already moved on with another woman. In contemporary variants of the Hollywood travel romance, female protagonists rarely encounter the potential for lasting love with local inhabitants of the tourist space, so dependent is the formula on the heroine's elevated hierarchical position as a result of her whiteness and projection of melancholy. Furthermore, the nostalgic element to the tourist zone, which in its inertia facilitates the protagonist's movement, guarantees that the heroine and any potential love interest are unable to coexist on the same temporal plane. 'I'm sorry that you're hurt but what did you expect?' Marcello

Figure 1.3 Katherine re-enacts her favourite Fellini scene in *Under the Tuscan Sun*.

asks Frances. 'We were never able to get together again even though we tried. These things must come naturally.'

Under the Tuscan Sun frequently pays homage to Federico Fellini's 1960 classic *La Dolce Vita* throughout the narrative. In polarising the diegetic material relating to *La Dolce Vita* with the natural, communal representation of Tuscany, this travel romance can distance its idealised lifestyle values from those based around consumerism, casual sex and female spectacle as employed in Fellini's film. Frances' British friend Katherine (Lindsay Duncan) becomes the embodiment of nostalgia for Italy's cinematic past, constructing her appearance with recourse to Fellini's heroines in her favouring of vibrant garments, long blonde locks stylised into waves, and dramatic, sweeping hats. While Katherine helps Frances acclimatise to her new environment, even suggesting that she buy the villa and indulge her 'terrible idea', it soon becomes evident that she utilises Italy as a space for indulging her own narcissism rather than adopting the philosophies of Tuscany to facilitate human connection as Frances does. Katherine informs Frances that Fellini once told her to live life spherically, in many different directions, while retaining a childish enthusiasm to ensure that good things come her way. Katherine uses this advice to live life to excess, such as by having her portrait painted by her young artist lover while draped in nothing but furs. While Frances eventually finds happiness, Katherine's final appearance sees her drunkenly swaying in a fountain in a melancholic parody of the iconic scene featuring actress Silvia (Anita Ekberg) in *La Dolce Vita*.

Katherine, while a sympathetic character and close friend to Frances, harbours separate values more akin to those of Marcello, whose name references *La Dolce Vita*'s lead actor Marcello Mastroianni. These characters exist in a realm of transient fantasy for Frances, operating in parallel to the film's construction of an authentic reality. While Frances will move forward from her existential crisis, Katherine will remain locked in melancholic temporal suspension, her unattainable dreams represented by her interpretation of *La Dolce Vita*, with the values held by the superficial characters in the film sitting uncomfortably close to those Frances has left behind in the US.

PROBLEMATISING BENEVOLENT FEMINISM

Under the Tuscan Sun and *Eat Pray Love* may attempt to soften social commentary with recourse to religion and the plight of the female individual in neoliberal America, but these texts are also dependent on the cult of celebrity, and indeed the politicisation of celebrity, to tell their stories. As David P. Marshall points out, the celebrity brand is not utilised merely to promote the entertainment vehicles in which these individuals appear, but also operate as 'channels' through which political, economic, and cultural occurrences are understood (Marshall 1997: 6). Audiences utilise these celebrated individuals to forge and navigate their own identities amidst complex social terrain, while stars themselves often capitalise on their branded image to effect political expression and campaign for change. The religious discourse and iconography permeating these films thus resonates with a media culture that frames celebrity political intervention and activism in terms of Christian mythology, with stars such as Bono and Angelina Jolie framed through a salvation rhetoric that Spring-Serenity Duvall argues recalls the rhetorical framing of Christian missionaries prior to European colonisation (2009: 92). *Eat Pray Love* provides an interesting case study through which to emphasise this point not only by the choice of female star, Julia Roberts, but also through the celebrity image of the film's executive producer, Brad Pitt, founder of Plan B Entertainment. Pitt, one of Hollywood's most popular actors since the early 1990s, has become increasingly well known as one of the entertainment industry's leading political campaigners in the US. This is both as a result of his high-profile former relationship with Jolie, a United Nations Special Envoy with whom Pitt created a charitable foundation dedicated to investing funds in global humanitarian efforts, but also his interest in creating sustainable housing in the wake of Hurricane Katrina, an issue that led him into talks with President Barack Obama. Roberts, while perhaps not holding a philanthropic profile to rival Pitt, has also aligned herself with political causes having been involved with Gucci's Chime for Change programme, aiming to promote global female empowerment, as well as Extraordinary Moms, an initiative aimed at encouraging mothers to campaign for political change to ensure a better world for their children. The latter campaign saw Roberts chosen to interview then Secretary of State Hillary Clinton. These elements of the star personas associated with *Eat Pray Love* are critical given that this Hollywood travel romance requires its protagonist to 'give back' to the community that has worked to alleviate her melancholic state, thus signifying in relation to these celebrities' philanthropic efforts aligned with the political left in the US. This text thus provides a powerful ideological vehicle that perpetuates problematic discourses associated with celebrity humanitarianism, while strengthening the 'altruistic' celebrity brands of both Pitt and Roberts. In the film, Liz encounters a young Indian girl named Tulsi (Rushita Singh) who expresses her unhappiness at being forced into an arranged marriage by her parents, before meeting a Balinese woman Wayan (Christine Hakim), who has lost all her assets in a divorce. Liz's sympathy for this woman's plight results in her decision to organise friends around the globe to contribute money in order to help purchase a house for Wayan and her young daughter, Tutti (Anakia Lapae). As Liz reflects upon her journey, she muses that 'sometimes when you set out in the world to help yourself, you end up helping tutti', which, as coincidence would have it, is not only the name of Wayan's daughter but also the Italian word for everybody. Frances in *Under the Tuscan Sun*, after jokingly describing herself as 'the patron saint of horny teenagers', is rewarded with romantic love after she sets out to help a young couple in their relationship despite the girl's father expressing displeasure with his daughter's choice of romantic partner, a Polish migrant worker employed to renovate the villa.

The acts of generosity carried out by these female tourists, played by high-profile Hollywood stars, work to transform how communities view the American identity of these travellers abroad. Their value systems gradually transform from those favoured by their home country, in which an upwardly mobile lifestyle built upon economic privilege and conspicuous consumption is fundamental to personal success, to an ethos promising fulfilment through acts of care and kindness towards those society refuses to value. This transformation, while reliant on essentialist notions of women as harbouring a heightened capacity to nurture, is presented as the ultimate in feminist empowerment for the diegetic heroine, while also linking the capacity of Hollywood stars to act on the global stage to a perceived uniqueness and specialness, sanctioned in these texts via a process of divine intervention. *Eat Pray Love* presents gendered oppression as something shared by both the protagonist and the women she decides to help, despite the therapeutic capabilities of the tourist space, rather than presenting the American heroine as enjoying greater social freedoms. The protagonist's demarcation as exceptional, predicated as this is upon her race as well as country of origin, is key to her ability to reap therapeutic rewards. The protagonist therefore has a duty to recognise the exceptionality and specialness of those she wishes to help, so that they too are able enrich their lives through this supposedly symbiotic arrangement. The ideological drive of *Eat Pray Love* can perhaps best be summed up by Liz's monologue at the film's opening in which she describes the experiences of a psychologist friend who was asked to counsel a group of Cambodian refugees newly arrived in the US. While her friend displayed initial reluctance, uncertain as to whether she would be able to relate to these people's suffering, given their experiences of genocide and starvation, she soon found that all the women in the group wanted to talk about were their forlorn love lives. What this passage demonstrates is the inherent danger in these filmic narratives that present romantic fantasies built upon affective, symbiotic bonds between female traveller and encountered space. Because India and Bali operate as extensions of Liz's melancholia and because these oppressed women are seen through the lens of the white woman's view, their predicaments can really signify only in terms of similarity to what Liz sees as traumatic events from her own past – unhappy marriage or social exclusion as a result of divorce. For instance, witnessing Tulsi's wedding prompts a flashback for Liz as she recalls her own nuptials to Stephen. 'Funny thing about weddings', Liz's Texan friend subsequently muses, 'you end up thinking about yourself'. The film elevates female bonding as a source of healing for the American female while simultaneously disavowing the position of power and privilege occupied by the affluent protagonist. Oppression must be 'shared', meaning that forms the white woman cannot relate to through her own experience are elided in the text.

CONCLUSION

In the novel upon which the film *Eat Pray Love* is based, author Elizabeth Gilbert expresses her pleasure that the countries she wishes to travel to all begin with the letter 'I' – 'a fairly auspicious sign' she says 'for a voyage of self-discovery'. Indeed, the appeal of these Hollywood travel romances lies in the fact that these exotic lands operate as empowering, affective extensions of the melancholic white self, with the pseudo-symbiotic fusion of person and place allowing for a philosophical and spiritual 'transcendence' over neoliberal feminism's consumer-capitalist logic. Despite disavowing the position of privilege occupied by the female protagonist, the emphasis on gender works to obfuscate how engagement with foreign spaces is dependent on the cultural prestige afforded to the creative melancholic and middle-class whiteness, and how these texts in fact operate more broadly as fantasies of national rehabilitation for the United States. The films thus ultimately engage in a reimagining of the systems that the stories aim to critique through tales of middle-aged women seeking a feminist rediscovery of the self. These systems, of course, hold a high degree of political and cultural currency, and these texts at the extra-diegetic levels of production, marketing and commercial tie-ins are certainly embedded within them. Yet the fantasies are powerful ones, and help illuminate a US political environment currently negotiating not only the fluctuations of a neoliberal system, but also the branding of its own identity. When presented with stories about individuals negotiating their own pathways through these fluctuations, it is important to examine not only whose story is being told, but which social ideologies are perpetuated and challenged through a given protagonist's interactions with other characters in these stories. *Eat Pray Love*, as a highly problematic variant of the travel romance subgenre, aids in illuminating the ideologically questionable notions that a typical European travel romance like *Under the Tuscan Sun* is built upon. In these texts, the trope of feminist empowerment functions as a masquerade, with the growth of an already racially, economically and nationally empowered group dependent on the refusal to allow the growth of those aiding them in their journeys.

NOTES

1. Goldberg argues in *The Threat of Race* that the erasure of racial categories in daily social life in favour of an ideology of racelessness has resulted in relegating racism either to an attitude exhibited by the most bigoted, or to those who invoke race as a potential rationale when drawing attention to injustices (2009: 360).
2. Although an extended analysis is beyond the scope of this chapter, it is important to note that there is also a variation of the Hollywood tourist romance that aims to appeal to the teen market as exemplified by the popular 2005 film *The Sisterhood of the Travelling Pants*. Directed by Ken Kwapis and based on a novel of the same title by Ann Brashares (2001), this feature focuses on the journeys of four teenage girls whose shared connection is symbolised by the fact that they can all miraculously fit into the same pair of jeans. By individually writing about their travel experiences whilst wearing these jeans, the teens are more able to successfully navigate their journeys into womanhood. In contrast, *The Best Exotic Marigold Hotel* (John Madden, 2011) is a recent, highly commercially successful travel film exploring the lives of white British citizens in their sixties and seventies as they navigate the challenges of advancing age while at a retirement home in India. A sequel to the film, *The Second Best Exotic Marigold Hotel*, was released in 2015.
3. Utilising the work of Leslie W. Rabine, McRobbie points out that while the male presence is largely absent in images aiming to sell contemporary fashions to women, this presence is substituted by the fashion item as fetish object, ultimately reestablishing gender hierarchies despite the promise of liberation from these norms within the image.
4. Jennifer Guglielmo explores the issue of Italian whiteness in both the Italian and US context in the edited collection *Are Italians White? How Race is Made in America*. She notes the hierarchy of whiteness in Italy in discussing the historical role of the south as dark racial Other to the north (2003: 9), while also examining the ambivalent state of whiteness that the Italian diaspora inhabited upon arrival in the US. While Guglielmo states that according to the law Italians were white in that they could vote and own land, she also points out that racial discrimination occurred through segregation practices in public

institutions and through racist images of Italian people in the popular culture of the time (11).

5. Chomsky notes that governmental support, or lack thereof, for the unpopular Iraq war played a key role in US Secretary of Defense Donald Rumsfeld's distinction between Old Europe and New Europe. Old Europe, Chomsky states, consisted of those governments that refused to support the invasion, whereas New Europe consisted of nations that supported George Bush and Tony Blair despite the will of their population majorities (2010: 43). In Spain, Chomsky points out, polls at the time indicated support for the war was at a mere 2 per cent (44).
6. Maziar Peihani outlines these causes as well as their national and international impact in "The global financial crisis of 2008: an analysis of contributing trends, policies and failures" in *Banking & Finance Law Review* 27:3 (2012).
7. An interesting example of a character exhibiting a commercialist, and thus impure, rationale for visiting Italy occurs in *Letters to Juliet*. In this film, Gael García Bernal plays Sophie's love interest Victor, an immigrant to New York who harbours dreams of opening a successful Italian restaurant in the city. Victor's belief in the validity of the American dream results in him privileging work over his relationship with Sophie, who eventually finds love in Florence with an English traveller mourning the loss of his parents. Victor's fetishising of Italian culture is demonstrated through a hyperbolic performance of emotional excess that Sophie eventually learns to decode as inauthentic. The Tuscan countryside also provides the backdrop for the 2010 Abbas Kiarostami film *Certified Copy* starring Juliette Binoche, which explores questions relating to the authentic and inauthentic in romance, language, and art.
8. As noted on the book jacket of Elizabeth Gilbert's 2006 Penguin edition of *Eat, Pray, Love: One Woman's Search for Everything across Italy, India and Indonesia*.
9. Richard Dyer explains that the search for the authentic personality of the star constitutes an enduring aspect of our fascination with celebrity, in *Stars* (1998: 20).

CHAPTER 2

'Hoist the Colours!' Framing Feminism through Charismatic White Leadership in the Fantasy Blockbuster

Observable within the spate of fantasy films emerging over the past decade is a genesis of the melancholic white female figure, where an initial state of gendered despair and powerlessness is overcome through the simultaneous discovery of feminism and an innate leadership charisma that allows the heroine to restore social cohesion to the fantasy zone. This chapter analyses the characters of Elizabeth Swann and Alice Kingsleigh, the respective female protagonists of the *Pirates of the Caribbean* franchise[1] (Gore Verbinski, 2003; 2006; 2007) and Tim Burton's 2010 interpretation of Lewis Carroll's *Alice in Wonderland*. Burton's film was followed in 2016 by the James Bobin-directed sequel *Alice through the Looking Glass*, which has proven to be markedly less popular than its predecessor, yet utilises similar tropes that I will refer to throughout this analysis.

In these films, the melancholic state symbolises the potential for feminist empowerment in that it offers the white heroine the creative tools through which to engage in a reimagining of the world around her and her allocated role within it. The fantasy universe thus becomes a utopian space where the heroine can shed the restrictions of bourgeois white patriarchy and engage in modes of performance that allow her to experiment not only with gender roles, but the signifiers of her privileged race and class identity as well. These stories, in allowing their heroines to escape from aristocratic British societies in the eighteenth and nineteenth centuries, offer liberal Hollywood conceptualisations of England's past that are as much fantasy as the creative playgrounds the protagonists journey toward. The fantasy films, however, may offer a contemporary, popular means of indulging in forms of 'imperial nostalgia' (Rosaldo 1989) through the mobilisation of a proto-feminist aristocratic heroine whose relationship with colonial rule, presented as indomitably patriarchal in nature, is defined as ambivalent based on her biological sex and attitude towards gendered conditioning. Such heroines may appeal to us in that the transcendence of melancholia within their storylines provides a 'working through' of the contradictions inherent in postfeminist discourse, particularly as it operates in the contemporary Anglo-American context. The texts construct a knowing spectator, historically removed from the films' representations of female experience at the height of British imperialism and global power. Yet despite their historical setting, the texts are identifiable as culturally specific products of the postfeminist era due to narratives that frame feminism as an elusive, yet tangible reality to be 'discovered' through the modification of bodily comportment and relationship to space. Created in a contemporary social environment that has long perceived itself as beyond the need for political collective action to redress either race or gender discrimination, these Hollywood blockbusters can employ a sense of self-reflexivity and irony in their diegetic treatment of character interaction as informed by race and gender stereotyping. Yet the texts validate forms of colonial discourse through stories that align feminist empowerment with social control, with the ability to organise and lead groups of previously helpless people to victory in battle operating as a metaphor for personal growth in these coming-of-age tales.

Both *The Pirates of the Caribbean* franchise and *Alice in Wonderland* have been huge commercial successes, with *Pirates* to date having grossed over four billion US dollars at the box office and the first *Alice* film taking just over one billion dollars. The audience response to these big budget action-adventure spectacles may be attributed to several factors, including the storylines featuring heroic quests into magical worlds, lavish special effects, the popularity of star Johnny Depp, as well as director Tim Burton in the case of *Alice*, and the appeal of the proto-feminist heroines played by Knightley and Wasikowska, who were relative newcomers to the Hollywood scene at the time of the initial release of the films. Both Elizabeth and Alice are portrayed as troubled, melancholic fantasists – young women who have dreamed since childhood of escape from the boredom of their everyday lived realities and the restrictions placed upon them because of their gender. Like Judy Garland's Dorothy in the celebrated MGM musical *The Wizard of Oz* (Victor Fleming, 1939) or Manuela in *The Pirate* (Vincente Minnelli, 1948), who operate as cinematic precursors to these characters, the colourful utopian spaces that Elizabeth and Alice dream of are present within the subconscious and yet frustratingly beyond the parameters of mundane white civilisation. As young women on the verge of marriage to partners not of their choosing, these dreams seem in danger of imminent death as the last vestiges of childhood threaten to slip away. In both films, an encounter with the fantasy world made real offers an escape from the confining future role of aristocratic wife and mother. In the *Pirates of the Caribbean* franchise, which is loosely based on a Disneyland theme park ride, Elizabeth's adventures with the pirates on the high seas allow her to embrace an unruly lifestyle based upon the immediate gratification of desire, all the while distancing herself from an affluent white femininity that she grows to regard as performative and restrictive. While initially also experiencing sexism in the pirate world, Elizabeth finally earns the respect of the pirates after being elected King of the Brethren Court. As leader, she is able to protect the pirates' way of life by successfully leading her followers into battle against the villainous Lord Cutler Beckett (Tom Hollander) and the East India Trading Company. Through her engagement with piracy, Elizabeth transcends previously imposed physical limitations restricting her right to eat, exercise and travel, and as such is eventually able to re-signify her body in accordance with an active warrior ideal, thus transitioning from her previous role as decorative object.

Tim Burton's *Alice in Wonderland* demonstrates little resemblance to the Carroll classic, providing an innovative take on the original tale in envisioning a nineteen-year-old Alice haunted by her childhood visit to the fantastic realm of Underland. In this story, Alice's fall down the rabbit hole creates a suspension in the temporality of the 'real', allowing her to chart her own coming-of-age through the successful navigation of the fantasy zone. This nation is dependent upon Alice's prophesised arrival to ensure the happiness of its residents who are currently suffering under the cruel dictatorship of the tyrannical Red Queen (Helena Bonham Carter). Instead of having to abide by the rules set out for her in Victorian England, Alice learns to impose her own rules upon Underland and as such finds the courage to reject her suitor and continue her late father's work in proposing the expansion of trade routes into China. Like Elizabeth Swann, Alice's journey to empowerment is signified through her ability to demonstrate leadership in a foreign space, in this case by bearing arms to slay the Red Queen's jabberwocky and restore the White Queen (Anne Hathaway) to the throne. *Alice Through the Looking Glass* sees its heroine return to Underland upon learning that her share in her father's business is in jeopardy and that she may have to give up on her dreams of achieving 'the impossible' by parting with her beloved ship *The Wonder*. After entering Underland, Alice learns that to restore her despondent friend the Hatter (Johnny Depp) back to full health, she must go back in time and save his family from the wrath of the Red Queen. Alice's nemesis in the sequel is in fact Time itself, who is personified by Sacha Baron Cohen and is indicative of both her imperilled relationship to the constraints of gendered time and to Underland's troubled history of bloodshed and injustice, a fixed and shameful national past that seemingly cannot be changed. The *Pirates of the Caribbean* and the *Alice in Wonderland* films, in their distinction between an aristocratic white femininity as defined through the British heritage setting and feminist liberation as discoverable through interventions within the fantasy space, present strikingly similar examples of melancholic white womanhood in the fantasy genre.

FANTASY, FEMINISM AND WHITENESS

Hollywood fantasy film has experienced an astounding resurgence in popularity with cinematic audiences in the new millennium. Franchises including *The Lord of the Rings* (Peter Jackson, 2001, 2002, 2003) and the *Harry Potter* series have grossed billions of dollars at the box office, while associated tie-in merchandising consisting of action figures and video games amongst other paraphernalia has helped generate millions more. The renewed popularity of fantasy film has led to a surge in academic interest in fantasy as a genre, despite the difficulties involved in defining the requisite generic elements. David Butler in *Fantasy Cinema: Impossible Worlds on Screen* writes that the term 'fantasy' has been inconsistently applied within academia, film criticism and industry alike (2009: 16), hypothesising that the genre's exclusion from critical analysis in the past may be partially due to the fact that the label can be applied to such a wide variety of films (18).[2] Katherine A. Fowkes, in noting the prevalence of genre hybridity within the fantasy canon, concedes that generic boundaries are often not firmly set. Many fantasy films, she points out, demonstrate a close relationship with the science fiction and horror genres, while popular fantasy text *The Wizard of Oz* is recognisable as a musical and Ron Howard's mermaid tale *Splash* (1984) adheres to the conventions of both fantasy and romantic comedy (2010: 2). While Fowkes notes that fantasy film may specify itself through the appearance of specific iconography, including wizards, crystal balls and fairies (13), she hypothesises that in most of these texts, there exists a clear break between what the audience is to understand as the reference world of the 'real' and a magical alternate universe that 'discourages a solely psychological interpretation' of its existence (5–6). As such, fantasy cinema often contains the theme of escapism within the diegesis, with many films dramatising coming-of-age tales where the journey or quest within the fantasy space serves metaphorically in charting the personal growth of a young protagonist (Fowkes 2010: 9). While Fowkes' thesis regarding a requisite rupture between real and fantastic spaces on screen is not infallible – *The Lord of the Rings*, an important series in the filmic and literary fantasy canon, takes place entirely in the enchanted realm of Middle Earth – a vast number of fantasy films do indeed conform to the model, including *The Pirates of the Caribbean* and *Alice in Wonderland*.

It is not only the arguably progressive role these texts provide for contemporary feminism that interests me here, but also how these texts engage in this ideological work with recourse to white hegemonic power structures, despite the presence of a supposedly ahistorical, fantasy space. For an audience, analysing the representation of social inequalities predicated upon race, class and gender differences within fantasy cinema, and the relationship between these images and the cultures that produce them is perhaps somewhat difficult given the genre's tenuous connection to everyday lived realities. This dislocation manifests itself not only in the form of magical characters and events that are understood as impossible within the rules and laws that govern our world, but also through the spatial and temporal dislocation of fantasy zones from historical actualities. Within these films, the protagonists discover the real existence of magical worlds that previously only operated within the realm of imagination. While *Alice* clearly distinguishes boundaries between England and Wonderland, *Pirates of the Caribbean* capitalises on the ever-present threat the pirates pose to the residents of Port Royal through emphasising permeability between the two worlds. This trope helps create a more rigid distinction between an oppressive reality that perpetuates the melancholic state and the fantasy zone where feminist empowerment, and thus the cure, lie in wait to be discovered. This notion of feminism as both lost and yet discoverable identifies these texts as peculiarly postfeminist fantasies. For instance, while Dorothy in *The Wizard of Oz* seeks a more interesting and colourful world in her fantasy journey, she does not aspire to rule or lead the people within the discovered space in the way that Elizabeth and Alice learn to.

The *Pirates* and *Alice* films are firmly influenced by second-wave feminist rhetoric and associated discourses in relation to what constitutes empowerment. It is this relationship with the extra-diegetic historical and cultural transitions of the real that necessitate the inclusion of fantasy film in critical scholarship operating at the intersection between film and cultural studies. David Butler, discussing the common perception of fantasy as serving purely an escapist function with little meaningful social relevance (2009: 3), notes that while fantasy can provide 'idealistic solutions' to societal problems, it can also play a more progressive role in encouraging its audiences to re-engage with the familiar world in a more critical manner (99). Similarly, Victor Burgin, James Donald and Cora Kaplan's 1986 edited collection *Formations of Fantasy*, argues that fantasy creates a space for the articulation of subjectivities and political/ideological perspectives that would otherwise be silenced, if coded as 'real'. Our pleasure in these texts is brought about through the recognition of certain ideologies pertaining to the classification of bodies within everyday life, and through our understanding of such texts as allegories and fables for our times. Nevertheless, the genre does not have to engage with social oppression *directly* as the presence of the fantastic always guarantees some level of distance from the various forms of power that structure our lives. Furthermore, fantasy allows its audiences to map a variety of experiences of injustice and oppression onto stories that are open to broad interpretation. Francis Pheasant-Kelly, discussing the appeal of *The Lord of the Rings* films for a post 9/11 audience, suggests that although J. R. R. Tolkien alluded to Nazism in his portrayal of the wizard Saruman's villainous regime in his 1950s' novels, contemporary Western viewers are more likely to relate the ever-present danger of racialised boundary infiltration within the films with the threat of terrorism (2013: 26). Douglas Kellner, discussing the opening scene of *Pirates of the Caribbean: At World's End*, in which large numbers of people are hanged without trial for colluding with the pirates, identifies 'an obvious coding of pirates as terrorists and the established regime as oppressive and murderous' (2009: 163). Because *Pirates of the Caribbean* sympathises with persecuted outsiders, Kellner argues, it may be said to contain a 'subversive bent' (163).

While it is true that texts such as *The Lord of the Rings* and *Pirates of the Caribbean* have the potential to be read in a manner that is subversive and progressive with regard to the contemporary context, and while I will go on to argue that *Pirates* manages to destabilise white hegemonic power structures in ways that Burton's *Alice in Wonderland* never quite accomplishes, I also agree with Sue Kim in her critique of the problematic racial politics inherent in *The Lord of the Rings* films when she cautions against the urge to become overly selective in applying modern politics to the fantasy text. Kim notes that white semiology in *The Lord of the Rings* films is equated overwhelmingly with goodness and is mediated through English and Scandinavian cultural references, while darkness is identified as Southern and Eastern in origin and is aligned with the bestial and savage (2004: 875). Kim further states that the films are identifiable as products functioning within the logic of neoliberal global capitalism in that they both 'draw on and bury issues of race' (876), and cautions against reading for disruptive political potential at the expense of engaging more broadly with how and why racial ideological codings are utilised within the texts and in the larger cultural context. One could perhaps debate that *Pirates of the Caribbean* and *Alice in Wonderland/Through the Looking Glass* can engage in a greater degree of self-reflexivity in relation to views on contemporary race and gender, and indeed current global conflict, than Jackson's films given the lack of an historical textual referent in the case of the former and the lack of faithfulness to the source text in the instance of the latter. Yet in their construction of mythical pasts, these films also exhibit a nostalgic yearning for racialised, historical forms of international social control even as they present the rationale for an individual's intervention into a foreign zone as unmarked by national politics in the 'real' space of the protagonist's home.

This intervention is predicated upon the fulfilment of the character's destiny, and, in *Pirates of the Caribbean* and the *Alice in Wonderland* films, the simultaneous discovery of the heroine's long dormant feminist potential. J. E. Smyth, writing again on Jackson's *Lord of the Rings* films, queries whether the retreat into fantasy and analogy becomes a mode through which whites can maintain the viability of imperialist discourse, pointing out that the 'old empires' are valorised within the films through the sought-after wisdom of Gandalf the wizard (Ian McKellen) and the elves (2004: 20). Certainly, genres that deal in the fantastic are not devoid of racial allegory, for as Guerrero reminds us, science fiction, horror and fantasy are in fact dependent on defining the monster or outcast as 'different' and 'other' in familiar terms to drive their narratives forward (1993: 56–7). These definitions must be recognisable to the audience, but do not have to operate entirely in accordance with their historical contextualisation. These texts, in their representation of heroines whose progressiveness is dependent on regressive racial politics, engage in forms of what Rosaldo has termed 'imperialist nostalgia' in that they simultaneously mourn the passing of certain facets of imperial rule while concealing the role of whiteness in such forms of domination (1989: 108). 'Aristocracy' here on the one hand operates as ideological shorthand for an outdated whiteness in need of modification, but on the other naturalises the white woman's superiority and potential for leadership. To be aristocratic is to occupy the position of the ultimate white European ideal, or as Ghassan Hage puts it, to have 'a natural access to high civilisation' (2003: 50), with the aristocracy providing a continual source of fascination and debate in contemporary Anglo-American culture even as its members occupy different roles in relation to the national. However, in analysing these simultaneously progressive and regressive heroines in terms of their relationship with the always interconnected politics of gender, race and class, it is possible to begin to engage in an exploration of the currency of whiteness within postfeminist popular culture, rather than merely noting that whiteness operates as the default position for a typical postfeminist heroine.

ARISTOCRATIC FEMININITY: COSTUME, BODILY RESTRICTION AND MELANCHOLY

When the audience is first introduced to Elizabeth Swann and Alice Kingsleigh, these two young women in their late teens from aristocratic British families are both preparing for lavish social occasions that may potentially double as engagement ceremonies. Having to abide by the patriarchal dictates of the household, both daughters are expected to accept marriage to high-ranking gentlemen to ensure the continual association of their families with abundant wealth and privilege, while safeguarding the white, upper-class bloodline. Both women are associated with spectacle and hyper-visibility, and are required to perform socially for the public's gaze in accordance with idealised models of delicate and restrained bourgeois femininity. However, Elizabeth and Alice demonstrate a profound melancholia and unhappiness with their social situation, a state of affairs the films choose to represent primarily through the protagonists' discomfort with feminine fashion. Upon her father's return from London, Elizabeth is presented with a peach corset as a homecoming gift. As she is laced into the garment, Elizabeth grimaces, gasps and declares that 'women in London must have learned not to breathe!' Just prior to receiving a proposal from Commodore James Norrington (Jack Davenport) later in the evening, Elizabeth's corset causes her to faint and tumble over a cliff edge into the ocean, narrowly avoiding the rocks on the way down. It is this event that precipitates her first encounter with Captain Jack Sparrow (Johnny Depp), an infamous pirate of the high seas who saves Elizabeth from drowning and immediately knows that the corset caused the accident. As Antonija Primorac has pointed out, the corset frequently operates in contemporary historical drama as a signifier for feminine repression; she argues that the costume piece functions as a 'metaphorical cage' imprisoning the heroine's sexuality, desire, and agency (2012: 43). It is the encounter with Captain Jack and his alluring adventurous and transient lifestyle that therefore provides the key to the female protagonist's emancipation. Although Elizabeth concedes to her lady's maid that Commodore Norrington is 'a fine man, what any woman should dream of marrying', she secretly harbours an illicit crush on the blacksmith Will Turner (Orlando Bloom), whom she knows to be of pirate blood.

Alice Kingsleigh similarly expresses discontent with the gendered roles of Victorian England through her constant critique of the fashion choices supposedly embraced by young upper-class women. The film immediately sets up a generational opposition of values in an early sequence during which Alice and her mother Helen (Lindsay Duncan) travel in a small carriage to what – unbeknownst to Alice – will be her engagement celebration. The camera's tight framing captures Alice's bored and sullen expression as Helen declares her daughter to be improperly dressed. 'Who's to say what's proper?' Alice asks defiantly, declaring that she is against stockings before questioning the purpose and use value of corsets in proclaiming that 'a corset is like a codfish'. When Alice and her mother arrive at Lord and Lady Ascot's garden party, all the invited guests are uniformly dressed in pastel blues and whites, indicating their adherence to a strict social code that abhors expressions of individuality. The use of colour to indicate social conformity is a recognisable formal feature of director Tim Burton's work, with the block pastel colour scheme governing American suburbia in *Edward Scissorhands* (1990) foreshadowing the fear of difference that eventually leads to the exile of the protagonist, a creative outsider not unlike Alice.

Required to dance with Lord Hamish Ascot (Leo Bill), an uptight aristocrat chosen as a suitable marriage partner, Alice shares her queer vision of the male guests in dresses and the female in trousers, before wondering what it might be like to fly and thus presumably escape gender conventions altogether. Lord Hamish exhibits his preference for female passivity in informing his young bride-to-be that if she is ever in doubt as to whether her chosen conversational topic is appropriate, then it would be best to remain silent. In these fantasy films, costume changes in the supernatural realm thus have an

Figure 2.1 Alice faces the expectant gaze of the conformist crowd in *Alice in Wonderland*.

added significance. When women can wear trousers and thus run, jump, and most importantly fight, the costume change is automatically read as empowering because it shows the protagonist has been able to transcend the bodily limitations imposed on her in the real world. This play with gender roles operates as a postfeminist fantasy in speaking to contemporary constraints placed upon white, economically privileged young women, particularly in relation to the presentation of an ideally heteronormative feminine self and the associated intensified focus on corporeal discipline. The invocation of Time as an antagonist in *Alice through the Looking Glass* additionally speaks to Negra's argument that the postfeminist era characterises women's lives as marked by a fear of ageing prematurely and of potentially not reaching the milestones of marriage and motherhood. When Alice confronts her mother about selling shares in her father's trading company, Helen responds that everything she does is in Alice's best interests as 'time is running out', 'a sea captain is no job for a lady', and every woman must learn that 'you can't just make things however you want them to be'. Elizabeth and Alice's acts of cross-dressing, therefore, are also attempts to escape the female experience of having limited time in which to achieve one's goals. As Marjorie Garber has argued however, the appearance of cross-dressing characters can also indicate category crises existing beyond the realm of sex and gender, with resultant discomfort being displaced onto a figure already existing at the margins (1992: 17). In this manner, the films on the one hand speak to the gendered concerns of a female social group, engaging in a re-framing of 'feminism' and allowing for the fulfilment of thwarted wishes and desires. Yet these narrative depictions of nostalgic forms of social control are as dependent on the mobilisation of this liminal, cross-dressing and 'empowered' figure within the fantasy historical setting.

The utilisation of heritage tropes in *Pirates* and *Alice* constitutes somewhat of a twist to the way in which the heritage film usually circulates within postfeminist popular culture. As Antje Ascheid argues, period texts such as those based on the works of Jane Austen tend to operate in accordance with contemporary romantic comedy conventions. These films appeal to the postfeminist viewer, she suggests, in that they fetishise and exploit the British heritage setting to create historically distorted narratives that centre on the female protagonist's struggle for independence, emotional fulfilment and ultimately romance within a strict patriarchal environment (2006). As Roberta Garrett adds, films such as *Sense and Sensibility* (Ang Lee, 1995) and *Pride and Prejudice* (Joe Wright, 2005) 'have offered a feminist-inspired take on 19th century classics – foregrounding sisterly love, women's restrictive social conditions and plucky heroines valiantly resisting oppression' (2007: 131). Heritage cinema can thus entertain a postfeminist audience concerned with 'having it all', both professional and personal independence as well as romance, through films that dramatise these concerns while locating feminist struggle safely within the historical setting. While heritage costuming does indeed function as both metaphor and masquerade[3] for the postfeminist melancholic heroine in the fantasy blockbuster, working both to confine her to gendered social performance and to obscure her true desires and ambitions, it is the fantasy zone that offers her the independence and emotional fulfilment that the initial milieu will not and cannot provide. In keeping with the conventions of the heritage picture, female desire becomes the prime motivating factor that drives the narrative (Cook 1996: 77), yet romance with an idealised male does not here constitute the ultimate goal. In fact, the transgression of gender, race and class boundaries allowed for within the fantastic realm creates an atmosphere somewhat hostile to heteronormative romantic intentions as the female protagonist becomes increasingly dedicated to her political ambitions. In *Alice in Wonderland*, Alice's commitment to fulfilling her destiny of liberating the people of Underland takes precedence over all her social requirements in England, ultimately leading her to reject Lord Hamish's proposal of marriage. Though Elizabeth Swann and Will Turner do enter into a romantic relationship by the conclusion of the third *Pirates* film, Will's debt to a supernatural ghost ship, *The Flying Dutchman*, means the couple can only spend one day per year together. Elizabeth's purpose, following the pivotal role she plays in protecting the pirates from Lord Beckett's schemes, is ultimately one of social control. Because she literally possesses the heart of the *Dutchman*'s captain, she can exert control over the seas on which the ship travels. The heritage setting therefore does not constitute a world *within* which the heroine can achieve her desires, rather it operates as a historical fantasy built upon the extreme values of white bourgeois patriarchy. The heroine's escape from this construction of the past allows her to create an *alternative* feminist fantasy vision based upon a set of utopian social values that the supernatural world must learn to conform to.

Both Elizabeth and Alice are afflicted by emotions of grief and loss, as their dreams of being able to choose their respective futures seem unlikely to manifest because of their status as exchangeable objects on the marriage market. Nevertheless, because the fantastical space that will liberate them within the course of the narrative has been present in their subconscious for many years, their dreams are granted validity and possibility. The heroines are disenchanted with their social status not only because they find the feminine role constricting, but because they exist in a perpetual melancholic state, continually haunted by the possibility of a magical social realm that may offer them an alternative mode of being. Freud argues that the melancholic continues to identify with his or her lost object, with the loss of the object equating to a loss in the patient's sense of self (1917/2000). Elizabeth and Alice may be described as melancholic owing to the continual and encroaching presence of Underland and the pirate world within the psyche. The re-entry of the adult protagonists into the fantasy zone marks the beginning of their urgent struggle to free themselves from the mental tyranny of these lost places by discovering their hidden psychological and cultural meaning, as the heroines are forced literally to navigate their coming-of-age through journeying beyond the known world.

Furthermore, Freud articulates that despite often being unaware of the significance of this lost object, the melancholic will appear self-reproaching, demonstrating a pronounced lack of interest in the surrounding world as well as an inability to love (1997/2000: 283). Complaining about Alice's visual representation in the film, *News of the World* film critic Robbie Collin declared that Wasikowska's Alice 'is not a heroine – she looks like she's *on* heroin' (AAP 2010, original emphasis). Indeed, Alice does appear almost deathlike in pallor, with darkly rimmed eyes, a thin build and sullen demeanour that is reminiscent of the 1990s' 'heroin chic' fashion trend popularised by designers such as Calvin Klein and models like Kate Moss. It should be noted that director Tim Burton frequently employs a similar aesthetic, though primarily influenced by German Expressionism, to convey the sense of his protagonists as alienated outsiders, mere ghosts sleepwalking in societies that demand performances of them that they can never quite deliver. Within the film, the rationale provided for Alice's tired and wan appearance is her troubled sleep patterns. Ever since she was a small child, a recurring dream has plagued her about a place called Wonderland. Though her late father frequently indulged little Alice's nightly fantasies, reassuring her that all the best people are 'round the bend', she discovers the magical realm to be increasingly incongruous with the life she is expected to lead as she grows older in Victorian England.

Alice recognises femininity as a performance, exhibited primarily through her disdain for feminine clothing, yet she is expected to embrace the fashions that everybody else does. Prior to Lord Hamish's proposal, various guests at the garden party set out to frighten Alice into accepting the offer by reminding her that beauty does not last forever and that she could be in danger of ending up mad and alone like her Aunt Imogene (Frances de la Tour). After Alice confesses to Imogene that she may be going mad as she has just sighted a white rabbit in a waistcoat, her aunt declares that she won't be bothered with the matter as she is waiting for her royal fiancé who must 'tragically' renounce his throne to marry her. Wonderland is therefore not merely a fantastical space that Alice must learn to navigate; it also represents her only avenue of escape from a Victorian femininity that requires that she get married or risk insanity as a result of subsequent social alienation. Interestingly, *Alice through the Looking Glass* invokes this history of gendered madness in having the Ascots commit Alice to an institution after they discover her muttering about having to locate a time-travelling device called the chronosphere. At the bleak, shadowy and sterile institution, Alice is told by Dr Addison Bennett (Andrew Scott) that she is 'excitable, emotional and prone to fantasy', and therefore appears to have 'a textbook case of female hysteria'. The doctor's overly eager and physically aggressive approach to treating Alice, as well as the sounds of female patients shrieking off-screen, marks the medical centre as a patriarchal space where men can punish women for their deviation from gender norms. Furthermore, Dr Bennett's dishevelled appearance and the fact that viewers are likely to recognise the actor from his turn as the psychotic Moriarty in the BBC's popular *Sherlock* series (2010–), characterise the doctor (and the ideas that he represents) as considerably less sane than Alice. Here, the gendered history of madness and neuroses is invoked as a means of contemporary feminist critique. Alice is justifiably melancholic when she in England, but she is certainly not mad, and her escape from the institution back to Wonderland represents a key victory against entrenched sexism in her home country.

Like Alice, Elizabeth Swann in *Pirates of the Caribbean* is haunted by a fantastical space of alterity that simultaneously offers the prospect of feminist liberation. The film opens with a young Elizabeth accompanying Commodore Norrington, her father Governor Weatherby Swann (Jonathan Pryce) and Joshamee Gibbs (Kevin McNally) on a sailing expedition. While journeying, they come across a flaming ship and a boy clinging to debris in the surrounding waters. Elizabeth discovers that the boy, Will Turner, is wearing a gold pirate medallion and removes it from his possession to allow him a better chance of being taken in and cared for by her family. Although Elizabeth enthusiastically proclaims that it 'would be rather exciting to meet a pirate', the ship's crew do not share her opinion, with Norrington informing her that pirates are 'vile, dissolute' creatures who should all be hanged. Elizabeth is thus immediately set up as having liberal viewpoints at odds with the vast majority of Port Royal's British residents, as she sees pirates as exciting and interesting rather than dangerous, and because she protects Will, who is very likely to be a pirate's child. Following this prologue to the first film in the franchise, we are introduced to the adult Elizabeth in close-up as she awakens after having been startled by a dream. She then opens a drawer in her bedside cabinet and retrieves the pirate medallion, fixing it around her neck and gazing at her reflection in the mirror before her father enters and surprises her with the new corset. The encounter with the pirate world is simultaneously situated as an important moment in Elizabeth's past and as a fantasy that has accompanied her into adulthood. Like Alice, Elizabeth has dreams that consist of another world briefly encountered as a young child, and also like Alice, she is desperately unhappy performing the femininity required of her in the real world. Because these protagonists are identified as melancholic, they are represented as having a special *connection* with a fantastic space, whose inhabitants can be read as both queer and non-white. While this special connection allows these heroines to appropriate selected elements of the encountered fantasy culture, the control they are required to exert and the privileges they obtain within the magical space mean that they never completely abandon the advantages that come with being both white and upper class.

LIBERATION FROM WHITE HETERONORMATIVITY

In *Pirates of the Caribbean* and *Alice in Wonderland*, the protagonist's commitment to the political liberation of others is predicated upon postfeminist fantasies of corporeal liberation. These texts speak to a neoliberal postfeminist present in their framing of the affluent, white, female heterosexual body as hyper-spectacle, subject to the constant scrutinising gaze of the many, rather than the disciplinary male gaze alone. If, as Anita Harris argues, young, white, middle-class women bear the burden of achievement in neoliberal Western societies (2004: 1–3), then perhaps such audience members can identify with these heroines who are similarly selected as social role models for their performances of ideal femininity. The heroines of the fantasy blockbuster are not then so different from the heroines of the Hollywood travel romance, whose filmic narratives formed the case studies of the previous chapter. Like Liz in *Eat Pray Love* and Frances in *Under the Tuscan Sun*, Elizabeth and Alice are perceived as successful examples of femininity and as such are admired in their respective social circles. Yet these young women grow to resent their social position, and like Liz and Frances, their journey abroad allows them the freedom to experiment with their bodily capabilities in a way not allowed for within the initial setting. All these films speak to postfeminist discourse in situating the body and the eventual modification of its signifying systems as not only constituting the key site of initial oppression, but as integral to the success of one's journey to empowerment.

Although this privileging of the corporeal as a source of empowerment speaks to contemporary postfeminism, the means through which these heroines achieve this is unusually subversive in relation to these exact same ideologies. As McRobbie reminds us, the gender contract required of young white women in Western neoliberal countries is a heteronormative one, valorising marriage and the nuclear family unit and encouraging exaggerated performances of femininity in the public sphere (2009: 50, 67). For Elizabeth and Alice, however, their very survival in the fantasy zone requires the embrace of queer modes of being. In *Alice in Wonderland*, the creatures of Underland are in much doubt as to whether the seemingly subdued and passive Alice Kingsleigh can in fact be the *real* Alice of prophecy, with the Hatter declaring that she is 'hardly Alice', is always 'too small or too tall', and has lost her 'muchness'. Burton's Alice is not a pre-adolescent girl who has to navigate her way through a nonsensical world, but rather a young woman whose prolonged absence from the mystical realm has helped to further intensify her designated status as a person of future great importance to the nation. Alice's transcendence over her melancholic state and subsequent transition from passive spectacle to active agent has to come with a shedding of femininity and an immediate agreement to don the traditional accoutrements of masculinity. Here her personal growth is considered complete when she agrees to wear armour and carry a sword, a transition that ultimately allows her a renewed command of foreign space and place. 'I choose where to go from here,' she claims. 'I make the path.' Tellingly, when Hatter does recognise Alice as the 'real Alice', he gender-confuses her, proclaiming 'I'd know him anywhere!'

The subversive play with gendered identities and sexuality is even more pronounced in the *Pirates of the Caribbean* series, which sees protagonist Elizabeth Swann having to adopt a number of guises in order to navigate the high seas. When Elizabeth, wanting to save Will from a charge of piracy, sets out to find Captain Jack by stowing away on board a pirate ship she has to dress as a boy because of the pirates' superstitions about women. This marks a rejection of her initial identity as an aristocratic woman and is also a strategy that allows her to begin to take control of the seas. Through exploiting the pirates' fear of women by setting up a message from a ghostly widowed maiden, Elizabeth ensures that the ship heads for Tortuga. Elizabeth, in taking charge of the ship and by extension taking charge of her entire journey, is transgressing the feminine position in favour of a masculine relationship to space – an endeavour that marks a reversal in traditional gender roles, as she is the one to rescue Will. Much of the comedy of the franchise, as Martin Fradley argues, comes from its 'self-consciously queer dynamic' (2011: 294). He explains that the series utilises the mythological figure of the pirate to play with sex and gender conventions, pointing out that the pirate as cultural construct is always an outcast or socially liminal figure who rejects the normative and here operates as 'a queer outlaw exploring uncharted territories of the heterosexual matrix' (301). Elizabeth Swann's performances of femininity in the pirate world, Fradley writes, are highly self-reflexive, citing a scene where she pretends to faint from the heat to break up a fight over the heart of Davy Jones. The same self-reflexivity is also evident in *Alice in Wonderland*, with the rationale for the Red Queen's cruelty being her jealousy of the White Queen, her younger sister, who found greater favour with their parents due to her ideally feminine beauty and charm. The despotic Red Queen's inability to adequately perform gender roles results in a perpetual insecurity that leads to her selecting only physically deformed subjects as members of her Royal Court. In *Alice through the Looking Glass*, the Queen's tendency to deform her guards (who are made of vegetables) by eating their body parts leads to these employees releasing Alice and the Hatter after their capture. It is the Red Queen's inability to cope with the social ostracism that occurred following an accident where her head swelled to abnormal proportions that leads to her cruel behaviour and ultimately weak leadership. Alice, while similarly an outsider who has been unable to perform an idealised feminine role correctly, is just and compassionate, and as such holds values and leadership qualities that benefit Underland in times of crisis. This queer reading of the films is lent ideological weight when one considers the star images of those given top billing. Fradley notes that Johnny Depp consistently plays sexually ambiguous characters, citing his roles in Burton films such as *Ed Wood* (1994), *Edward Scissorhands* and *Charlie and the Chocolate Factory* (2005), though it is worth also noting his fascination with playing Native American characters as in *The Brave* (Johnny Depp, 1997) and *The Lone Ranger* (Gore Verbinski, 2013). Fradley additionally states that Keira Knightley's roles in films such as *Bend it Like Beckham* (Gurinder Chadha, 2002) have emphasised her boyish, androgynous femininity (2011: 306–7).

When Elizabeth Swann dramatically declares fatigue and 'faints' due to the heat, however, she is not merely distancing herself from femininity, but the aristocratic whiteness that demands such a performance as predicated upon race and class privilege. This distancing from an old kind of performance, made possible in the fantasy zone, destabilises the ideologies of white hegemony that are so adhered to in Port Royal and works to prove as unfounded white male fears for her safety and preservation of virtue. It is worth noting a contrast in characterisation here, however, for while Elizabeth can utilise her previously imposed identity in games of strategy, given that the pirate world also functions as an extension of her melancholic subconscious, this is not the case for the pirates who are never allowed this gap between self and mask. Furthermore, Elizabeth is always contrasted as orderly and civilised in relation to her 'wild' double Tia Dalma (Naomie Harris), a West Indian voodoo priestess who, in goddess form, has the power to unleash fury upon the seas, causing havoc and destruction in her wake. The pirates, though undoubtedly coded as queer, are simultaneously marked as racially Other by the British inhabitants of Port Royal in accordance with recognisable Hollywood stereotypes. The British consider the pirates to pose both a sexual and economic threat to white civilisation, a fact that Jack Sparrow displays awareness of when he informs Navy representatives of his plans to 'rape, pillage and pilfer my weasly black guts out'. Jack here engages in a 'naming' of whiteness, an act that critical race theorist George Yancy argues is subversive in that it aims to disrupt 'the wonderful capacity to live anonymously' that only white people enjoy (2012: 4). Yet although Jack knowingly reflects back at its creators their characterisation of his kind, from what we see of the pirates in the first film, these stereotypes are largely accurate. They are individualistic, greedy squabblers who for the most part are unable to unite to achieve a sense of purpose. This fact, along with their bewildering banter, works to render them harmless and ineffectual – hardly the threat the British Navy fears.

The representation of the pirates as selfish, prone to bickering and unable to share also works to characterise them as infantile, a way of representing the 'savage' typically employed to justify a people's subjection to colonisation. As William B. Cohen points out, British and French colonial powers often modelled the coloniser/colonised relationship on the parent/child familial hierarchy, with colonial subjects perceived as in need of growth and guidance by the 'presumably more advanced states of Europe' (1970: 427). Although the pirates are played by actors of various racial backgrounds, they seem to operate at the intersection of two stereotypes that Bogle found available for black males in Hollywood cinema – the buffoon and the buck. In this fantasy film, blackness operates as an attitudinal projection by whites and to a degree functions outside of a real sense of space and time, even though historically contextual racial attitudes are referenced.[4] Bogle states that the harmless and childlike buffoon eased white anxieties about the black male, while the brutal buck heightened and played on this fear through his representation as 'oversexed and savage, violent and frenzied (in his) lust for white flesh' (1973: 13). When Jack saves Elizabeth from drowning and brings her to shore in *Curse of the Black Pearl*, the soldiers of the Royal Navy misread the pirate's intentions: after he removes Elizabeth's corset, they promptly draw their swords. This scene demonstrates the Englishmen's fear at the pirates' perceived inability to control their carnal appetites as well as their anxiety at possible sexual interaction between the 'races'. In fact, the pirates' unbridled lust for the travelling white heroine is a source of comedy throughout the franchise. After Captain Barbossa kidnaps Elizabeth, the buffoonish pirate duo Pintel (Lee Arenberg) and Ragetti (Mackenzie Crook), gleefully inform her that if she refuses the

Figure 2.2 Captain Jack Sparrow is a rock star pirate in *Pirates of the Caribbean.*

captain's offer to eat with him then she will have to dine naked with the crew. In *At World's End*, Elizabeth stands over a grate while the pirates push and shove each other in an attempt to see up her dress. These scenes are self-reflexive ones and are played for laughs, with the pirates usually depicted as comedic rather than aggressive. Additionally, Pintel and Ragetti have an equally ridiculous mirror-image pair in the Royal Navy, Murtogg (Giles New) and Mullroy (Angus Barnett). Although that pair are not lustful, they are inept and ineffectual, and as such their characterisation functions to question the validity of the divisions between self and Other that the Navy has worked so hard to construct.

The pirates, however, are likely to invite a greater degree of audience investment given the contrast of their action-packed, adventurous world to the mannered, civilised and ultimately rather boring Port Royal. The majority of developed characters, with the exception of the villainous Lord Cutler Beckett, are either pirates or come to sympathise with their plight, and the franchise functions as a blockbuster star vehicle for Johnny Depp, who plays the now culturally iconic character of Captain Jack Sparrow. This notorious and morally ambiguous pirate, whose costume and make-up were designed by Depp in homage to Rolling Stones guitarist Keith Richards (cast as Jack's father Captain Teague in *At World's End*) is a rock star of the high seas with the best lines and escapes. This alignment between Jack Sparrow and the popular musical genre is interesting for the inevitable issues it raises in relation to the appropriation of ethnicity and queer sexuality for commercial gain. Jack is the ultimate hedonist, whose love of rum, sex and adventure draws parallels with the image of the narcissistic rock 'n' roll icon, who typically proclaims to live a lifestyle of liberty and excess while adopting performance styles designed to challenge social morality and conformity.

Rock 'n' roll has a rhythm and blues influence and it was commonplace for bands like the Stones to appropriate ethnic musical styles to give their songs an added flavour – to retain a freshness and point of interest in an ever-expanding market and ultimately to keep selling records and concert tickets. Although the films paint Jack Sparrow as a womaniser with a girl in every port, his eyeliner, flouncing strut and pouting demeanour nevertheless invoke a queer, campy sensibility. It was the 1960s and 1970s, the era of the Stones, that saw rock 'n' roll performers begin to explore gender fluidity in their lyrics and stage performances, with Mick Jagger incorporating glittering costumes and feminine bodily signifiers into his act. Perhaps the pirate is somewhat like Depp himself, who while often queered through his filmic performances has been simultaneously noted for a rock 'n' roll life of excess off-stage, as well as volatile relationships and numerous engagements to Hollywood actresses and models. While Jack Sparrow poses a threat within the diegesis because of his ambiguous ethnicity and sexuality, this threat is always mediated through the lens of rock 'n' roll star performance. Such a trope elevates the character as a star of the high seas while also working as a distancing device in that it is frequently unclear as to whether Jack is performing or not, or whose side he is on. Jack is less able than Elizabeth and Will to liaise between the stakeholders of Port Royal and the pirates, as these characters hold currency in both worlds. Yet he differs from the other pirates in his self-consciousness and self-awareness. Jack needs piracy to maintain his infamy and to fuel his celebrity status. As such, he *over-performs* piracy through the telling of highly exaggerated stories about his various daring adventures, such as the time he roped together two sea turtles as a means of escape from a desert island. Jack uses potentially damaging stereotypes about pirates as a source of empowerment, but the character also points to how Otherness can be appropriated to create an air of transgressive mystique through either constructed characters within popular media, or stars in the music and motion picture industries.

Because Underland exists as a separate realm in the *Alice* films, its magical creatures are unable to pose any real threat to the English aristocratic way of life. Furthermore, unlike the disruptive, pillaging pirates, the inhabitants of Underland are remarkably dependent and passive – desperately in need of the teenager's aid in imposing order upon their chaotic community. Alice sees the potential of Underland, for as the wise caterpillar Absolem (Alan Rickman) informs her, the term 'Wonderland' was initially invented by her younger self as an affective term designed to represent her feelings of awe and amazement upon first encountering the space. Alice's arrival in Underland in the first and second films is presented as both necessary and urgent, with the creatures fervently enquiring as to whether she is the 'real' Alice, prophesied to arrive in Absolem's Oraculum. Wonderland is a melancholic dreamscape that, not unlike the foreign countries in the tourist films, functions to restore a sense of agency and empowerment to a protagonist who sees the gendered restrictions in her daily life as overly restrictive. Yet Wonderland is simultaneously a nation that is on the brink of despair – a wasteland whose inhabitants live in terror of the Red Queen's tyrannical, murderous dictatorship. The Red Queen is spoilt and childlike, which works to constitute Underland as similarly immature and in need of development – a problem that Alice must rectify as she experiences her own coming-of-age. Small in stature and speaking with a prominent lisp, the Red Queen spends her days eating jam tarts, playing games and throwing frequent tantrums when things do not go her way. She is manipulative, prone to declaring herself unloved when others attempt to flout her orders, and professes an adoration of 'tiny things', for instance the miniature music box depicting a beheading that the enamoured Time gifts her as a present. The Red Queen's despotism is aligned with her desire to live perpetually as a child, with her initial youth having been destroyed by the accident that resulted in her swollen head and by her parents' alleged favouritism of her younger sister Mirana. Though the White Queen is not villainous, she nevertheless performs an exaggerated variant of white femininity that to a degree destabilises the idealised expectations that arise from gendered and racialised behavioural conditioning. With her mask of white face powder, bleached blonde hair and wide-eyed gaze, the White Queen gesticulates in amplified, graceful flourishes, her voice never wavering from its saccharine tone. The subversive potential of the White Queen's characterisation however, is undercut given that Alice's personal journey and transcendence of her melancholic state relies upon the assumption that there *is* a correct way to perform white femininity. Alice must learn to master her literal growth by modifying her intake of magical potions and cakes, a symbolic task that ultimately empowers her in finding an appropriate performative balance that allows her to stay true to herself while also aiding in the maintenance of social harmony and order.

If, as Kellner states, it is possible to read a critique of Bush politics in *Pirates*, then the opposite must surely be the case for a film like *Alice*, which utilises not only the appropriation of 'difference' but also intervention into foreign rule as a metaphor for the melancholic heroine's location of feminist empowerment within the postfeminist context. This is not at all to suggest that this film, or other similar Hollywood blockbusters, are created in support of certain administrations or policies within the US, but rather that certain political ideologies are inextricable from historically contextual beliefs pertaining to race and gender, and thus are reproduced through means that are not necessarily obvious or indeed conscious. The rationale for Alice's intervention has its basis in the fact that Underland is a place that lacks an 'appropriate' standard of governmental law. This is the reason the inhabitants of Underland suffer a low quality of life and it is also the reason the nation initially appears incomprehensible to Alice. The madness of the Hatter in this film can be directly attributed to his anger at the presumed demise of his family on Horunvendush Day – the date of the Red Queen's murderous coup in which she seized control of the lands with the aid of her jabberwocky. As it transpires, Alice is destined by the Oraculum to slay the jabberwocky and return the White Queen to the throne – an act of justice aimed at restoring peace and order and creating a higher standard of living for her newfound fantastical friends. Underland's residents cannot achieve this result without Alice, who becomes the embodiment of a righteous and benevolent superpower whose knowledge as to the correct course of action becomes indispensable to the ailing nation. Zillah Eisenstein notes that because colonisation allows the colonisers to perceive the world only from their viewpoint, they can construct false universal truths (2004: 28). In accordance, Underland, as is the case with Oz in *The Wizard of Oz* or the pirate world in *Pirates of the Caribbean*, is always understood as an extension of the female protagonist as the question persistently remains as to whether the supernatural realm is real or a merely a subjective, melancholic projection.

Alice in Wonderland is fundamentally a story of feminist liberation with the chaos of Underland initially acting as a psychic impediment to the empowering affective potential of wonder. Sara Ahmed in *The Cultural Politics of Emotion* calls on feminists to release their feelings of anger and pain at their subjection to an emotion with more creative potential, that of 'wonder'. Wonder, Ahmed states, 'allows us to realise what hurts, and what causes pain, and what we feel is wrong, is not necessary, and can be unmade as well as made. Wonder energises the hope of transformation, and the will for politics' (2004: 181). What *Alice in Wonderland* does, then, is tell a feminist story built upon the transcendence of gendered melancholy through the discovery of the political potential of wonder. Yet it does so ultimately in favour of a rather conservative agenda, as Alice's empowerment depends upon her invasion and conquering of Underland, which doubles as a metaphor for her fears. The text depends upon colonial discourse and the mythos that Western powers are to set the standards of peace, democracy and justice, in order to tell its allegorical tale. Such a mythos is of course still evident on the world stage today. As Eisenstein notes, US interventions into Iraq and Afghanistan were predicated on divisions between 'the West and the rest', with so-called freedom operations acting as 'pseudonyms for empire building' that ultimately created disorder and pain rather than democracy (2004: 15). Within the fantasy universe that is Hollywood film, however, post-invasion opposition and unrest can be neatly elided. Imperialism, the promise of providing a white, stabilising force to the unruly and untamed world, brings no pain to the inhabitants of the fantastical space, who approve of Alice's arrival not only as necessary but in fact as destiny. Alice can exercise her power and might within the smaller nation because it is her God-given right to do so, a mythic rationale commonly provided for war by larger nations intent on expanding their land and resources.

When Alice accepts her destiny and infiltrates the Red Queen's castle, she constructs a fraudulent history in claiming she is from the fictional town of Umbridge, an act that obscures the real power she holds as an English citizen. This disavowal of national power through the mobilisation of a feminist heroine continues when Alice returns home and embarks upon her chosen career path as a merchant seaman in the hopes of accumulating wealth through trade with China. While Alice's interventions in Underland are motivated by a sense of justice and oppression empathy, she does not gain from her victory merely in terms of personal growth but also financially. It is, after all, her love and appreciation of 'difference' that identifies her as an ideal candidate through which to promote Britain's financial interests abroad. The *Alice* films, therefore, do not exhibit the same critical stance in relation to global capitalism that other texts within this book do, yet they do obscure the power relations inherent within matters of international trade in presenting Alice's every journey abroad as an empowering act of gender transgression. When Lord Hamish takes over the trading company, the audience is to believe that he would make a poor ambassador for the nation due to his racist and sexist attitudes, attributing his fervent belief in Alice's 'strangeness of mind' to her frequent acts of 'going native'. Alice's decision to attend the Ascot party dressed in the robes of a Chinese empress aligns her with an idealised future of whiteness, in which the embrace of racial difference supposedly correlates to equality in international relations. The outmoded views of the scandalised party guests become relegated to a problematic past that Alice, because of her interactions with Time, knows she can only hope to learn from rather than change. Alice's bid for leadership, while gesturing toward a desire for social equality and inclusiveness, nevertheless resonates with the rise of plutocratic forms of neoliberal feminism advocated by female corporate bosses such as Facebook CEO Sheryl Sandberg and *Huffington Post* founder Arianna Huffington. Discussing Sandberg's 2013 best-selling book *Lean In: Women, Work, and the Will to Lead*, Catherine Rottenberg explains that Sandberg primarily associates gender inequality with a lack of female representation at the higher echelons of government, corporation and industry (2014: 423). Rottenberg argues that change is characterised in an 'internal, solipsistic and affective manner', where the possibility of a collective feminist politics is disavowed in favour of advocating an individual drive for power (426). While the *Alice* films certainly equate the protagonist's feminist credentials with her suitability for political and economic leadership, they nevertheless exhibit discomfort with Alice's implied desire for economic influence. Tellingly, Alice's desire for financial gain is not shown to be primarily driven by patriotism or economic greed, but by her need to retain her father's legacy and support her family into the future, such as in the second film where she is able to prevent the sale of her mother's home.

THE POSTFEMINIST UNVEILING OF CHARISMATIC AUTHORITY

While neither Elizabeth nor Alice is accepted in her new world right away, each script posits a turning point where the heroines are elevated above their newfound social group and, as a result, their transition from passive spectacles to active authorities. It is this representation of *authoritative* white femininity that distinctly marks the characters as having been successful in 'discovering' feminism outside the confines of white upper-class identity. In *Curse of the Black Pearl*, the narrative depicts Elizabeth as a figure at the mercy of the male characters. She is kidnapped, locked away, rescued and at times denied access to the action. Although at the film's conclusion, she fights against Barbossa's cursed crew, she is unable to convince the other pirates to help her. Once kidnapped by Barbossa however, she discovers a certain similarity in their predicaments. Gazing hungrily at the feast set before her in the captain's cabin, Elizabeth refrains from eating as she is still adhering to the rules of aristocratic white femininity. It is Barbossa who informs her that these rules have no currency in the pirate world. 'There is no need to stand on call to impress anyone,' he states. 'You must be hungry,' causing Elizabeth to tear into a piece of chicken and as such begin to shed her prior identity. Barbossa then informs Elizabeth of the Aztec curse that has been placed upon his crew – a punishment for their materialistic greed – which means they can no longer gain pleasure from acting upon their desires. Elizabeth is also unable to act upon her desire to eat or love, and so an empathetic bond is formed between her and Barbossa. Since, unlike Barbossa and his crew, Elizabeth's barriers are only of the social kind, this dinner marks the point where she begins to realise that social barriers may be permeated or even exploited. It is not until the second film, where Elizabeth dresses as a boy and exploits the pirates' fear of women by manufacturing a message from a 'ghostly maiden', that this character really begins to assume control over both her literal and symbolic journey. Elizabeth's newfound ability to 'pass' in the pirate world, whether as a member of the opposite sex, a pirate shipmate, a trapped goddess or a villager in 'the Orient', is nevertheless consistent with the model of the white traveller able to organise the world in his own image. To state 'his own image' is not a grammatical slippage, as Elizabeth assumes a form of power more consistent with white masculinity than femininity, and as such her newfound performative power invites a reading as liberating and ultimately, within the terms of the film, as feminist.

These heroines, however, do not merely make a transition from passive spectacles to active authorities, as there is something *special* about their eventually granted authority that marks it as different from traditional patriarchal forms of white, colonial control. This special authority depends upon the concept of a 'lost' feminism and is alluded to at the films' beginnings, which introduce the melancholic attachment of the female protagonist to her magical space. This melancholia is caused by the restrictive expectations placed upon the feminine role, but also indicates a unique ability to craft new futures based upon a new set of rules and conditions that may empower the self and, by extension, benefit others. In these films, Wonderland and the pirate world become tangible realisations of feminist potential, preventing the protagonists from passively accepting their societal position. The magical space is both the heroine's lost object and a potential source of liberation, and in turn she is the source of liberation for the oppressed inhabitants of the magical world. Therefore, the relationship is symbiotic. This relationship, however, also depends upon the female protagonist's elevation above the pirates/residents of Underland, who must agree to defer power to her. For this to happen, something must differentiate the female character from those in the magical world even though her journey requires the rejection of her previous identity. In *Pirates of the Caribbean: Dead Man's Chest*, the audience comes to realise this difference following an exchange between Jack and Elizabeth, who is worried that she may desire the pirate captain despite professing to find him repulsive. In one scene, Jack informs Elizabeth that they should get married as they are in fact very similar, theorising that soon she will be unable to resist on account of her longing to act on selfish impulse. Elizabeth denies this perceived similarity, pointing to Jack's lack of honour, decency and moral centre. Although Jack is quite correct in imagining that Elizabeth covets the liberty his lifestyle offers, her reply indicates what she perceives to be the difference between the pirates and people like her and Will, who engage in acts of piracy to benefit others. Elizabeth's moral centre, her willingness to fight in the service of a greater good, is what elevates her above the pirates who are all out for themselves.

It is Elizabeth's 'civilised' upbringing that problematically marks out her moral superiority and it is she who instils this sense of honour in the pirates in order to unite them. When we are first introduced to the Brethren Court, the government made up of pirate lords, it is clear that the organisation is a farce. No decision is ever made because each lord will always push his or her agenda, and no king can ever be elected because each lord will only ever vote for himself. It is Jack's strategic decision to vote for Elizabeth instead of himself that results in her being crowned leader and it is in this role, another performance of gender transgression, that Elizabeth is able to gain the respect of the pirates. Defining charismatic authority, Max Weber states that this type of power rules by virtue of a gift not accessible to everybody and also by virtue of a mission that must be obeyed and followed (1946/2006: 61). This mission is an anti-colonialist one, as Elizabeth is fighting for the pirate way of life in opposition to the evil Lord Beckett, who has declared that as the blank edges of the map are being filled in, the pirates must find a place in his new world or perish. Yet her mission also requires that the previously anarchic pirates learn to follow a leader. Dyer argues that charismatic appeal is at its strongest when it offers a sense of order and stability amidst social upheaval (1998: 31) and it is Elizabeth who becomes the ultimate symbol of cultural unification as the pirates prepare for battle. Elizabeth's eventual success in the war mission, following a speech in which she instructs the pirates to 'hoist the colours', ultimately earns her much respect and admiration.

Alice's charismatic authority is recognised much earlier than Elizabeth's as her very arrival in Underland is marked as a fulfilled prophecy and as such has deeply religious undertones. Alice is the embodiment of a global power player on the one hand, but she is also crucially a messiah. Underland waits for her as though it is waiting for the return of a Christ-like figure who can reintroduce the possibility of Eden, who can bring light to dark, and who can enlighten those who have lost hope. In fact, Alice does not have much of a choice in the matter. Like Joan of Arc, it has been prophesised that she will carry out this task for a higher purpose, and so her charismatic authority is inextricably related to her task of carrying out a divine mission. Just as Dyer's study of whiteness explored how Christian ideology was and is utilised to inform and maintain the hegemony of whiteness (1997), in invoking the concept of the saint with the divine mission, *Alice in Wonderland* naturalises the colonial authority Alice exercises through a religious discourse that marks her out as Chosen. In fact, it is Alice's refusal to comply with gender norms at the beginning of the film that marks her out as special and so her latent feminist potential becomes a crucial aspect of her 'charisma' – the indefinable special quality that empowers Alice and endows her with the right to act upon Underland as she does. Furthermore, if charismatic authority must reside outside the bureaucratic system as Weber hypothesises, then it makes sense that those endowed with it in these Hollywood blockbusters are women. The melancholic heroine is liberated from her mental state in her recognition that political disenfranchisement based on identity categories other than gender merely function as an extension of the oppression that she herself is experiencing. The discovery of feminism, arising as it does from the creative fantasy play that melancholia allows for, must come from the realisation that to be a feminist, one must also become an activist involved in erasing other forms of social disadvantage.

It is the ambivalence as to what constitutes 'feminism' within popular postfeminist philosophy, and the inextricable relationship of this philosophy to facets of neoliberal ideology, that frequently allow fantasy film to adopt a simultaneously progressive and regressive function in relation to white hegemony. Fantasy film, as discussed earlier, is a genre that mobilises familiar racial stereotypes in order to characterise Otherness, while also being a genre that frequently manages to sustain imperial discourse in the form of magical analogy (Smyth 2004: 20). Yet Hollywood fantasy may also, and

Figure 2.3 Alice is a saintly Joan of Arc figure in *Alice in Wonderland*.

indeed simultaneously, encourage its audiences to reflect critically upon the role played by larger Western powers in contemporary international conflicts. It is the trope of melancholic white femininity, framed through an imaginary construction of heritage Britain, which allows these films to distance themselves from models of patriarchal, bourgeois whiteness and associated forms of aggressive nationalism. In fantasy cinema, feminist power equates to social power, which in turns functions to produce new and timely forms of nationalism that rehabilitate and redirect forms of white, Western imperial control rather than deposing it. Yet in having these heroines overcome their melancholia and discover feminism in a foreign space that operates as both a functioning culture and a utopian feminist dream, the films allow for the creation of a new model of whiteness that can only ever masquerade as benevolent. This benevolent whiteness recognises all forms of political disenfranchisement as an extension of sexist oppression, symbolised through the question as to whether Underland and the pirate world are mere melancholic projections of the white female self. The films therefore produce an authoritative whiteness, as the heroine's discovery of a 'correct' feminist performance is gauged not only through how well she manages to organise struggling social groups but how invested her 'subjects' are in her superiority and leadership.

Although the figure of the warrior woman has been a key pop-cultural site through which to navigate the changing state of feminism in the West, this figure also has traditionally functioned as a national allegory. Marina Warner explains that concepts including liberty, justice and victory have historically been allegorised through female figures, with generations of men able to project their 'longings, terrors and *fantasies*' (my emphasis) onto iconography that appears 'in public commissions and in the edifices where authority resides' (1985: 37). The bodies of armed maidens, Warner points out, are typically chaste due to their possession of an idealised combination of innate virtue and strength, with the Sword of Justice not representing an executioner's weapon but rather the ability of humanity to distinguish between right and wrong (160). Elizabeth Swann's inability to devote her life to her romantic relationship and Alice Kingsleigh's rejection of romance altogether, as well as the queering of both heroines, must additionally be read in this allegorical context. The armed maiden, Warner states, exercises sovereignty over the heart (53), as she is primarily a warrior 'for the cause of righteousness', her 'secondary sexual characteristics sheathed and shielded by breastplates, jock-straps and pelvic girdles' (173). Furthermore, the image of the armed maiden may become synonymous with national identity, powerfully amalgamating the ruler and the ruled, as in the case of Britannia (Warner 1985: 41–2). Elizabeth and Alice are individuals who 'come of age' through their discovery of feminism within the supernatural world, yet in instigating political reform in their respective social milieus they become both icons and *embodiments* of rehabilitated national leadership.

It is perhaps on television, however, that we can observe the most literal, contemporary and currently iconic example of the discovery of feminist empowerment as not only sanctioned by virtuous whiteness, but aided through an engagement with the racial Other that allows the heroine to read her previous performance of white femininity as complicit in her feelings of oppression and restriction. Based on the best-selling novels of George R. R. Martin, HBO's highly successful fantasy series *Game of Thrones* (2011–) sees several contenders vie for the right to rule on the Iron Throne by engaging in brutal power plays of deception, treachery and violence. One of these characters, the blonde and fair Daenerys Targaryen (Emilia Clarke), begins her journey on the patriarchal continent of Westeros under the guidance of her sadistic and conniving brother Viserys (Harry Lloyd). The aristocratic siblings are the last surviving members of their family, who once ruled Westeros but have since been banished into exile and are forced to live on the good graces of the Magister Illyrio. Daenerys is initially introduced to us as passive and non-emotive, a voiceless pawn in her brother's schemes to regain power. Assessing his sister's naked body prior to selling her to the warrior Khal Drogo (Jason Momoa), Viserys orders her not to slouch, reminding her that she needs to 'be perfect' in order to ensure the commodity exchange of her body for an army. He informs her that Drogo, leader of the dark-skinned yet apparently multi-ethnic nomadic Dothraki tribe, is a 'savage' and 'one of the finest killers alive'. Viserys, invested as he is in the belief that whites are aligned with mental superiority and enterprise, claims he 'knows how to play Drogo', while the wedding ceremony between Daenerys and the Khal distinguishes between

Figure 2.4 Daenerys Targaryen is hailed as a 'mhysa' in *Game of Thrones*.

the clean and orderly Targaryens and the primitive Dothraki, who engage in rituals of feasting, sex and death.[5]

Unexpectedly however, Daenerys finds love with the Khal and in assuming her role as Queen of the tribe also begins to embrace an identity free from the tyranny of her brother and his schemes. Following the Khal's death, she miraculously becomes 'mother' to a group of dragons, symbols of Targaryen rule, and embraces her future destiny as ruler of the people of Westeros. Owing to her experiences of oppression, Daenerys is a compassionate leader and forms her army by liberating abused slaves and encouraging them to fight for her as free men. Feminist empowerment here is directly aligned with an abolitionist sentiment, and is formed through the affective bond of 'oppression empathy' with victims of other forms of social injustice. Nevertheless, the moral superiority of the Mother of Dragons and her right to lead these people is rarely questioned. Season Three of *Game of Thrones* culminates in a powerful scene during which the liberated slaves of Yunkai hail Daenerys as their 'mhysa', which while sounding very much like 'messiah' in fact means 'mother' in the native tongue. Daenerys is lifted above the cheering masses, her white-blonde hair and blue costuming contrasting sharply with the thousands of brown arms that clamour to touch her. The central framing and lighting here utilised to illuminate Daenerys as a figure of uniqueness and specialness recalls Dyer's arguments regarding the usage of lighting to privilege white individuals. White women, Dyer suggests, are frequently lit to suggest an association with ethereality, purity and ultimately the heavenly. 'Idealised white women are bathed in and permeated by light', he notes. 'It streams through them and falls onto them from above. In short, they glow' (1997: 122).

The melancholic female protagonist's narrative trajectory in the fantasy text involves locating an elusive 'feminism', the discovery of which coincides not only with the realisation of her personal empowerment but also with the realisation of her ability to empower others in allowing them to realise that their oppression too may be overcome. Yet social power cannot be exercised unless one is acknowledged in the first instance as having a greater claim on which to exercise it, and in these films the heroine's success in her mission directly correlates to how prepared others are to invest in her ability to guide them on their path to social harmony. In fact, for the films discussed in this chapter, feminism *is* leadership, with the triumph over sexism here made possible only through a privileged race and class positioning that constitutes an *already* greater claim to such leadership. In this manner, melancholic white femininity is mobilised as a type of compromise for white hegemonic power structures undergoing an imagistic fracturing that contemporaneously speaks to the problematic nationalism of certain Western powers. The feminist white heroine of the final filmic frames is no longer melancholy, yet she speaks the promise of new forms of whiteness marked by a feminine benevolence, compassion and social understanding that pleads for a new strategic direction in foreign interventionism, which will remain firmly based upon principles of white entitlement and control.

NOTES

1. Although there has now been a fourth *Pirates* film entitled *On Stranger Tides* (Rob Marshall 2011) and a fifth entitled *Dead Men Tell No Tales* (Joachim Rønning and Espen Sandberg, 2017), my analysis will concentrate on the first three films in the series in which Elizabeth Swann is a prominent character.
2. Although academic analysis of fantasy film as a genre has become more popular in recent years, there have been past studies exploring the psychic and social meanings behind the mobilisation of 'the fantastic' within associated cinematic genres such as horror and science fiction. The chapters in James Donald's edited collection *Fantasy and the Cinema* (1989) are examples of work in this area.
3. Pam Cook in *Fashioning the Nation: Costume and Identity in British Cinema* argues that because heritage drama serves the needs of both present and future, its presentation of history functions as a form of masquerade, with the semiotic elements of *mise-en-scène* operating as 'intertextual sign systems with their own logic' (1996: 67).
4. In *Against Empire, Feminisms, Racism, and the West*, Zillah Eisenstein argues that 'blackness' can function as a white cultural construction in the form of projected attitudes toward people deemed Other (2004: 70).
5. Richard Dyer discusses the association of whiteness not only with cleanliness and orderliness, but also with civilisation and enterprise in *White* (1997: 210).

CHAPTER 3

Neoliberalism, Female Agency and Conspicuous Consumption as Tragic Flaw in Woody Allen's *Blue Jasmine*

The camera captures an anxious woman sitting alone on a park bench in San Francisco, her incoherent monologue having initiated the abrupt departure of a fellow urbanite reading a newspaper beside her. Voicing aloud what appear to be fragmentary reminiscences of a high society life spent in the comfort of every imaginable luxury, the woman quietly informs her absent listener that she has seen 'Danny', who is getting married. 'I can wear the Dior dress I bought in Paris,' she muses. 'Hal always used to surprise me with jewellery. Extravagant pieces. I think he used to buy them at auction. This was playing on the Vineyard ... "Blue Moon" ... I used to know the words. Now they are all a jumble.'

The woman's visual presentation also conveys something of a discord between outward appearances and conflicting internal emotions. Pristinely dressed in a white Chanel jacket with black trim, her hair is damp and matted, her face betraying signs of recent tears. As the final credits begin to roll, the cinematic audience is left to wonder what the future holds for this dishevelled and anxious creature, the forgotten lyrics to 'Blue Moon', which tell of one who stands alone with neither love nor dreams to comfort them working to bespeak the tragic nature of these witnessed circumstances. The 'creature' under discussion here is none other than the protagonist of Woody Allen's critical and commercial success *Blue Jasmine*, a film that chronicles the downward spiral of a Manhattan socialite who suddenly finds herself both homeless and penniless following her husband's incarceration for fraudulent business activities and his subsequent suicide. *Blue Jasmine* insinuates that its protagonist's mental illness and corresponding inability to successfully participate on the labour market is largely explained by her need to construct an idealised sense of self through the pursuit of luxury goods. This is a practice that allows her to continually disavow the possibility of an ethical agency that she possesses, yet exercises wrongly throughout the course of the narrative. A darling on the American awards circuit, *Blue Jasmine* was lauded as a return to form for Allen and garnered a number of prestigious prizes, including the Academy Award for Best Actress for Cate Blanchett. It is also a film likely to be of special interest to the feminist critic interested in the cultural trajectory of the postfeminist sensibility in its emphasis on the affluent white female subject and its alignment with the political imperatives of neoliberalism. This sensibility, as Negra and Tasker point out, is enabled by 'optimism and prosperity' (2014: 1), and in the wake of the global financial crisis Jasmine operates as a social outcast who exemplifies value systems that have temporarily been deemed morally reprehensible, based as they are upon the overvaluation of economic income and enthusiastic participation in consumer capitalism. Jasmine is certainly a melancholic, yet the film suggests that her melancholy is *misplaced* in that she yearns for a past lifestyle of decadence and frivolity that the film suggests is not only unethical but importantly also unearned, having been acquired through Jasmine's strategic decision to marry into wealth.

This chapter argues that *Blue Jasmine*'s narrative and its protagonist Jasmine French must be understood as signifying at a temporary period of ideological weakening for neoliberalism and its associated political rhetoric in the wake of the 2008 global financial crisis. It is this moment of instability that allows for the privileged race and class status of the postfeminist representational subject within this film to be configured as an ethical *problem* to be debated, even if on superficial or temporary terms, rather than a conditional aspect of the aspirational ideal. The politics of gender, race and class evident in *Blue Jasmine* can aid us in understanding the contemporary evolution of the relationship between neoliberal discourse and societal opinion as to what constitutes female agency by exploring how these images shift in accordance with fluctuations in the popularity of governmental ideology. Jasmine is given the chance to work through her state of melancholic anxiety via engagement with her sister's working-class milieu, yet unlike the characters of the travel romance or fantasy film is unable to renegotiate aspects of her identity that she believes justify her social superiority. *Blue Jasmine*'s examination of capitalist greed and conservative neoliberal principles are filtered through a lead character who simultaneously becomes a mouthpiece for this rhetoric and an embodiment of its related value systems in her refusal to discard old designer pieces, an act of defiance that becomes symbolic of her adherence to the 'old ways' of doing things. The story's social critique is thus dependent on its representation of gendered variants of consumer capitalism to explore the financial and psychological consequences of an individualist neoliberal philosophy that disavows the socio-economic limitations facing the working class. These consequences too are portrayed as individualised and gendered, being framed primarily through the character of Jasmine's adoptive sister Ginger, who frequently declares that Jasmine has been favoured in life due to 'better genes'. While the negotiation of neoliberal governmentality in relation to class privilege may be welcome, the film's debate is ultimately not about systemic financial failures and corresponding social inequalities, but about the ethical and moral conduct of affluent white women, as framed through their consumption habits. It is for this reason that *Blue Jasmine* is a prime case study through which to explore the political precariousness of gendered melancholia in relation to neoliberal and postfeminist discourses. The broader power dynamics of late capitalism and finance culture are not critiqued holistically, but rather reframed through the scapegoating of a quintessentially postfeminist character.

The film introduces its protagonist Jasmine as she disembarks from a first-class aeroplane cabin with her Louis Vuitton luggage, having regaled a reluctant elderly passenger with a grandiose monologue about her first meeting with husband Hal (Alec Baldwin) and their subsequent travels abroad. We are immediately introduced to Jasmine's love of the luxurious lifestyle through these tales, as well as to her controversial viewpoints, particularly in relation to her disdain for education and employment. 'I wasn't learning anything at school,' she explains to her fellow passenger as to why she did not graduate from college with an anthropology degree as intended, before pointing out that doctors put both her parents in early graves. 'Could you picture someone like *me* as an anthropologist?' she scoffs. The comment is indeed pertinent, as the film takes an anthropological approach in analysing Jasmine's character as constructed through elaborate social performance, comparing and contrasting her past behavioural patterns in New York to her present-day interactions in San Francisco, where she frequently encounters opposition to her elitist viewpoints. Jasmine is represented in this opening scene and throughout the film as preoccupied with self-image and other people's perceptions of her, and her self-presentation works to encourage responses of adulation through her style of dress, stories of opulent living, and performative gestures that suggest an upper-class 'habitus' (Bourdieu 1984/2010). The film, however, immediately distinguishes Jasmine's fantasy image of herself as an idealised figure worthy of adulation from the reality of her effect on others, with the woman she has been speaking to shown later complaining to her husband that her flight neighbour 'could not stop babbling about her life'. Jasmine's narration of her past additionally allows the audience to catch a glimpse of what her future may have held had she continued with her studies and adopted a conventional middle-class lifestyle, as opposed to meeting Hal and subsequently becoming a New York socialite. Jasmine's first encounter with Hal, the film suggests, constituted a fork in the road at which she took a miscalculated turn, yet her arrival in San Francisco presents another such opportunity for reinvention – to 'start afresh' as Jasmine puts it. Despite Jasmine's role in the loss of Ginger and her ex-husband Augie's lottery winnings – Augie played here by controversial comedian Andrew Dice Clay, known for engaging in misogynistic humour –

Ginger invites her to move in for a time until she can get back on her feet. The story follows Jasmine as she moves into Ginger's apartment, where she speaks feverishly of having to 'hide everything from Uncle Sam' and insists that her second-hand designer goods are unsaleable, reporting her frequent cruel comments about Ginger's home, job and partner and further descent into alcohol and prescription drug abuse. Jasmine expresses disgust at Ginger's lifestyle, believing her sister to have failed in taking the necessary measures to improve her economic situation, but sees the potential for an improvement in her own perilous circumstances when she begins dating a wealthy diplomat named Dwight (Peter Sarsgaard), although she must lie about her past to win his affections. When the truth is finally revealed, along with the fact that it was Jasmine who informed the FBI about her husband's activities due to anger over his intention to leave her for a teenage au-pair, a disgusted Dwight abandons her and Jasmine is left alone, clinging to her delusions of grandeur.

This plot of course bears a striking resemblance to the famed Tennessee Williams play *A Streetcar Named Desire*, first performed on Broadway in 1947 and later made into an award-winning film directed by Elia Kazan and starring Marlon Brando and Vivian Leigh in the title roles of Stanley Kowalski and Blanche DuBois. The role of Blanche is a sought-after one in theatrical circles, having been immortalised by several prominent female stars over the decades including Jessica Tandy and Tallulah Bankhead, with Vivian Leigh winning an Academy Award for her performance in the 1951 film adaptation. Not coincidentally, Blanchett's role as Jasmine came following a successful stint as Blanche in the Sydney Theatre Company's 2009 interpretation of the classic production directed by Liv Ullman. This performance further cemented her reputation as an actress of unusually high calibre given the emotional extremities required to perform the part successfully, and also strengthens the parallels between the themes of *Streetcar* and Allen's film. Like *Blue Jasmine*, *Streetcar* utilises a simultaneously melancholic and delusional female protagonist to explore the mythic construction of the white, upper-class self and its relationship with US national identity. Although the play specifically explores the disjuncture between the antebellum South's racially and sexually conservative values and the impact of Eastern European immigration on an inevitably transforming cultural milieu, the broader social themes inherent in the story have allowed for a number of adaptations over the decades in accordance with a changing sociopolitical climate, as well as a variety of characterological interpretations with regard to the text's key players.[1] *Streetcar*'s treatment of the relationship between American citizenship and the role whiteness played for immigrants in ensuring access to political, social and economic privileges[2] thus haunts Allen's film, even as the subject matter is updated and modified for contemporary concerns and sensibilities. The famous play follows Blanche, an ageing and penniless Southern Belle who arrives in working-class New

Orleans to live with her sister Stella, who to Blanche's dismay has married a man she perceives as rough, brutish and uncouth, and whom she describes as an 'animal' and 'subhuman'. Likening Stanley's poker gatherings to a 'party of apes', Blanche professes that a love of art, poetry and music constitute markers of evolutionary refinement, while her sister would benefit by not 'hanging back with the brutes'. George Crandell observes that though Stanley is a Polish-American immigrant, Blanche draws upon racialised discourses that conflate his status as a 'cultural alien' with that of the Africanist presence in the US through associated stereotyping of black masculinity as 'physically threatening, inarticulate, lacking intelligence, full of desire and sexually potent' (1997: 343). Stanley's struggle, Crandell points out, is to assert a valid claim to American citizenship by disavowing his ethnic heritage when he emphatically declares that he is 'not a Polack' but 'one hundred percent American, born and raised in the greatest country on earth'. It is the fact that Blanche constantly reminds Stanley of his social and ethnic differences, Georges-Michel Sarotte hypothesises, that leads him to expose her masquerade and ultimately destroy her (1995: 147).

Although, as David Roediger points out, 'working-class formation and the systematic development of a sense of whiteness went hand in hand for the US white working-class' (2007: 8), *Blue Jasmine* misses the opportunity to explore profoundly the neoliberal construction of a 'post-racial' present through an extended examination of the interlinkages between race and socio-economic inequality. As such, *Blue Jasmine* downplays the racial themes that are so prominent within *Streetcar* in favour of a more pronounced treatment of capitalist inequality and class oppression. This is not to suggest that these themes within *Streetcar* are entirely absent within Allen's film, but rather that they exist in a manner that 'ghosts' what the text centres on as its more pressing subject matter. While *Blue Jasmine* emphasises the socio-economic disparities that have shaped Jasmine's condescending attitude towards Ginger, the San Francisco environment is also markedly populated with an Italian-American and Polish-American presence that is absent amongst the white, Anglo-Saxon coterie that makes up Jasmine's friendship group. The film as such provides a subtle commentary on the relationship between white privilege and contemporary investments in the concept of the American dream as related not only to class hierarchy, but perceptions of difference amongst Northern European cultures towards white working-class ethnicities. When Ginger visits Jasmine in New York, she pointedly informs husband Augie that Jasmine's friends will not tolerate his 'stupid Polish jokes', a reminder to both Augie (and the audience) of the culture of ethnic exclusion that underlines Jasmine's claims to superiority and correlates specific forms of whiteness to both economic currency and cultural capital within her social environment. As Bonnett states, whiteness is an idealised construction designed primarily by and for

Figure 3.1 Jasmine reluctantly spends the day with Ginger, Chili and Eddie in *Blue Jasmine*.

the bourgeoisie, with the working-class positioned marginally in relation to its privileges as dependent on the fluctuating symbolic and socio-economic structure of the capitalist system (2000: 30). When a penniless Jasmine visits San Francisco, she exhibits not only disgust with her surroundings but also a level of physical revulsion when in proximity to Ginger's partner Chili (Bobby Cannavale), an Italian-American mechanic, and his friend Eddie (Max Casella). Upon meeting the pair at Ginger's introduction for the first time at an outdoor café, Jasmine recoils when Chili kisses her on the cheek and quickly retracts from Eddie's handshake, noticeably wincing at Chili's description of his friend as 'a sad excuse for a blind date'.

Jasmine's visible discomfort at being in the presence of the two 'grease monkeys', as Ginger terms their profession, along with her desire to maintain strict boundaries of personal space and her refusal to abandon her designer wardrobe, all speak to a will to maintain a sense of social superiority through bodily integrity and cleanliness. Correlations such as those between whiteness, purity and cleanliness, as Shannon Sullivan explains, form modes of bodily performance that perpetuate habits of white bourgeois privilege and in turn reproduce social, political and economic benefits for that same group (2006: 4).

Jasmine however, like Blanche DuBois, has been cast out by her former community and has thus been stripped of the various forms of social power that in the past have allowed her to reproduce hierarchical modes of interpersonal performance with no significant degree of interrogation from others. Her melancholic yearning for her affluent New York lifestyle manifests itself in a series of gestures that now constitute empty signifiers, dislocated as they are from their 'correct' social context, and leave Jasmine open to a level of critique that she has never before experienced. Like Blanche, whose name translates as 'white woods', Jasmine functions within the diegesis to dissect the 'psychological habits and fantasies that the American middle-class has about itself' (Owens quoted in Kolin 2000: 2). Blanche, in mourning for her days on the plantation Belle Reve (meaning 'beautiful dream'), is a typical Williams heroine in that she lives by a set of social arrangements that constitute a nostalgic ideal as opposed to an historical lived truth (Emmet Jones 1961: 111). Kazan, in his written notes for the character, describes her as an 'emblem of a dying civilisation, making its last curlicued and romantic exit'. Blanche's belief in her own inherent specialness, what the director describes as the character's 'tragic flaw', becomes all the more pronounced in a harsh world that does little to accommodate her fantasies (Kolin 2000: 10). Although Jasmine does not represent a 'dying civilisation', she does come to exemplify an economic system built upon competition and risk that has flourished in its relationship with the mythos of the American dream, but has experienced ideological fracturing in recent years as a result of its failure to expose the corruption and inequalities at the core of its own ethos. The upwardly mobile white woman, then, in becoming segregated from her social group and engaging in a series of performances that no longer make sense given her difficult circumstances, comes to stand for the weaknesses and hypocrisies of such a system and bear the criticisms of those who have experienced its hardships. As with other films analysed within this book, the failures of white hegemonic power structures as related to neoliberal capitalism in *Blue Jasmine* are projected onto a burdened white woman. In this film, however, the white woman does not serve as a vehicle through which key modifications in value systems are conducted in order to assuage mistakes made in the national past. Instead, it is Jasmine, as the very embodiment of neoliberalism's competitive, individualistic ethos, who must be discarded for others to live their lives free from harsh economic judgement. A key means by which the text can achieve such a gendered critique is to implicate Jasmine's investment in consumer items in her failure to act ethically and empathetically, particularly towards family members.

GENDERING THE FAILURES OF NEOLIBERALISM'S CULTURE OF COMPETITION

Blue Jasmine's tragedy rests on its protagonist's inability to realise that her investment in the luxury purchases associated with an affluent lifestyle constitutes a commodified, false sense of agency and by extension a pseudo-feeling of empowerment. Her dependence on consumer items equates to a reliance on modes of social performance that have suddenly become unviable and now demand a renegotiation of their terms. The film's exploration of contemporary American femininity must be situated in the context of a recessionary media culture that Negra and Tasker argue engages in a public gendering of the roles of production and consumption (2014: 3), with the postfeminist consumer operating increasingly as a figure of excess as well as of admiration

(4). Postfeminist culture's key preoccupations, which include an emphasis on female affluence and self-fashioning, are, they state, enabled by economic positivity, opportunity, and health (1). Jasmine French operates as an extreme caricature of this normalised, consumer-driven sensibility, which calls on women to engage in self-management practices to appear younger, thinner and more fashionable and, importantly, to compete with one another for personal gain. Jasmine has previously viewed herself as a strategic actor in relation to her socio-economic privilege and initially claims that she can simply 'reinvent' herself, yet she has failed to realise the extent to which she has depended on Hal for both her financial position and her reputation. Relics from Jasmine's New York past, namely designer clothing and jewellery, therefore, become objects that allow her to persist in her fantasies and delusions – to repress the memory of the catastrophic fall from grace that she has suffered. Jasmine continues to wear her designer clothing throughout her time in San Francisco, pointedly informing Ginger that while jewellery appears to be a priceless investment it is actually very difficult to sell and that she would be unable to sell her Louis Vuitton luggage as no one would want second-hand items bearing her initials. In *Streetcar* too, as Brenda Murphy points out, Blanche's flawed investment in the fantasy of the Southern Belle archetype is 'encoded materially' through her reliance on physical objects that help ensure the survival of old traditions, for instance her use of cologne to evoke her previous existence at Belle Reve, or her request for love interest Mitch to search her purse for keys, which Murphy describes as a 'gesture of helplessness and intimacy' (1992: 39). Yet it is Blanche's wardrobe that occupies a key source of tension with brother-in-law Stanley, who in one scene rummages through his sister-in-law's luggage and points to her love of furs and diamonds as evidence of a desire to deceive Stella through a falsification of finances.

Blue Jasmine borrows the play's symbolic treatment of the relationship between feminine consumer culture and fantasy, and re-contextualises this treatment within a contemporary setting that positions Jasmine in relation to a particular set of lifestyle choices that Hilary Radner has termed 'neo-feminist' practice (2011). Neoliberal feminism, Radner explains, works to define the feminine primarily in relation to the capitalist economic system by promoting upward mobility and self-fulfilment as achievable through a strategic engagement with consumer culture (6). Within this culture, the body and the cultivation of one's appearance and habits constitute principle *resources* in the name of individual survival within a profit-driven society (Radner 2011: 11). *Blue Jasmine* functions as an indictment of such a society in its attempts to engage in a disentangling of the relationship between female agency and the consumption of fashion and lifestyle objects by charting the downfall of a woman who takes her investment in postfeminist consumer culture to extremes. At its ideological core then, *Blue Jasmine* is perhaps not dissimilar from contemporary recession-era reality television programmes such as *The Real Housewives* franchise, which Michael J. Lee and Leigh Moscowitz astutely argue 'creates rich women as objects of cultural derision', inviting its audience to 'judge the extravagance of female scapegoats harshly in tough economic times' (2013: 65). The pair point out that the show utilises an ironic tone in illustrating how money destroys friendships, self-awareness and competent mothering, to produce a 'provocative, recession-era, postfeminist drama about rich women too crass to be classy, too superficial to be nurturing, and too self-obsessed to be caring' (65). Lee and Moscowitz hypothesise that such a series, like Woody Allen's film, functions as a contemporary cautionary tale about upwardly mobile white femininity within a popular culture landscape that typically celebrates the appearance-conscious, consumerist, bourgeois woman (67).[3] During the pre-awards promotional circuit for the film, actress Cate Blanchett described Jasmine as a 'grand character' suffering the 'tragic flaw' of epic delusion, a fault that ultimately leaves her without a centre, any sense of self or concept of *agency*.[4] The actress's comments here thus speak to ambivalence as to what the terms 'feminism' or 'female empowerment' mean today. It is Jasmine's constant posturing, her belief that an idealised outward appearance equates with social worth and personal value, that contributes to her downfall. Not only does Jasmine upon her arrival in San Francisco refuse to change her style of dress or her attitude toward low-income earners, scorning Ginger's ideas as to how best obtain paid employment and regaling her and her friends with tales of sailing adventures off St Tropez, Cannes and Monaco, she also habitually continues imaginary conversations with her past contacts from New York. These conversations, which chronicle Jasmine's feelings of shame at having to work for a living and the hurt she has experienced as a result of being excluded from her friendship group, become increasingly fraught with anxiety as she faces growing struggles with her mental health. For instance, when Jasmine complains to Ginger that she cannot commit to working in a job that is 'too menial', she recounts her experiences of having to sell shoes on Madison Avenue to the women she used to host at dinner parties. Recalling an incident when her former close friend Erica Bishop became embarrassed and pretended not to see her working behind the counter, Jasmine becomes distressed, chewing her fingernails, and uncontrollably shaking as she splutters, 'I *saw* you Erica!' These episodes prevent Jasmine from being able to assess her past mistakes with any degree of rationality, but also work to convey her continual investment in a neoliberal competitive ethos which, as William Davies argues, is 'a world organised around the pursuit of inequality' (2014: 30).

Jasmine's failure to reconnect with her sister is built upon a melancholic bond with her previous lifestyle and a corresponding refusal to redefine her ideas as to what constitutes agency or social empowerment. Jasmine perceives Ginger not as a family member with whom she shares a close personal relationship, but rather as a *co-competitor* who, through 'hard work' and careful strategy, she has until this point succeeded in surpassing in the game of life. While Ginger explains to her sons that their mother preferred Jasmine due to her superior genes, Jasmine complains to her friends that she always feels guilty around her sister because of the different life paths they each have taken, although additionally blames Ginger's lack of self-esteem and poor taste in men as key reasons for why she is not living a more comfortable lifestyle. 'What's wrong with your self-esteem?' Jasmine chastises Ginger after her sister reveals that she has reunited with Chili. 'You always marry losers because you think that's what you deserve and that's why you're living like this!' This exchange notably follows a scene detailing the breakdown of Jasmine and Hal's relationship in New York, where Hal informs his distraught wife that he is leaving her for a teenage au pair.

Jasmine can refuse to interrogate her own choices, it would seem, as her wealth indicates that she has always made the correct decisions for succeeding on the terms of neoliberal capitalism, given that correctness is typically defined through the quantitative rather than the qualitative. Neoliberal governmentality, Davies explains, is based upon an 'ethic of competitiveness' (2014: 30), through which the economic, social and political spheres are not treated as separate entities but rather evaluated collectively according to 'a single economic concept of value' (21). Its emphasis on substituting the quantitative for the qualitative in foregrounding statistics, facts and figures, he adds, acts to allow for a greater ease in decision-making by utilising numbers as opposed to more complex moral argumentation when taking political action, thus 'emptying politics of its misunderstandings and ethical controversies' (8). Governments, businesses and indeed individuals working within the neoliberal system are required to adopt strategies for boosting competitive performance (Davies 2014: 67), even if their choices may ultimately be destabilising or destructive (157). Jasmine and Hal, members of an economic elite favoured by the terms of neoliberalism and its emphasis on competition and inequality, engage in decisions based upon the best actions to take to increase their personal fortune, which allows them to overlook ethical shortcomings inherent in the manner in which they choose to do business. Similarly, when Jasmine chooses to marry Hal, she initially overlooks both his unlawful business dealings and his flirtations with other women and chooses instead to focus on his evident ability to accumulate wealth. Neoliberalism's emphasis on individual responsibility, which David Harvey summarises as built fundamentally upon the principle of defining both the wellbeing and failures of individuals in entrepreneurial terms, allows Jasmine to blame Ginger for her decision to invest with Hal rather than Hal's business model itself. Personal freedoms in the marketplace are encouraged, yet it is individuals as opposed to the state who are held responsible for their welfare, health and education (Harvey 2005: 65).

Ironically Jasmine, too, is responsible for her ultimate homelessness when she chooses to tell Ginger that she is leaving to accept Dwight's marriage proposal, which has since been revoked. The film's conclusion thus paints Jasmine as a less sympathetic figure than Blanche DuBois, who suffers a complete mental breakdown after being raped by Stanley and is escorted from Elysium Fields by psychiatric professionals. Chili, who is *Blue Jasmine*'s closest male equivalent to the Kowalski character, by contrast does not ultimately attempt to destroy Jasmine, but instead endeavours to tolerate her behavioural idiosyncrasies and insults because of his love for Ginger.

Neoliberal ideology, however, as Overbeek and Van Apeldoorn point out, must be understood, as 'a project in motion, *continuously* contested, a process of countless rounds of struggles and negotiations with oppositional forces' (2012: 6), which is currently undergoing such a period of contradiction and instability following the 2008 global financial crisis and the rise of new powers on the international stage (2). This instability may operate in favour of conservative governmental agendas, with the authors pointing out that austerity measures are often utilised as opportunities to gain public support for privatisation and marketisation reforms (3). Nevertheless, the postfeminist sensibility as outlined by Gill, Negra and others, must be understood as fluctuating in accordance with these political occurrences, with the representation of the 'feminine ideal' subject to such directional shifts. The upwardly mobile, affluent white woman may become an icon of the neoliberal system when it is in good health, but she is also a highly visible and significant figure when it is not. These observations don't suggest that there is no contestation regarding the terms of female agency within popular media, in fact quite the contrary, but they do indicate that such textual dissention may very well be recuperated on the terms of neoliberalism and late capitalism. This is one of the reasons why it is important to chart closely the representational evolution of various 'postfeminist tropes', and when analysing feature film, to consider how a female protagonist's narrative trajectory is facilitated through her engagement with less centralised characters, especially those characters not favoured by the terms of neoliberal logic.

Neoliberalism's struggles and negotiations impact upon the representation and appeal of the postfeminist sensibility, and this in turn can aid us in analysing the importance of socio-economic privilege to this pervasive cultural construct. The negotiation of neoliberal hegemony in *Blue Jasmine* is dependent on the filtering of broad and complex issues through an individualised, gendered framework, where the protagonist, in many ways an ideal neoliberal female subject, is forced essentially to stand trial for perceived 'abuses' of the system. Jasmine French is forced to confront her previous investment in hyper-capitalism, and its impact on her construction of an ideally feminine self, by engaging with the working-class inhabitants of Ginger's San Francisco environment. It is Jasmine's disdain and neglect of Ginger that allows the film to tell a story about a greedy and corrupted postfeminist subject, rather than a greedy and corrupted corporate environment. Jasmine's negotiation of her value systems outside the affluent New York environment she inhabits therefore raises interesting questions for scholars examining female representation in contemporary media in accordance with neoliberal discourse, as it demonstrates a marked shift in the treatment of a social type typically fêted in Anglo-American popular culture. In Imogen Tyler's book *Revolting Subjects*, which discusses social abjection in the neoliberal British context but which also makes many arguments easily applicable to other neoliberal economies, the author draws upon Harvey in noting that neoliberalism is fundamentally a class project (Tyler 2013: 8). Arguing that this form of governmentality centralises upon class struggle and stigmatisation as well as the manifestation of anxiety and fear through the generation of crisis rhetoric (8),[5] Tyler points out that national insecurities come to be projected onto social scapegoats who are 'imagined to be a parasitical drain and threat to scarce national resources' (9). Utilising the example of a gendered figure of social disgust, the 'chav', Tyler primarily examines the 'white trash' character of Vicky Pollard from *Little Britain* (BBC: 2003–7), who she notes 'moved relentlessly through public culture on a wave of mockery, contempt and disgust' (165). The projection of social disgust onto an affluent, white woman, then, is thus symptomatic of neoliberalism's temporary ideological fracturing. While the lived experience of bourgeois whiteness undoubtedly continues to confer considerable political, social and economic benefits upon this group, and while this cultural type is unlikely ever to face the public revulsion experienced by a single mother on welfare, a film like *Blue Jasmine* aids in providing a fantasy scapegoat and an imaginary class 'role reversal' for an American public disillusioned in the wake of the Wall Street crash.

Across mainstream media texts, particularly in popular film, it is still uncommon to find nuanced, sympathetic portrayals of those not favoured by neoliberalism's political terms and when represented, such characters are commonly defined in relation to the white, middle-class social ideal. Working-class women are far more likely to be visible in independent as opposed to commercial cinematic fare, or viewed through the scrutinising lens of reality television as opposed to prime-time drama. Beverley Skeggs points out that the reality 'makeover' format, in particular, often depicts working-class women whose appearance standards are found to be lacking and in need of expert guidance from upper middle-class women in possession of the 'correct' knowledge as to the right and wrong ways to engage in consumer capitalism (2009: 628). The negotiation of self in *Blue Jasmine* thus takes place within a broader cultural context that negates the realities of socio-economic disadvantage as predicated upon one's race or class, and would normally situate the protagonist Jasmine as a centralised and idealised figure to be emulated. In *Blue Jasmine*, it is the affluent, white woman who is unaware of the inappropriate nature of her consumption practices, while Ginger and her friends, as well as the cinematic audience, are invited to adopt the judgemental, scrutinising gaze.

WOODY ALLEN'S SOCIAL COMMENTARY AND PSYCHOLOGISING THE CRISIS OF THE ECONOMIC ELITE

Blue Jasmine, as an auteur project, may not be the typical object of study for a piece of scholarship exploring the mechanisms of the postfeminist sensibility. Yet the fact that *Blue Jasmine* is an auteur project is significant in that it dislodges the icon of the female consumer from media domains where she is more likely to be celebrated by female fans, and situates her within an environment imbued with a higher level of cultural 'gravitas', where her portrayal must serve the personal vision of the director as artist and is thus likely to attract a greater degree of critical appraisal. While the validity of French New Wave theories on the cinematic auteur have been debated within the academic context, the concept has become a powerful commercial branding tool within various film industries and is designed to invest products with a mark of quality and prestige – an equivocation more easily achieved when the auteur in question is male. Sam B. Girgus describes Woody Allen as a 'cultural symbol', a 'Gatsby figure' charting transformations in the American experience through work characterised by an intellectual and literary aura (2002: 27). The presence of the postfeminist sensibility here, then, may be said to operate as a key marker of a contemporary shift in the American experience as viewed from Allen's valued and privileged vantage point, in accordance with his unique brand of cultural commentary often directed at New York's insulated, upper middle classes. Leonard Quart points out that although Allen often takes aim in his films at the 'insecure, shallow, narcissistic, name-dropping world' (2006: 16) typically consisting of academics, artists or media workers, the New York that he chooses to depict often excludes African-American or Hispanic peoples, as well as the poor of the city. This 'carefully selected' milieu, Quart suggests, allows Allen to focus on the private turmoil of his characters and modes of cultural criticism as opposed to social or political criticism (16). The mode of cultural criticism Allen employs within this film, however, cannot be extrapolated from the creation of social and political *meaning* even as the wider political context for Jasmine's actions is minimised. Additionally, while *Blue Jasmine* is a recognisable addition to Allen's canon in terms of its themes and preoccupations, the treatment of the subject matter is considerably darker, lacking the humorous self-deprecation and gentle, teasing critique of the middle classes that characterises Allen's earlier work. This key tonal shift identifies the film as a text with a particularly important contribution to make in relation to its commentary on contemporary US value systems.

Blue Jasmine is a typical Allen vehicle in its focus upon the neurotic individual consumed by narcissistic tendencies,[6] yet the film is unusually politically minded in its moral interrogation of Manhattan 'elites'. As a result of continual juxtapositions between Jasmine's past self in New York and her contemporary self in San Francisco, the audience is not only frequently invited to pass judgement as to how her prior statements and actions have informed her present-day attitude and predicament, but also on how her previous choices have shaped the social pain of those within her newfound environment. The film makes heavy use of dialogue hooks and motifs to cue the audience to draw such parallels. In an early scene for instance, Ginger retrieves her two sons from Augie's care and informs him that Jasmine is coming to stay as she has fallen on hard times. Augie, having lost thousands of dollars because of Jasmine's suggestion that he invest in Hal's business ventures, immediately voices his opposition to Ginger's generosity and exclaims that Jasmine must have known about the criminal activity, being clearly happy to look the other way 'when all the diamonds and minks were flying in'. This scene is immediately followed by one where Jasmine is shown at her New York home partaking in an outdoor summer luncheon with the wives of wealthy businessmen. 'I never pay attention to house affairs,' Jasmine claims, before adding that she signs papers without reading them as she is 'very trusting'. 'It's called looking the other way,' a female friend pointedly and knowingly replies, introducing a line of dialogue that will recur frequently throughout the film.

Jasmine's anxiety and neuroses in present-day San Francisco come to be seen as mere extenuations of what has always been her tendency to 'look the other way' as opposed to engaging with the unsavoury reality of any situation that may threaten her privileged lifestyle. Jasmine's questionable ethics are thus raised by Augie early in the piece, with her love of lavish consumer items like 'diamonds and minks' directly implicated in her mistreatment of close family members. The New York elitist environment does not constitute an object of cultural fascination in and of itself for Allen within this film, as the location is permeable rather than insulated and can be interrogated continually through temporal juxtaposition and through the transient character of Jasmine.

Jasmine's downfall is inextricably related to her inappropriate negotiation of consumer capitalism, yet the fallout from her lifestyle choices goes far beyond the individual or familial, entering the realm of the sociopolitical and offering ripe material for a moral commentary on US value systems. In telling this story, the film relies upon tropes associated with the tragic dramatic

Figure 3.2 Jasmine discusses her tendency to look the other way while lunching with wealthy friends in *Blue Jasmine*.

form. Jasmine, it must be noted, is not an entirely unsympathetic figure. The audience plays witness to her genuine attempts at navigating the job market and to her emotional pain upon learning of Hal's numerous infidelities. Hal is the true villain of the piece yet does not have to experience the ramifications of his actions because of his jail cell suicide, a narrative device that allows the film to explore its heavy moral themes predominantly through a female figure who consumes to excess. 'There's a tragedy to her clinging to these threadbare things,' Blanchett stated in a *Vogue UK* interview in reference to Jasmine's designer wardrobe. 'One of the primary industries in America is fantasy and there's a naivety behind that. And I think that makes Jasmine an anti-hero of her time in her own way' (Alexander 2013). Blanchett's comments here aptly illustrate the slippage that occurs in the film where the individual pain of the female consumer becomes indicative of a broader tragedy within America's value systems and the concept of the American dream. If Jasmine's characterisation is consistent with that of the tragic figure, then she is also guilty of the crime of *hybris*, which N. R. E. Fisher describes as the deliberate assault on the honour of another in order to gain pleasure in one's subsequent feelings of superiority (1992: 1). Typically perpetrated by members of the upper classes, *hybris* intends to make clear to another that they are not honoured or valued, leading to feelings of shame in the victim (8). This is exemplified by Jasmine's continual ill treatment of Ginger despite dependence on her hospitality, and indeed by Blanche's treatment of Stella in *Streetcar*. *Blue Jasmine* is a modern-day morality tale exploring issues of honour, guilt and shame in the wake of the financial crisis, which the film references in utilising investment fraud as a catalyst for narrative proceedings. Jasmine is a quintessential tragic figure in that she is 'characterised by a miscalculated confidence and its consequences' (Felski 2008: 2), her future bleak and yet unavoidably set in stone as a result of what has occurred in the past.

While the creation of Jasmine as a melancholic and ultimately tragic character invites the audience to pass judgement on her past actions as contributing to her fractured relationships with other characters and her own unravelling mental state, the film is also notably consistent with a recent turn toward individualising and *psychologising* the failures of neoliberalism. In accordance with the filmic melodrama's stylistic preoccupations, *Blue Jasmine* utilises a moody jazz and blues soundtrack to intensify Jasmine's frequent episodes of emotional turbulence,[7] both as an illustration of inner pain and her openly expressed anxieties, and also drawing yet another parallel to *Streetcar*. Kazan's film employs a similar musical jazz score to narrate the downfall of Blanche DuBois and to highlight her melancholic alienation in the multicultural environment that is Elysian Fields. Yet as Elisabeth R. Anker explains, melodrama is not only a filmic or literary genre, but also a genre of national political discourse, that 'casts politics, policies and practices of citizenship within a moral economy' (2014: 2), and is able to be harnessed by the political left or right.[8] *Blue Jasmine* can thus utilise the formal codes of filmic melodrama, with its conventional emphasis on the psychic life of a member of the white upper classes, in order to create a politicised, subversive and yet *individualised* commentary on neoliberal governmentality. Running concurrent to coverage of the economic breakdown, Davies explains, was not only concern about the morality of important financial, political and social institutions,[9] but also an increasing amount of attention being paid to rising 'epidemics' of anxiety, depression, and addictive behaviours (2014: 2). Davies points to the former Chair of the Federal Reserve Alan Greenspan's confession that he made a mistake in trusting the 'self-interest' of lending institutions (164), enquiring as to whether an institution can indeed exercise self-interest, and noting the use of psychological rhetoric as a means to avoid a more radical critique of the economic system (158). As Davies argues, 'if the limits and failures of market-based techniques and rationalities can be attributed to minds, selves or brains, then neoliberalism itself can be modified in view of contingent calculative anomalies, but also preserved as a particular tradition of practice' (158). The manner in which individuals exercise choice, Davies argues, has as a result become an important empirical question, which has led to forms of economic psychology that attempt to gauge national happiness and wellbeing through data (167), with new policies designed to counteract psychological irrationalities (165).

This is in keeping with Barbara Ehrenreich's observation that the ideology of positivity is pervasive within the United States (2009: 4), and underpins dominant modes of thinking within the intersecting worlds of health, psychology, religion and business. Such rhetoric attributes personal failings to a negative outlook (8) and works to discourage dissent and critique (187). Ehrenreich points out that an ideology of optimism played a key role in contributing to the economic collapse, as American corporate culture had embraced an environment of 'mysticism, charisma and sudden intuition' as opposed to a 'dreary' rationalism (184). Furthermore, Ehrenreich implicates the fervent American belief in opportunity and upward mobility as a key reason for why so many engaged in risky borrowing practices and spending habits (181–2). Anxiety and depression, which may be common afflictions given the uncertainties and inequalities of the neoliberal economy, are, Davies states, 'reduced to set of neuro-chemical imbalances' that may be healed not only by pharmaceuticals but also by various forms of social interaction such as gardening, dancing or singing (2014: 168).

Blue Jasmine literally psychologises and genders the failures of neoliberalism by the film's intense focus on the morally problematic choices of one character and the impact of these past individual decisions on her present-day health and wellbeing. In doing so, the film can detract from a critique of Hal's corrupt business dealings, the details of which remain vague throughout the piece although they bear a strong resemblance to real-life scandals such as the Bernie Madoff Ponzi scheme,[10] and instead chooses to illuminate the perceived pathogenic potential of a woman's decision to invest in a neoliberal postfeminist ethos. Jasmine's decision to relocate temporarily to San Francisco has the *potential* to act as a social curative for her particular form of burdened white womanhood, in the same manner that communal bonding serves a restorative function in the travel romance or indeed the fantasy adventure, yet the film ultimately chooses to cast her as a tragic figure, emblematic of the supposed ideological homelessness of neoliberal consumer capitalism. While the film does not plead a case for the rehabilitation of neoliberal governmentality, its failure to deal with the political complexities of the subject matter and its insistence on gendering and psychologising the material indicate an avoidant mode of social critique that is perhaps not dissimilar from Jasmine's avoidance of her own economic circumstances.

NEOLIBERAL RHETORIC AND GENDERED CLASS VIOLENCE

Jasmine, who in marrying Hal experiences a substantial rise in wealth and prestige, expresses disgust with those she sees as having failed to 'better' themselves both economically and socially. It is this attitude that provides the basis for the gendered class violence within the film, with Jasmine positioned as a figure of hypocrisy when she continues to perpetuate these views even as she herself becomes unemployed and destitute. It is the representation of gendered conditioning as inflected by class position that allows the film to examine the importance of class to the postfeminist sensibility, but also allows it to utilise 'female privilege' as the primary device through which to explore the human cost of capitalist greed. Despite Ginger's hospitality and willingness to forgive her sister for her past errors in judgement, Jasmine continues to voice her opinions on what she perceives to be Ginger's lack of ambition, as evidenced by her supermarket job and poor taste in boyfriends. These verbalisations, along with Jasmine's refusal to sell her designer wardrobe, aid her in maintaining a façade of wealth and entitlement. Ginger is the only character in the film willing to take pity on Jasmine and see the potential for her redemption, an aspect of character that the text suggests is due simultaneously to Ginger's inherent moral virtue and her misplaced idolisation of her adoptive sibling. Advocating a combined economic and cultural model of class analysis, Fiona Devine and Mike Savage point out that the interrelationship between class and culture does not require the presence of a coherent or distinctive class identity, but is rather born out of 'the way in which cultural outlooks are implicated in modes of exclusion and/or domination' (2000: 195). Skeggs, explaining how internalised class judgements impact upon the negotiation of femininity by young working-class women, determines that because respectability is not seen to be the domain of the working classes it becomes a sought-after object (1997: 1), facilitating the need for various improvement practices to simulate fantasies of middle-class elegance and sophistication (84). Proximity to the correct knowledge and practices, as defined by the middle and upper classes, functions to generate a damaging awareness of one's own wrongdoings (Skeggs 1997: 15). In a scene prior to Hal's arrest, Ginger visits Jasmine in New York where she proudly proclaims to new husband Augie that her sister's 'got taste', asking Jasmine to take her shopping because she 'always could pick clothes'. Jasmine, however, expresses her displeasure at Ginger's visit, informing a friend while on a shopping excursion that her sister 'was never too bright', while complaining to Hal that she has had to neglect her yoga classes as Ginger is 'such hard work'.

Ginger's desire to obtain Jasmine's approval is not confined merely to her choice of clothing but, as noted earlier, also extends to her choice in romantic partners. Upon her sister's arrival in San Francisco, Ginger becomes doubtful as to the suitability of her new boyfriend Chili after Jasmine opines that he is 'another version of Augie, a loser', and instead begins seeing Al (Louis C. K.), a man she meets at a party that Jasmine has insisted she accompany her to, and whose name bears a close resemblance to that of Jasmine's ex-husband. Asking Jasmine if she thinks Al is a 'step up' from Chili, Ginger is ultimately hurt when it transpires that Al has neglected to inform her he is married, which culminates in her realisation that compliance with Jasmine's value systems may not lead to personal contentment. Prior to her disappointment with Al, Ginger is invested in the allure of the postfeminist sensibility and its accordant emphases on affluence and consumerism as aiding in promoting the 'right' modes of feminine dress and conduct. Ginger's realisation that she does not

Figure 3.3 Jasmine's homelessness doubles as a 'casting out' of the postfeminist sensibility in *Blue Jasmine*.

need to 'class pass' to lead a happy life coincides with the vindication of both Augie and Chili's statements that Jasmine is a 'phoney'. It is perhaps at this juncture that the film's critique of the American dream becomes most apparent, with Gwendolyn Audrey Foster noting in *Class Passing* that 'the desire for class mobility seems as normative and opaque as the American dream itself' (2005: 3). Foster points to the contradictory discourses at the heart of this nation-building narrative, which on the one hand promises upward mobility as a reward for hard work and determination while simultaneously encouraging citizens to engage in displays of hedonistic consumption (22), an ethos that the film suggests women like Jasmine invest in to their ultimate detriment. Tellingly, it is Ginger who is the most naïve with regard to Jasmine's performative displays throughout the film, with Augie and Chili always able to detect a degree of falsity. Augie exasperatedly informs Ginger that Jasmine could not have been married to a 'a guy up to his ass in phoney real estate' for years without knowing about his illegal activity, while Chili reminds her that there was no financial support when Jasmine had immense wealth and Ginger was bartending and waitressing. Ginger's characterisation as particularly susceptible to Jasmine's falsehoods intensifies the film's gendered focus on the immorality of particular investments in consumer capitalism, with a story about investment fraud becoming a story about the fraudulent construction of the feminine self. The revelation of Jasmine's inauthenticity and her ultimate homelessness exposes the postfeminist sensibility as a construct to be identified and cast out, an exposure that can only occur if women choose to invest in alternate modes of femininity.

Besides becoming a symbol for the ills of consumer capitalism, Jasmine, in her calls for Ginger to become an autonomous agent and manage her life more appropriately by improving her social and financial prospects, operates as a spokesperson for neoliberal rhetoric. Her espousal of conservative viewpoints that define agency and success largely in financial terms allows her to cling to a personal ideal of rigid class hierarchy that has in the past positioned her atop a pedestal. Jasmine disavows any obstacles in Ginger's path toward achieving wealth other than what she perceives to be her sister's weakness of will, a logic that works to absolve both her and Hal of the role they have played in the loss of Ginger's money. As Wendy Brown states, neoliberalism 'carries responsibility for the self to new heights: the rationally calculating individual bears full responsibility for the consequences of his or her action no matter how severe the constraints on this action' (2005: 42). 'You can't always blame your genes!' Jasmine exclaims to Ginger one evening. 'You have to work hard and not settle!' Jasmine here espouses the neoliberal viewpoint that socio-economic inequalities provide no barrier to individual agency or success as defined on the terms of the capitalist system, a point that is echoed later in the film when she reminds Ginger's sons to 'tip big' when they eventually come into wealth, thus assuming the system rewards the many rather than a select few. In making such condemnations of her sister's choices, Jasmine echoes neoliberalism's branding of wealth inequality as but the outcome of failed individual decision-making, a pervasive mode of perception that Tyler argues works to frame economic inequality as a 'psycho-cultural' issue, thus legitimising the punishment of the poor (2013: 162).

All of Jasmine's pronouncements and judgements on this topic, however, are contextualised and rendered hypocritical in relation to her own difficulties in navigating the labour market as a result of both her financial situation and failure to complete her university education. When Jasmine is questioned about what she plans to do to support herself, she proclaims that she wants to study rather than engage in anything menial, while Ginger reminds her that such courses cost money. Jasmine's anger at Ginger for blaming her genes comes during an evening of significant stress when she is struggling to study for a computer course and Chili begins to challenge her about her past behaviour toward Ginger and her lack of employment. Jasmine's neoliberal rhetoric, then, is yet another aspect of her fantasy persona, becoming a means of insulating herself from both the unethical nature of her past actions and her lack of career prospects in the present moment. Jasmine, the film suggests, is in no position to advocate any mode of socio-economic organisation or navigation as she has only achieved financial comfort through marriage. Her belief in neoliberal ideology vindicates her position of privilege and allows her to indulge in the pleasures of consumption without experiencing guilt over the social inequalities that afford her this lifestyle. By the film's conclusion, Jasmine has ironically become a victim of her own belief system, failing to navigate a tough economic climate on her own and failing to appreciate forms of human bonding that lie beyond the entrepreneurial. Although Jasmine will perpetually 'look the other way' rather than acknowledge unethical acts that may threaten her lifestyle, Ginger and Augie are shown to act with moral integrity, as is shown when Augie notes the importance of 'having a friend's back' before Ginger warns Jasmine of Hal's closeness with modelling agent Raylene (Kathy Tong). Ultimately, the challenge of negotiating neoliberal postfeminism outside its required context of socio-economic privilege allows Jasmine the *opportunity* to reconnect with family and build new friendships, but she fails to seize this chance.

BLUE JASMINE AS FASHION TEXT AND THE POLITICS OF FEMALE LABOUR

Blue Jasmine, however, appears invested in the very systems it aims to critique, in that the film operates not only as a tragedy drama or auteur prestige project, but also as a variant of the 'fashion film', which Pamela Church Gibson explains is a text where fashion occupies a presence that is both 'central and celebrity-linked' (2013: 83). The role of designer fashion as spectacle does partially undercut the ideological work of the film's narrative, and this point proves the value of Church Gibson's call to 'look sideways' (11) at a text's alliance with other media forms such as fashion and advertising when engaging in ideological analysis. Yet it also works to illustrate how the film demonises only a particular *type* of female consumer, rather than female engagement in consumer capitalism altogether. Although Jasmine is vilified for her love of luxury products, part of the pleasure of the film for many audience members would undoubtedly lie in the array of designer garments on display from fashion houses including Chanel, Carolina Herrera and Oscar de la Renta, which helps account for the attention paid to the film and its star by leading fashion magazines such as *Vogue* and *Harper's Bazaar*. The film thus opens up a profound space of discomfort for the female viewer who is simultaneously invited to take pleasure in the film as a fashion text, while judging Jasmine harshly for her lack of self-awareness and disregard for others. Female audience members are therefore encouraged to interrogate their own pleasure in consumer capitalism in relation to their individual investments in the postfeminist sensibility and to question whether they have struck an appropriate balance between production and consumption. Cate Blanchett as a star text becomes an important focal point through which the film can undertake this ideological work, not only because of her commercial alignments with the fashion industry but also owing to her particular category of stardom and her much-publicised political convictions, which importantly differ markedly from Jasmine's. Blanchett is a star well-known for her glamourous sartorial choices[11] and has spoken of her expertise in fashion as allowing her to craft an authentic performance as Jasmine while also enabling an additional level of creative input into the picture in its entirety (Alexander 2013). The actress's fashion expertise thus allows her an authorship role over one aspect of the text and imbues her with a level of creative *agency*, while Jasmine's investment in fashion and other luxury products can only ever provide her with at best a misdirected or false sense of agency, and at worst an unethical agency. While Ginger is redefined by the text as 'respectable' in a cultural context that typically presents working-class women as objects of scorn or renders them invisible, Jasmine is defined as 'not respectable' on the basis that she hasn't earned the right to consume in the first place. Jasmine is shown to be dismissive of both education and paid labour from the film's opening and upon her arrival in San Francisco, where she insults Ginger by expressing her reluctance to 'bag groceries' while offending Chili's friend Eddie by exhibiting her disdain for the nursing profession.

Blanchett, on the other hand, belongs to what Christine Geraghty describes as the most prestigious category of stardom – that of the star as performer. These stars, Geraghty explains, are distinguished from celebrities in that their 'skill, craft, and talent are placed in the forefront of their image lexicons and put on display in their performances' (2000: 187). Due to the considerable international acclaim her work has thus far amassed, Blanchett has a significant degree of artistic and economic influence not only within the Hollywood film industry, but also in her role as cultural icon and arts ambassador in her home country of Australia, where she often provides political commentary on the importance of the arts to the nation state. An invited speaker at former Labor Prime Minister Gough Whitlam's funeral, Blanchett took the opportunity to praise Whitlam's goal of the 'creation of a society in which the arts and the appreciation of spiritual and intellectual values can flourish', while describing herself as a grateful beneficiary of his policies relating to free tertiary education, healthcare and maternity stipends (ABC News 2014). This speech, met by rapturous applause, not only importantly demarcates Blanchett from Jasmine in terms of her leftist politics, but also illuminates how Blanchett functions as an influential celebrity text through which, because of the cultural value placed upon her labour, political articulations and calls to action can be made. Blanchett thus belongs to a privileged *class* of celebrity, a class that has a voice, can be mobilised to political effect, and is of course not indistinguishable from social class. The contemporary negotiation of privilege inherent within the construction of the postfeminist sensibility, then, does not necessarily constitute an outright vilification of the privileged female consumer, but is predicated upon a more complex relationship between her participation in the labour market and her participation in consumer capitalism, an interesting point to consider when addressing the class politics in which a text such as *Blue Jasmine* is embedded. Jasmine is a tragic villain because of her conservative neoliberal viewpoints, her utilisation of altruistic activities as vanity projects, and most importantly her engagement in consumer capitalism as defined by her failure to generate income. Hal and Jasmine, then, both spend money that they have not rightfully earned, with illegal business activity and the reluctance to engage in paid work treated as an almost equivalent socio-economic and ethical failing. As Dwight accuses Jasmine upon discovering the lies that she has told in relation to her personal history, 'Your ethical behaviour is equal to your husband's!' The audience is here invited to sympathise with Dwight, an innocent victim of Jasmine's lies and schemes, and to participate in the masculine bias that informs the film's critique of neoliberal ideology.

CONCLUSION

The postfeminist sensibility is dependent on neoliberal discourse for its signification, and favours an upwardly mobile, affluent and typically white female subject who will participate in the labour market, engage in consumer capitalism and eventually embrace motherhood. Yet when modes of neoliberal governance are seen to fail, for instance in the fallout from the global financial crisis, the relationship between neoliberal rhetoric and the postfeminist sensibility must accordingly be modified to allow for the emergence of new discourses facilitating the recovery of the state. In *Blue Jasmine*, the US Government is shown to act swiftly and appropriately both in the arrest of Hal and in the repossession of the couple's belongings, while Hal's death allows the narrative to explore the aftermath of the incident primarily through Jasmine. It is she who becomes the embodiment of societal sickness in exhibiting an extreme imbalance in her production and consumption responsibilities and through her overt melancholic attachment to a previous lifestyle built upon corruption. Although the text invites the audience to question whether Jasmine could utilise her engagement with Ginger to transcend her melancholic state and craft a more promising future for herself, Jasmine's investment in the status her prior identity afforded her ultimately proves too great for her to surmount. A consideration of the film as a fashion text, however, indicates that it cannot act as a straightforward vilification of the female consumer, a crucial aspect to consider given how dominant and influential neoliberal feminism has become over the last two decades. Furthermore, the text's exploration of societal value systems through the affluent white woman's negotiation of the postfeminist sensibility is dependent upon her interaction with a woman disadvantaged by the neoliberal ideology she believes in. The role of Ginger in this text is to aid the postfeminist subject to see the errors of her prior ways – an endeavour that may or may not prove successful, and ultimately may be superficial, given that this role does little to displace the centrality and narrative dominance of the white, upper-class protagonist. If such treatments of postfeminism are becoming more frequent, then more attention needs to be paid to exactly how politics of race and class are informing these shifts in gender representation within mainstream Hollywood and celebrity texts.

NOTES

1. Philip C. Kolin in *Williams: Streetcar Named Desire* discusses the fact that there also have been subversive treatments of the play that destabilise the race and gender politics of the text and liberate it 'from the racially imposed constraints of a white theatre culture' (2000: 120), for instance, the 1955 Ebony Showcase Theatre production directed by Paul Rodgers that featured an all-black cast, and the 1991 queer/camp adaptation *Belle Reprieve*.
2. As explored by Cheryl I. Harris in her influential article 'Whiteness as property', published in the *Harvard Law Review* in 1993.
3. Citing vilified historical women and fictional characters including Marie Antoinette, Cruella de Vil and *Dynasty's* Alexis Carrington, Lee and Moscowitz argue that the caricature of the selfish and materialistic 'rich bitch' works to fuel class antagonisms and promote traditional gender roles. Interestingly, the authors point to the failure of a similarly themed reality show focused on men entitled *Househusbands of Hollywood* in order to illustrate their point that audiences are more likely to vilify female socialites as opposed to their male counterparts (2013: 65).
4. Discussed as part of the *Academy Conversations* segment on the film, held at the Academy Theatre Lighthouse International on 23 July 2013.
5. It is worth noting here that Tyler, in examining the plight not only of the economically poor, but also of asylum seekers, Gypsy travellers, socially alienated youth and people with disabilities, employs a highly intersectional approach in her analysis of those disenfranchised by the politics of neoliberalism.
6. See Barbara Schapiro's article 'Woody Allen's search for self' in the *Journal of Popular Culture* (1986) for a discussion of this topic.
7. Thomas Elsaesser discusses the psychologising function of music in the family melodrama in 'Tales of sound and fury: observations on the family melodrama' (1987/2012: 441).
8. Although Allen's film in its vilification of a specific female social type could hardly be classed as a radical socialist critique, it is interesting to note that Anker explores the melodramatic rhetoric of the political left as characterised by what Walter Benjamin has termed 'leftist melancholy'. Leftist melancholy, Anker explains, exhibits an attachment to older forms of Marxist critique that promised and yet failed to deliver freedom from capitalist oppression (2014: 205). Although Jasmine's individual melancholy works markedly differently within this text, it could be argued that the film's lack of broader social critique and importantly its inability to imagine alternative social structures beyond the neoliberal system permeate the film with certain characteristics of leftist melancholy.
9. Davies here discusses British events including the 2011 *News of the World* incident where journalists were found to be engaged in the criminal hacking of phones and the 2012 Libor scandal in which major banks were discovered to be falsely inflating and deflating interest rates.
10. Bernard Madoff, founder of Wall Street investment firm Bernard L. Madoff Investment Securities LLC, pled guilty in 2009 to eleven federal felonies and admitted to defrauding investors of billions of dollars' worth of funds. Hal's fate in *Blue Jasmine* may resonate with viewers familiar with the scandal, given that Madoff's son Mark committed suicide by hanging two years following his father's arrest.

11. A number of Blanchett's recent films have garnered attention for the use of dramatic and extravagant costuming in order to convey character, including the Cannes Film Festival favourite *Carol* (Todd Haynes, 2015) and the blockbuster hit *Cinderella* (Kenneth Branagh, 2015), in which Blanchett wore a selection of 1940s *femme-fatale*-inspired gowns in her role as the wicked stepmother Lady Tremaine.

CHAPTER 4

Paranoid Attachments to Suburban Dreams: Reading Pathological Femininity in *Gone Girl* and *The Girl on the Train*

In 2012, Gillian Flynn's psychological thriller *Gone Girl* was released to widespread critical acclaim. Centring upon the post-recessionary marriage breakdown of young couple Nick and Amy Elliot Dunne and Amy's subsequent suspicious disappearance, the book requires its readers to invest in Amy's diary confessionals as evidence of her loveless marriage and victimisation at the hands of a frustrated and potentially violent husband. The twist of the criminal investigation comes as Amy reveals herself to her reader as something of a fraudulent gothic heroine – a woman whose desire to frame her husband for murder is born out of the insufficient rewards garnered by her dutiful adherence to a distinctly neoliberal and postfeminist construction of self. For Amy, or 'Amazing Amy' as her parents' series of books nickname her childhood alter-ego, success is equated with the admiring gaze of the upscale crowd and the perception of the 'Nick and Amy' brand as the most perfect or the happiest. For 'what is the point,' she asks, 'if you are not the happiest?' Amy's determination to amass a public outpouring of grief for her mediated story of suffering, and ideally a conviction of legal guilt for Nick, is thus an elaborate punishment for her husband's anti-competitive laziness and his implicit threat to leave her for a younger adherent to the postfeminist masquerade. Flynn is an 'expert angler', Alison Flood writes for *The Guardian*, her unreliable narrators 'baffling, disturbing and delighting in turn', while the novel is 'an early contender for thriller of the year' (2012). Janet Maslin in *The New York Times*, meanwhile, describes *Gone Girl* as 'wily, mercurial, and subtly layered', comparing the novel's 'discrete malice' to the works of Patricia Highsmith (2012).

As is customary when a distinctive formula proves both a critical and commercial success, new titles are released in an attempt to capitalise upon the wave of audience taste. One of the more high profile of these contenders has been Paula Hawkins' 2015 offering *The Girl on the Train*, in which the alcoholic lead Rachel Watson's unreliable narration creates uncertainty in the reader as to her potential involvement and culpability in the disappearance and death of local woman Megan Hipwell. The book immediately drew comparisons to its predecessor, with Suzi Feay in *The Guardian* commenting that the Hawkins novel contains 'clear echoes' of *Gone Girl* character tropes (2015), while Heidi Pitlor in *The Boston Globe* cites the two bestsellers as indicative of a new era of 'complex and mighty heroines' (2015). Both novels were soon adapted for the cinematic screen, with David Fincher's *Gone Girl* opening in 2014 and featuring Ben Affleck and Rosamund Pike as its dysfunctional suburbanites, while Tate Taylor's *The Girl on the Train* opened in 2016 and starred Emily Blunt as the abject heroine. As in *Blue Jasmine*, both Amy Elliot Dunne and Rachel Watson exhibit melancholic attachments to elite lifestyles and neoliberal postfeminist philosophies that have offered fraudulent promises of happiness and contentment. The refusal to alter one's investment or to see it as anything other than an ideal mode of being is aligned with a depiction of the heroine's melancholic state as harbouring an inner mental precarity and potential capacity for violent psychopathology. If Jasmine's misplaced melancholia is implicated in her ultimate mental decline and capacity for linguistic violence, then Amy and Rachel's capacity for physical violence raises the stakes of the neoliberal postfeminist project and its hegemonic negotiation considerably.

Rachel and Amy's melancholic attachment to neoliberal postfeminist philosophy is familiarly aligned with both societal pressure and frustrated artistry. Rachel exhibits a longing for her previous lifestyle as spouse to Tom Watson (Justin Theroux) in an upscale New York neighbourhood to such a degree that she repeatedly undertakes train journeys past her old home to catch a glimpse of her ex-husband and his new wife Anna (Rebecca Ferguson), and to fabricate fantasy narratives about those who live nearby. If, as Lucie Armitt suggests, 'melancholia is a trap sprung by endless returns to the site of trauma' (2007: 25), then the neighbourhood where Rachel suffered physical and emotional abuse at the hands of her husband becomes a key site of both repetitive return and obsessive fascination. Its significance to Rachel's fractured mental state constitutes a mystery that can be solved only through a belated realisation of the suburban marriage as a fraudulent site of contentment. 'My husband used to tell me I have an overactive imagination,' Rachel's narrative voiceover tells us as she gazes from the train window. 'I can't help it. I mean, haven't you ever been on the train and wondered about the lives of the people who live near the tracks?' Rachel's obsessive surveillance of the upper middle classes serves as a deflection of the wary and disgusted gaze of her fellow commuters who notice her ruddy complexion, bleary-eyed appearance and unsteady gait. Her appearance operates at a significant remove from the Rachel of the past that we have witnessed in flashback, who favoured soft knits in cream and beige neutrals as opposed to heavy overcoats in black and dour grey, and who had a perfectly

Figure 4.1 Megan's suburban melancholia in *The Girl on the Train*.

made-up appearance. When a woman holding a baby sits next to Rachel on the train, she becomes wary of Rachel's interest in her son after sighting a bottle of spirits in her handbag. While Rachel understands that people can see that she is 'not the girl [she] used to be', she fails to understand the real history behind her transition from an object of middle-class success and admiration to a figure of social abjection, and her former husband's culpability in this psychological transformation. Rachel's love of sketching, however, provides a means of working through these regressive memories, with her final sketch an intricate evocation of a statue of three women holding hands, symbolising Rachel's newfound awareness of feminine melancholia as a potentially shared state and the importance of female solidarity. Tellingly, Rachel's earlier imaginings of Megan Hipwell's life theorise that while her husband is likely to be a doctor or an architect, Megan (Hayley Bennett) is probably a painter or something 'creative'. While Rachel believes that Megan has the perfect life, their shared affinity for the creative arts creates an alignment between the two women and alludes to Megan's own unhappiness and discontent within a town that she perceives as 'boring' and 'routine'. Rachel's theory that Megan is a painter foreshadows what the spectator comes to learn of Megan's free-spiritedness and disregard for social conformity – personality traits that ultimately play a role in her demise.

Amy Elliot Dunne in *Gone Girl* is also an example of a stifled creative – a frustrated 'A1 girl' (McRobbie 2009: 15), whose cognisance of the postfeminist masquerade's socio-economic benefits drives her to commit murder in a bid to maintain her elevated social position. Like *The Girl on the Train*, *Gone Girl*'s psychological impetus lies in its bid to uncover the darkness and duplicity

Figure 4.2 The commercialisation of 'can-do' femininity in *Gone Girl*.

inherent within a seemingly ideal marriage. The film opens with Nick's subjective musings as he casually strokes his wife's hair while she lies on his chest, seemingly contentedly. 'When I think of my wife, I always think of her head,' he confides. 'I picture cracking her lovely skull, unspooling her brains, trying to get answers. The principles of any marriage: what are you thinking? How are you feeling? What have we done to each other?' This interior monologue betrays Nick's failure to understand his wife, and the violent thoughts that arise from such a failure, while also implicating him as the likely instigator of the narrative's central crime. Amy, we learn, has a 'type A' personality – Ivy League-educated, 'standoffish', and without many friends. Her parents are overly invested in what they perceive to be their daughter's superior beauty and brilliance, having accumulated significant wealth from a series of children's books that centre upon the adventures of a blonde, pig-tailed child who excels at everything she does. At a party held to celebrate Amazing Amy's fictional marriage, Amy takes Nick on a tour past iconic examples of the book series, wryly pointing out that while she was cut from the volleyball team in junior year, Amazing Amy made varsity, and when she quit learning the cello, her cartoon counterpart became a prodigy. When Nick exclaims that Amy's parents plagiarised her childhood, Amy notes that this is not in fact correct. 'They improved upon it,' she states, 'and peddled it to the masses'.

It is this gap between Amazing Amy's embodiment of the perfected self and Amy Elliot's acknowledgement that she is both 'real' and 'flawed', that give rise to her refusal to accept anything less than an outward appearance of happiness and success. 'Amazing Amy', as symbol of a pervasive social construction of ideal femininity, is always ripe for image exploitation. Amy, like Rachel Watson, is creatively inclined, yet exhibits frustration that her writing skills have been limited to creating personality quizzes for women's magazines. The anniversary games that she creates for Nick indicate an affinity for women's literature and foreshadow the importance of female authorship to her manipulation of national sentiment. In the library, Amy hides clues that Nick must solve to gain romantic and sexual rewards. 'God bless Jane Austen!' he cries as Amy initiates sex at a study table between the rows of books. Amy's creative capacity signals a dissatisfaction with postfeminist image construction, but unlike some Hollywood films featuring melancholic heroines, it is not employed in the pursuit of renegotiating the relationship to postfeminist whiteness to positive effect. Instead, Amy endeavours to utilise her creative skillset in a bid to maintain and capitalise upon her idealised social status, with Nick's praise of an iconic female writer indicating his naivety as to the potential power of his wife's games and fabrications.

SUBURBAN TALES AND POST-RECESSIONARY PRECARITY

Both *Gone Girl* and *The Girl on the Train* are recent additions to a canon of American films that critique suburban ideology and its perceived emphasis on tranquillity, order and conformity. Such texts seek to expose what Robert Fishman calls the 'Bourgeois Utopia' (1987), a term that he argues champions 'leisure, family life, and union with nature', while concealing how such principles operate on a basis of exclusion (4). While the construction of suburbia was predicated upon white, middle-class values, and systematically excluded those not belonging to this group, both films choose to foreground the isolation of the female protagonists from the public sphere as a more central issue. As Fishman argues, while the bourgeois utopia exalted the role of middle-class women within the family, it also 'segregated them from the world of power and productivity', with self-enforced segregation reflecting 'the alienation of the middle classes from the urban-industrial world they themselves were creating' (4). Following the couple's job losses in *Gone Girl*, it is Nick's decision to move himself and Amy from their New York apartment to suburban Missouri that deepens his wife's frustration with their marriage, while the quiet, picturesque houses and bored, gossip-hungry housewives provide the perfect ingredients for her mass-mediated tale of domestic discord and woe. The production decision to relocate the setting of *The Girl on the Train* from the gritty outskirts of London to the affluence of suburban New York situates the film version of the story within this cinematic lineage, while also strengthening the symbolic relationship between New York as a cinematic sign and the fracturing of neoliberal postfeminist philosophies. It is the segregated and suffocating nature of the suburban environment that facilitates Rachel's total dependence on her husband, allowing Tom to control her to such a degree that she is eventually fired from paid work because of her drinking habit. The removal of both women from the public sphere undermines the gains afforded them by the second-wave feminist movement and situates them within an environment commonly imagined in American popular culture as permeated with 1950s' domestic ideology. Discussing the recent proliferation of film and television shows that take American suburbia as their setting – such as *American Beauty* (Sam Mendes, 1999), *Little Children* (Todd Field, 2006), *Mr and Mrs Smith* (Doug Liman, 2005), and *Weeds* (Showtime: 2005–12) – David R. Coon points out that these texts frequently draw upon the concept of the suburban façade (2014: 18). While suburban life appears on the surface to be 'harmonious and fulfilling', there is within these narratives a gradual peeling away of the layers that constitute familial performativity to reveal 'hidden desires, secrets, and problems that threaten to disrupt the tranquil suburban existence' (18). The traditional architectural emphasis within suburbia on community as a shared space, with tightly packed developments and the introduction of design elements such as the sliding glass door and picture window (Coon 2014: 74), allows these texts to serve as ideal venues for an exploration of the distinction between the public and private, and the performance of public and private selfhood (78). This collapse of the public façade that accompanies a new precarity of postfeminist ideology and the A1 girl's realisation that her optimism and attachment to such ideology is 'cruel' (Berlant 2011) are culturally imagined as contributing to her mental break. In these films, the protagonist's intelligence, promoted within neoliberal rhetoric as a social asset, become newly threatening within the private sphere, as it is an attribute that proves difficult to contain and control. Female intelligence is also threatening within the public sphere of the films as it is a tool that threatens to 'leak' beyond the perimeters of the suburban environment and disenfranchise white masculinity.

Familiar criticisms within fictional suburban films and television shows that these developments that are subject to heightened surveillance and thus are not conducive to individual growth and creativity have a basis in sociological critique of the 1950s and 1960s. As Coon points out, best-selling books such as David Riesman's *The Lonely Crowd* (1950) popularised the idea that social status within suburbia was largely predicated on conforming and 'blending in' rather than celebrating difference (9). Yet mediated dramatisations of suburbia are also dependent upon a shared knowledge of these spaces as simulated, drawing upon a pop-cultural lineage of suburban representation and often exhibiting significant levels of intertextuality. Timotheus Vermeulen, for example, notes that the popular film *Pleasantville* (Gary Ross, 1998) is a parody of the *idea* of the 1950s' sitcom, with contemporary representations of suburbia signifying more prominently in relation to the Republican Party's invocation of the 1950s as a nostalgic ideal than to the sociopolitical complexities of the decade and its cultural products (2014: 27). It is the exposition of the suburbanite's public self as elaborate façade that allows this setting to serve as a perfect venue through which to renegotiate postfeminist selfhood as a form of masquerade that carries both benefits and costs, and contributes to the banality of gendered routine. The partial temporal collapse of 'suburbia' as mediated simulacra allows the narrative to draw comparisons between the characters' predicaments and pre-second-wave gender ideals, exploring the continuing cultural value of, for instance, the stay-at-home wife in the postfeminist and post-recessionary context. Furthermore, the suburban film's manipulation of an iconography of setting serves to set the stage for the female characters' manipulation of the cultural significance of gendered icons, for instance Amy's library clue trail, which utilises Jane Austen as a tool of marital reward. Austen's persona, and the thematic material inherent within her writing, provides clues as to Amy's dissatisfaction with gendered public performance, while also alluding to the text's dystopic imagining of the pathological potential of female authorship within the public sphere.

As in *Eat Pray Love* and *Blue Jasmine*, the global financial crisis of 2008 provides a key catalyst within these psychological thrillers for a renegotiation of the postfeminist sensibility. As Kirk Boyle and Daniel Mrozowski point out in their examination of US 'bust culture', the recession has served as a backdrop or plot catalyst for increasing numbers of film and television programmes over the last decade, from corporate dramas such as *Up in the Air* (Jason Reitman, 2009) and *The Company Men* (John Wells, 2010), to television comedies and 'dramedies' like *2 Broke Girls* (CBS: 2011–), *The Middle* (ABC: 2009–) and *Girls* (HBO: 2012–) (2013: x). The recessionary narrative is also a fixture of the horror genre, with April Miller noting that media discourses accompanying the economic collapse often metaphorically invoked horror tropes, and characters.[1] The collapse of the US housing market and subsequent home foreclosures, Miller argues, finds its genesis in filmic narratives where the domestic space becomes a site of anxiety and dread, subject to external invasion and 'possession', such as Sam Raimi's 2009 film *Drag Me to Hell* (2013: 31). *Gone Girl* and *The Girl on the Train*, in their attribution of murder and violence to the suburban residents themselves rather than supernatural forces, and their emphasis on ambiguous psychology and suspense over gore and shock value, are more likely to be dubbed gothics or thrillers than horrors. Yet as Emily Johansen's reading of Flynn's novel argues persuasively, to live under neoliberal capitalism is to live in gothic times (2016: 30). Neoliberal gothic novels like *Gone Girl*, Johansen argues, present the cruelties of capitalism as 'inevitable and inescapable', with such texts failing to imagine the emergence of alternative social structures (30). Grotesque and exaggerated gothic tropes become the norm, with the neoliberal emphasis on entrepreneurialism and individualism inevitably creating monsters of its ideal subjects and contributing to a 'sense of entropic decline' (31). Indeed, the film's establishing sequence, which involves a series of shots focusing on large suburban homes, local shops, and then Nick Dunne's introduction as he initiates his early morning routine by taking out the rubbish, bathes the neighbourhood in an ominous and eerie blue shadow. Atticus Ross and Trent Reznor's musical track entitled 'What Have We Done?' overlays the scene with low, foreboding notes coupled with high-pitched, eerie synthesised sound in a distorted arrangement reminiscent of Angelo Badalamenti's score for David Lynch's *Twin Peaks* (ABC: 1990–1). The musical reference here to this cult favourite, which dramatises the secret lives and unsavoury dealings of small-town residents in the wake of the murder of teenaged girl Laura Palmer, further imbues the depiction of everyday suburban life with an underlying dread, and is likely to arouse tension in the viewer as to what is to come. As Reznor told CBS News, Fincher requested that he create a piece of music 'that might appear to be perfect or pleasant on the outside, but have it sort of rot inside' (Lusk 2014).

Gone Girl situates its post-recessionary narrative in the context of the colloquially named 'he-cession', which as Michelle Rodino-Colocino argues, emphasises male white workers as the hardest-hit group of the economic downturn and works to prevent an intersectional and systemic understanding of its impacts (2014: 343). Rodino-Colocino cites conservative economist Mike Perry's renaming of the global financial crisis as the '2008 male recession', and his attribution of the growing male unemployment rate to a 'lipstick economy' that rewards sensitivity, collaboration and intuition as evidence of this media trend (343–4). Amy is the more economically empowered in the relationship within this film, with the couple depending largely on her trust fund. It is after Nick is laid off from his job and is reduced to spending his days on the couch playing video games that Amy notes he has become 'lazy' and somebody she 'did not agree to marry'. Penning a diary entry in the mode of her personality quizzes, Amy questions her reader as to the best way to test a marriage for weak spots. 'Add one recession and subtract two jobs,' she confides. 'It's surprisingly effective.' Gazing from their apartment window at a New York cityscape that now appears hostile to the couple's quest for economic security and upward mobility, Nick and Amy promise each other that they will not allow themselves to become like those 'awful couples' they know – the husbands who treat their wives 'like the highway patrol, to be outfoxed and avoided', and the wives who treat their husbands 'like dancing monkeys to be trained and paraded'. What Nick fails to realise is that in times of economic health his marriage was also a game of performance, albeit with lower stakes. As Johansen points out, Nick's ultimate failing is that he is not as good a performer as his wife (47). His penchant for playing Monopoly with his sister Margo (Carrie Coon) serves as both a metaphor for the importance of capital accumulation within his marriage, and his misreading of the extent of Amy's investment in neoliberal postfeminist philosophy and its emphasis on material success. The goals and stakes of Monopoly, a game associated with familial leisure time, bestows victory on the players best able to expand their real estate empire and control other players financially. Nick and Margo's playing of the game to pass the time indicates a lack of awareness as to their own status as 'pawns' in Amy's elaborate schemes, but also their role as peripheral players within a capitalist economy – an economy that the text imagines as favouring middle- and upper-class white women.

While *The Girl on the Train* does not invoke its post-recessionary context as explicitly as *Gone Girl*, Rachel's unemployment and her alternating idealisation and jealousy of the affluent Megan, who appears to 'have it all', is likely to resonate with viewers familiar with a hostile job market and precarious employment conditions. The male characters in *The Girl on the Train* hold a greater balance of economic power within their respective marital relationships, although the film's suspense lies in the question as to whether the female characters wish to usurp this power and destroy their economic and/or marital comfort. Nevertheless, the comparative lack of socio-economic power held by the three female leads of *The Girl on the Train* provides a clue that the tale is 'authentically' gothic, as opposed to *Gone Girl*, in which Amy's diary construction of her victimisation serves to obscure the real power that she holds.

THE POSTFEMINIST GOTHIC HEROINE AND THE ELUSIVE *FEMME FATALE*

The thrill of both *Gone Girl* and *The Girl on the Train* lies in the representation of female melancholia as potentially harbouring the capacity for a violent psychological break. Melancholic white femininity in an era of neoliberal postfeminist anxiety is produced culturally as an ambivalent and potentially dangerous state, depending upon the afflicted sufferer's understanding and negotiation of it. The questions these films posit thus relate to whether Amy Elliot Dunne and Rachel Watson can be understood as gothic heroines, or if they are merely masquerading as such, concealing a will to harm that has arisen following the optimistic fantasy's brutal puncturing. Such narrative and thematic questions are made possible by contemporary ambivalence as to exactly what feminism is, and the myriad media narratives that may be understood as comprising forms of popular feminism. *Gone Girl* and *The Girl on the Train* exhibit a particularly close relationship with the genre of 'postfeminist gothic', a formula that has proven popular with contemporary consumers of both novels and cinema. Benjamin Brabon and Stéphanie Genz, writing on the post-second-wave development of gothic fiction and film, attribute dominant definitional understanding of the gothic to the literary scholar Ellen Moers, and describe the typical narrative as centring on 'an innocent and blameless heroine threatened by a powerful male figure and confined to a labyrinthine interior space' (2007: 5). Sarah E. Whitney, discussing the emergence of postfeminist gothic fiction in the US by writers such as Alice Sebold, Patricia Cornwall and Sapphire, states that this strain of literature centralises issues of gendered violence and pain, subverting postfeminist culture's 'victim-resistant' and 'empowerment-oriented' rhetoric (2016: 2). Whitney argues that this body of work asks its readers to acknowledge that being a woman in contemporary US society still carries considerable risk, and so works to critique depictions of the postfeminist world as happy, bright and 'candy-coloured' (2). Postfeminist gothic cinema, too, enjoys popularity with audiences at the multiplex, with Helen Hanson describing films such as *Sleeping with the Enemy* (Joseph Ruben, 1991), *Deceived* (Damian Harris, 1991) and *What Lies Beneath* (Robert Zemeckis, 2000) as examples of the genre. These female-addressed thrillers, Hanson argues, typically locate the female protagonist within a domestic environment and an 'unhappy or dysfunctional heterosexual relationship', in which the heroine becomes convinced that her husband harbours a terrible secret relating to a woman in his past and may be trying to kill her (2007: 175). While Hanson states that the fearful femininity of the postfeminist gothic heroine has not traditionally been understood as a form of masquerade (182), cultural anxieties relating to female melancholia in the present moment and uncertainties relating to the future of feminist politics have allowed for increasing levels of play with the genre. Such genre play relies upon a media-literate audience familiar with the various codes and conventions of mediated popular feminism, and the interaction of these audiences with postmodern entertainment texts that present the 'real' psychological states of female characters as discoverable through a set of clues.

The ambiguity as to the victim/avenger status of the female protagonists in *Gone Girl* and *The Girl on the Train* rests upon ambiguity as to their respective desires in relation to neoliberal postfeminist culture. Do these characters wish for an uncomplicated acceptance into the dominant ideological paradigms offered by neoliberal postfeminism, or will they reject these paradigms and embrace an uncertain future? Amy is the more economically empowered marital partner in *Gone Girl*, yet it is also her glamorous femininity that serves as a clue that she may not be the gothic heroine that she claims to be. As Hanson notes, the suffering gothic heroine typically presents an 'unspectacular femininity', with 1940s' variants of the character often made to feel 'bookish' and 'gauche' in comparison to their sophisticated husbands (2007: 188). Amy parodies the familiar characterisation of gothic femininity through diary entries that emphasise a growing fear of her husband. She claims that Nick uses her for sex and threw her violently against a bannister following an argument over whether they should have a baby. 'What scared me was how much he wanted to hurt me more,' Amy confides in voiceover as her past self is witnessed cowering against the staircase. 'What scared me was how much I am afraid of my own husband.' She later narrates her experience of buying a gun at a homeless dwelling on Valentine's Day while dressed all in pink, informing her reader that it will help her to sleep better, which further demonstrates her reliance on the reader's knowledge of appropriate feminine performance and female domestic vulnerability. In *The Girl on the Train*, Rachel's alcoholism serves as a plot device through which the audience is invited to question her interpretation of past events, and assess whether she is an innocent bystander in Megan Hipwell's death or a perpetrator of violence herself. The use of flashbacks to create competing memory archives of significant events in Rachel's past and the repeated use of motion blur to indicate both her intoxication and unreliable vision work to problematise the audience's identification with Rachel and their allegiance to her investigation.

In both films, the use of subjective flashbacks proves to be deceptive and the characters' relationship with the image, whether in relation to their visual recall of the past or to images of literary or cinematic feminine 'types', is troubled. When Amy finally reveals the fabricated nature of her planted evidence and the role this will play in her wider revenge scheme, she is depicted wearing a headscarf and sunglasses as she drives along the freeway basking in her newfound liberation. Amy's visual representation, as well as how the act of driving here functions as metaphor for female emancipation and escape, recalls the 1991 Ridley Scott film *Thelma & Louise*, which features Susan Sarandon and Geena Davis as two friends fleeing from lives defined by male violence. While driving, Amy engages in a feminist monologue of sorts in which she criticises defining features of the postfeminist sensibility as well as women who mould themselves into idealised feminine fantasies to please their male partners. Admitting that she pretended to be a 'cool girl' by drinking canned beer and watching Adam Sandler movies, remaining sexually available and maintaining a size two figure, Amy highlights her need to renegotiate the power dynamics within their relationship after learning that Nick can simply trade her in for a 'newer, younger, bouncier cool girl' the moment he tires of her charade. It is important to note that Amy is not anti-charade or anti-performance – she does, after all, eventually return to Nick and attempt to reconstruct their image as an affluent, contented suburban couple. She is, however, opposed to not being in control of her own image and/or to becoming a victim of the implicit power dynamics inherent within the terms of the contracts she enters into with others. While viewers may initially sympathise with Amy, and even agree with the sentiments expressed in her 'cool girl' speech, they are likely to become increasingly disturbed by the character as more is revealed about her history with men and the lengths she will go to in the pursuit of 'winning' at life. Amy's reunion with Nick is preceded by a graphic murder scene, during which she violently stabs her infatuated ex-boyfriend Desi Collings (Neil Patrick Harris) in a ploy to clear Nick's name and instead frame Desi for her abduction and sexual abuse. The invocation of *Thelma & Louise*'s gender politics, in which

Figure 4.3 Amy evokes the heroines of *Thelma & Louise* in *Gone Girl.*

both characters are the genuine victims of rape or attempted rape, sit uncomfortably in a text where the female protagonist frequently fabricates instances of sexual assault to punish men and maintain her status as a quintessentially postfeminist 'A1 girl'. In a narrative context that emphasises female power and achievement and presents white middle-class men as the ultimate victims of neoliberal postfeminist philosophies, Amy's appropriation of popular feminist iconography invites a reading as sinister, given that it works in the service of punishing a dominant social group that is recast in the film as marginalised. It is worth noting that *The Girl on the Train*, which questions yet ultimately reasserts the gothic heroine's embodiment of contemporary social truths, was not received nearly as well as Fincher's film,[2] in which social fears relating to the pathogenic potential of the postfeminist sensibility is not only acknowledged, but spectacularly vindicated.

Amy and Rachel are unreliable narrators, allowing the characters to signify within a cinematic history in which women's voices, as Mary Ann Doane argues, have frequently been subject to a loss of consistency, coherence and unity (1987: 173), with male characters able to reinterpret or subvert female narration (151). The role and primacy afforded to the female voice within the two films becomes a further point of notable divergence in relation to gender politics and ideological drive. The twist of *The Girl on the Train* comes when Rachel realises that her inaccurate recall of events can be attributed to her husband's psychological tyranny and emotional abuse. Her ability to speak, and thus to provide evidence in a murder case, has been severely compromised by the unequal power dynamics inherent within her former marriage. While Rachel's vocal coherence is corrupted by Tom's desire to control the women in his life, it is his former boss Martha (Lisa Kudrow) who restores Rachel's memories and allows her to speak the truth of Tom's nature to his new partner Anna. Martha, who explains to Rachel that she fired Tom for his attitudes toward women in the workplace, reassures her that she did 'nothing wrong' and speaks to the feminist sympathies of the text in that she stands as a positive example of female professional power. By contrast, *Gone Girl* treats the rise of the female professional within the public sphere – particularly the female journalists fronting current events talk shows – as contributing to a dystopian primacy of the female voice that appears over-eager in its desire to apportion blame to 'failing' male subjects. If Amy's spectacular femininity and comparative economic power in relation to her husband Nick provide important clues that she may not qualify as an 'authentic' gothic heroine, then so too does her voice, which remains cold and emotionless even when recounting tales of past victimisation and distress. Rosamund Pike's cultivated tones and lower vocal register, along with her visual resemblance to the Hitchcockian blondes of classical cinema, is perhaps a reason why she was favoured for the role over other candidates like Reese Witherspoon, whose higher-pitched tones and association with romantic comedies made her a less obvious fit for the lead, though she served as a producer on the piece. Amy's controlled and aloof narration comprises a 'misfit' with the genre of writing through which we initially learn about her married life – the confessional, intimate, affective mode of diary writing. The importance of the diary is a further 'joke' relating to the audience's presumed familiarity with postfeminist media culture and popular contemporary femininities, given the primacy of the diary as a mode of address in texts aimed at girls and women. While *Bridget Jones's Diary* is perhaps the most well-known example, *The Nanny Diaries* (Shari Springer Berman and Robert Pulcini, 2007) is another notable film that prioritises the subjective confessional mode, while *The Princess Diaries* (Garry Marshall, 2001), *The Carrie Diaries* (The CW: 2013–14) and *The Vampire Diaries* (The CW: 2009–17) are all examples of postfeminist media products aimed at the teen market. Amy's diary entries mock a postfeminist media culture that sells 'intimate' modes of feminine address to consumers in the pursuit of market dominance. Yet the entries also mock the cultural importance placed upon female diaries, autobiographies and memoirs as important historical documents that construct alternative 'herstories', such as the journals of writers Sylvia Plath and Katherine Mansfield, or archives dedicated to women's writing, like the Harvard University Library's 'Women Working' collection. *Gone Girl*'s critique, then, is levelled not only at postfeminist media culture, but also at feminist methodologies designed to bring women's creative labour in the private sphere into the domain of public record.

Amy's grasp of melodramatic and confessional tropes emphasise her initial appeal to female consumers of postfeminist fiction, film and television within the diegesis and likely also to be external to it. It is the character's self-referential and satirical knowledge of the importance of genre as she addresses her reader that contributes to the success of the shock plot twist and allows for the unravelling of the postfeminist masquerade. The text comments further upon strategies of consumption associated with the feminine in emphasising the role of infotainment, social media narcissism, therapeutic culture and gossip in Amy's quest to frame her husband. Catherine Lumby points out that while sensationalism and coverage of sex, violence and scandal have always played a key role in journalism (1999: 30), there are increasing concerns about the replacement of 'serious' economic and political analysis with entertainment stories, resulting in the subsequent emergence of 'trash culture' (15) and a 'feminisation' of mainstream news (McDonnell 2014: 26). Women are thought to be particularly susceptible to tabloid discourses, with Lumby noting that female consumers are constructed as 'an unpredictable and potentially voracious force whose desires are capable of threatening the social order' (86). Nick's agreement to pose for a smiling selfie with a local woman while at a meeting gathering volunteers for Amy's search backfires when the photo is publicly judged on *Ellen Abbott Live* as indicating a lack of concern for his wife's welfare. Female awareness in *Gone Girl* as to the power of new media technologies operates in contrast to *The Girl on the Train*, in which Rachel's drunken smartphone video of herself screaming 'fuck you Anna Boyd!' while in a pub bathroom raises further doubts as to her innocence in Megan's disappearance. Amy's plans are contingent upon her manipulation of neighbourhood women, one of whom she dubs the 'local idiot', and their willingness both to believe in the tales of her troubled life with Nick and, crucially, to share these tales with others. The journalist Ellen Abbott (Missi Pyle), who prides herself on being a champion of women's rights, is certain of Nick's guilt and influentially casts aspersions on his character. 'What is it about pregnant women, a woman carrying a life inside of her, that turns men into animals?' Ellen asks, before insinuating that Nick and Margo may have a closer relationship than is typical for a pair of siblings. When lawyer Tanner Bolt (Tyler Perry) encourages Nick to agree to a live television interview with Sharon Schieber to repair his public image following revelations of an extra-marital affair, Nick protests that he is 'sick of being picked apart by women'. Nevertheless, Bolt informs his client that the chat show host regularly attracts close to ten million viewers for her intimate couch-style interviews, and assures him that an on-air confessional is the best way to avoid the lethal injection.

The success of Amy's plan is thus a success allowed for by the perceived encroachment of feminine discourses into the journalistic sphere, where gossip-fuelled speculation and public perception are held to play a far greater role in the attribution of guilt than factual evidence. The 'feminist' agendas of journalists like Ellen Abbott are portrayed in the film as modes of narcissistic self-promotion, with the representation of the US news cycle not only serving to question the relevance of popular feminism, but positioning feminist politics as fabricated and potentially harmful. *Gone Girl*'s narrative, which imagines a collective female endeavour to get an innocent man sent to death row, thus plays into right-wing populist discourse promulgated by public commentators that label contemporary feminism as 'toxic' (Nolte 2017), full of 'man-hating nut-jobs' (Prestigiacomo 2015) and 'dead set on destroying the American way of life' (Yiannopoulos, quoted in Nash 2016). Postfeminist melancholia is unsuccessfully renegotiated within this film, with the resulting societal impact framed through familiar backlash narratives that present feminist ideology as comprising a dominant hegemonic order fuelled by hysteria, revenge and suburban boredom. The complexities of political economy and production cultures in relation to media industries are flattened and negated, with female broadcasters deemed solely responsible for deciding what topics are newsworthy and for interpellating viewers into their 'vindictive' ideological agendas.

SUBURBAN INSULARITIES: WHITE MELANCHOLIA AND THE INSCRUTABLE 'OTHER'

Although the primary victims in *Gone Girl* are presented as the white, middle-class men Amy enters relationships with – and, by extension, the white middle-class men who the text suggests are the primary victims of a feminist agenda – the film does take the opportunity to comment on the lack of visibility of economically disadvantaged women within US media culture. Amy's claims to victim status are invalidated in the film partially because she trades on her privilege, as opposed to recognising and attempting to renegotiate it as other cinematic melancholic heroines do. Nick and Amy's loss of their New York abode and relocation to suburban Missouri contributes to the growing hostility between the pair and a sense of aimlessness within their marriage. Problematising literary treatments of suburban life in the twentieth century, Catherine Jurca notes that these texts tend to position white, middle-class homeowners as plagued by a sense of homelessness (2011: 4), thus problematically aligning white affluence with spiritual and cultural displacement, and ultimately with subjugation rather than social dominance (4). The association of whiteness with subjugated femininity and spiritual homelessness can be seen in a range of texts that centralise the postfeminist melancholic, from the alienated, wistful heroines populating Sofia Coppola's films and fashion endeavours to Francis Mayes' stay in a halfway house providing emergency accommodation for depressed bourgeois professionals in *Under the Tuscan Sun*. As in tourist romances and fantasy films, the rejection of home in *Gone Girl* is associated with a bid for freedom from neoliberal postfeminist ideologies and the pseudo-abandonment of the 'trappings' of privilege. In this text, however, the rejection of the postfeminist masquerade is temporary, allowing Amy to stage her own death and observe the media condemnation of her husband from afar. As also occurs in the tourist romances and fantasy films,

Figure 4.4 Amy raises Greta's suspicions in *Gone Girl*.

Amy meets people away from home who do not share her privileges, yet does not utilise such encounters as part of a romanticised bid to shed her attachment to neoliberal philosophies. Instead, one such encounter serves as a point of missed connection in which Amy is not in command of the situation, but is instead unmasked and *interpreted* by a woman whom she perceives to be an irrelevant pawn.

After Amy flees her staged crime scene in Missouri, she disguises herself as a victim of domestic abuse from New Orleans and takes refuge at a group of cabins in the Ozarks. Here, she meets a young female traveller named Greta (Lola Kirke), an unemployed, transient woman and victim of physical abuse who queries if Amy shares her taste in men upon noticing the visitor's (self-inflicted) facial bruising. 'Let me guess,' she muses. 'He was trying to watch the big game and you just wouldn't shut up? Or you caught your boy rubbing up on some hot little skank and he apologised by busting you a good one!' Greta, however, is tellingly one of the few people able to see through the Amazing Amy media circus. When the pair watch *Ellen Abbott Live*, Greta laughs at the host's inflammatory rhetoric and declares that Amy seems 'uppity … a rich bitch who married a cheating asshole and paid the ultimate price'. When Greta later discovers Amy's cash supply and robs her, she scoffs at her threats to call the police and declares that Amy is obviously hiding something, having opted to wear fake glasses and dye her hair a mousy colour. Greta also voices her opinion that she does not think Amy has ever been hit before. This sequence not only highlights Amy's dependency on the socially advantaged to perpetuate and consume her constructed media narrative, but also creates a discordance between Amy's experience of burden and Greta's, whose life of disadvantage and abuse hardly invites the levels of national interest and sympathy that Amy's does.

Gone Girl thus comments on a media phenomenon known as 'missing white girl syndrome', which Sarah Stillman defines as 'round-the-clock coverage of disappeared young females who qualify as "damsels in distress" by race, class, and other relevant social variables' (2007: 492). Marian Meyers points to the relationship between social prominence and access to the news media, arguing that those of privileged race and class status tend to invite more extensive coverage. 'Violence against women who are poor and black', she states, 'is less likely to receive extensive coverage (or any coverage) than is violence against women who are white, middle-class and upper-class' (1997: 12). It is certainly true that young, affluent white women enjoy greater media visibility than do non-white or poor women, and invite more attention and sympathetic reportage in cases of violent crime. Yet in individualising and psychologising the failures of neoliberal governmentality, *Gone Girl*, like *Blue Jasmine*, misses a raised opportunity to engage in broader commentary on post-recessionary socio-economic inequality in the US, and instead chooses to scapegoat the protagonist (and women like her) who are held up as symbols of social and moral decay in contemporary America. Greta is a minor and underdeveloped character who escapes from her encounter with the film's villain relatively unscathed through sheer resourcefulness and 'pluck', unlike the affluent white men who are Amy's preferred targets. Desi Collings (Neil Patrick Harris), an extremely wealthy ex-boyfriend of Amy's, is tricked into partaking in her schemes before she brutally stabs him to death, while Nick must learn to adhere to Amy's demands and acknowledge his marital failures publicly to save his own life. The fact that Greta is not a 'target', but merely someone who gets in the way, precludes a deeper analysis of her situation and background, and implies that she is somehow peripheral to the fallout from the global financial crisis and the text's imagining of a subsequently dystopian US media culture that disenfranchises white men. Ultimately, the character of Greta raises interesting questions that are never answered or even sustained, with *Gone Girl*'s ideological drive ultimately in keeping with Negra and Tasker's assertion that recessionary media culture 'mobilises and gives new force to longstanding tropes of white masculinity in crisis' (2013: 346–7).

In *The Girl on the Train*, Rachel attempts to gain a better understanding of Megan and her relationships by visiting the psychiatrist Dr Kamal Abdic (Édgar Ramírez), with whom she believes Megan may have been having an affair prior to her disappearance. Unlike *Gone Girl*, white masculine crisis functions as something of a red herring, with Rachel's belief in Tom's innocence and inherent goodness initially allowing her to apportion blame elsewhere for Megan's victimisation and her own descent into mental illness. Dr Abdic, an immigrant and outsider within the insular suburban community, is to Rachel a source of both fascination and suspicion. In keeping with a typical function of characters within these films who do not fulfil the white, middle-class subject position, Dr Abdic is better able to understand the rationale behind Rachel and Megan's melancholic state than they do themselves, and he plays an integral role in healing both women. He also functions as a personification of enigmatic Otherness, whose presence and role in the film exposes malicious aspects of the white gaze while familiarly diagnosing the female gaze as a 'paranoid' one. Megan chooses to eroticise Dr Abdic and flirts with him to dissolve the ethical boundaries of their relationship, given that she sees sex as providing a key means of escaping her mental anguish. In the novel, Megan fantasises about her doctor's 'incredible dark honey skin' and muses that 'he has hands that I could imagine on me, long and delicate fingers, I can almost feel them on my body' (Hawkins 2015: 32). In the film, Megan behaves inappropriately in Dr Abdic's office, nuzzling his stomach and sucking on his fingers, before he warns that her behaviour will make it impossible for the pair to work together. While Megan eroticises signifiers of Dr Abdic's ethnic difference – in dreaming about his dark honey skin and long, delicate fingers – as a means of both repressing the memory of her dead child and escaping from her 'boring and routine' suburban existence, Rachel and Megan's husband Scott (Luke Evans) are quick to attribute blame to him. Dr Abdic's ancestry and country of origin are left deliberately opaque. He has an Arabic first name and Bosnian surname, while the character is played by a Venezuelan actor who breaks out into Spanish at a key juncture within the film upon reaching peak frustration with Megan. Dr Abdic is reluctant to disclose his familial background, replying that he is an American citizen when Rachel enquires about his accent. His perilous position as a reflection of white frustration and confusion is present within the film, though amplified further in the novel when Rachel asks Scott if the Indian artist Rajesh Gujral could have been the man she saw Megan kissing on the balcony. Scott replies that he knows someone else who may fit her description, musing that Abdic 'is not Asian, he's from Serbia or Bosnia, somewhere like that. He's dark-skinned though. He could pass for Indian from a distance' (2015: 123).

For Rachel, who initially sees the Megan Hipwell case as a 'distraction' from her own problems, Dr Abdic provides an ideal scapegoat who allows her to delay recognition of the true culprit behind Megan's disappearance – her affluent, white, seemingly 'normal' American ex-husband Tom. Abdic's only crime is that he is from 'somewhere else', and is thus to Rachel initially indistinguishable from any other inscrutable foreigner to be treated with cautionary suspicion, such as Rajesh Gujral. Her drinking allows her to live in a permanent state of melancholic suspension and subjective insularity, which manifests itself in a perception of the outside world as indecipherable. This is again observed in the novel when Rachel learns from the television news broadcast that Dr Abdic has been released without charge in the Hipwell case. Noting that she is almost at the bottom of the first bottle 'when it happens',

Rachel observes that the news ticker is flickering across the bottom of an image featuring a half-destroyed building, and she is unable to decipher whether this building is in Syria, Egypt or Sudan. Rachel's melancholic detachment from the outside world and her inability to make sense of it – as well as her reluctance to admit that patriarchal bourgeois whiteness may be perilous – is directly implicated in her false accusation of Dr Abdic. The insularity of the melancholic state thus proves an impediment not only to self-realisation or meaningful political action, but also to an engagement with the complexities of human conflict and the recognition of others' selfhood. The melancholic white woman is unable to completely detach herself from what Julie A. Wilson calls self-enclosed neoliberal individualism, which (following the work of AnaLouise Keating 2012) she defines as a form of boundary-fixing between oneself and the outside world that focuses exclusively and hyperbolically upon the human actor (2018: 3). Rather than drawing a boundary between oneself and the Other, however, the melancholic white woman of Hollywood cinema more typically sees the Other and her various encounters with the world around as extensions, or metaphors, for her state of crisis. The 'world's' pain must make sense in relation to the melancholic's experiences and her residual confusions, her disenchantment with neoliberal postfeminism rarely resulting in an ability to look beyond the self. This is a state of being and (not) seeing that in *The Girl on the Train* proves dangerous to those who have not been fully accepted by the white, middle-class inhabitants of New York suburbia.

It is Dr Abdic, however, who gets Megan to confide in him about her accidental drowning of her baby daughter Elizabeth as a new seventeen-year-old mother and her fears for her current pregnancy. It is also Dr Abdic who correctly points out that Rachel has come to him for help in recovering lost memories, although her rationale behind making the appointment is to uncover clues about Megan. Rachel's tearful recollection of her overwhelming sadness at her inability to bear a child creates a further parallel between her and the murder victim, and is a crucial step towards unlocking repressed memories of her husband's violence. Representation of the 'talking cure', particularly as a means of unburdening disturbed female patients, is by no means a new phenomenon in Hollywood cinema, although its appearance here is complicated by the power dynamic between Dr Abdic and his patients. The superiority of the medical gaze is problematised by Abdic's hyper-visibility within the suburban community, as predicated on his inscrutable nationality, and Scott and Rachel's initial persecution of him. As Glen O. Gabbard and Krin Gabbard note, the talking cure as a mode of psychiatric practice is over-represented in classical Hollywood cinema (1999: 27), pointing to the comparative rarity of such curative 'moments of catharsis' within real-life medical practice (28). Tellingly, the authors hypothesise that American films tend to focus on a specific historical moment within the development of psychoanalytic theory, in which Sigmund

Freud advocated the use of the talking cure as a means of treating hysterical patients, predicated upon his belief that the illness was caused by 'repressed traumatic memories' (28). Mary Ann Doane has influentially discussed the medicalisation of women in US films of the 1930s and 1940s, which she notes aimed 'to incorporate and popularise psychoanalysis as the latest medical "technology"' in 'a cluster of films which depict female madness, hysteria, or psychosis' (1985: 206). As in *The Girl on the Train*, female illness within these texts is signified in part by the protagonist's unkempt or unattractive appearance (Doane 1985: 208), her body becoming an element within medical discourse to be professionally decoded for clues to her backstory and identity (210). Doane argues that the doctor's gaze is a penetrating one (210), through which he 'exercises an automatic power and mastery in the relation, which is only a hyperbolisation of the socially acceptable "norm" of the heterosexual alliance' (226).

The representation of the talking cure in *The Girl on the Train* is clearly indebted to the recognisable Hollywood formula that Doane discusses, with Rachel and Megan's visits to Dr Abdic proving integral to their recovery. The viewer is never sure as to the extent and gravity of Rachel's mental illness, and it is Abdic who redefines her mental state for us as severely melancholic. Rachel needs to confront and overcome aspects of her past to realise her future potential. Because Rachel cannot let go of her trust in the perceived benevolence of the white male gaze and her investment in the postfeminist dream of 'having it all', she is in danger of permanently descending into hysteria. Yet Dr Abdic is not equivocally aligned with power and mastery in quite the same way that the medical professionals of Doane's study are, as he is uniquely qualified to diagnose not only pathological femininity, but pathological whiteness as well. His patients' inability to decode aspects of *his* background guarantees that he will provide greater insight into their lives than they do about his. Yet if Abdic's female patients are imperilled by violent, white masculinity, then he too is imperilled by Scott and Rachel's prejudice and the threat of the white US justice system. His job in applying the talking cure is not only to get Rachel and Megan to confess their painful pasts to him, as by doing so he is also gradually exposing the possibility that the white male gaze may be dangerous. Dr Kamal Abdic is a liberating and healing influence in these women's lives, in keeping with several other contemporary popular texts featuring melancholic white women. When he yells at Megan in Spanish during one of her appointments, she smiles victoriously at her temporary success in rupturing the performance of calm, bourgeois professionalism that she associates with boredom. Megan predictably embraces the Spanish outburst as exciting and passionate, but it also represents a moment of intimate truthfulness within an English-speaking suburban milieu characterised by treachery, lies and malevolent performances. Dr Kamal Abdic is thus actively engaged in realigning his patients' thinking as to who really constitutes 'the enemy within', yet his primary function is to heal white pain and improve white lives. His own grievances are never given a real airing within the text, his voice and experiences never allowed to rupture the mood of a film driven by female melancholia and the lead character's ongoing sense of anxiety and dread.

CONCLUSION

Gone Girl and *The Girl on the Train* are based on novels deemed to be part of the same literary craze for unreliable, and potentially pathological, female narrators whose thoughts and backstories help provide clues to solving suburban crime dramas. It makes sense, then, that the films upon which these narratives are based would be subject to critical comparisons, with many reviewers ultimately finding greater fault with Tate Taylor's film than David Fincher's reimagining of the Gillian Flynn text. Yet while these novels and films draw on similar tropes and likely appeal to a similar audience, their gender politics are markedly different. Both are narratives that could be said to resonate with a recession-weary audience knowledgeable of the failures of neoliberal and postfeminist ideologies, and both construct heroines whose melancholic attachments to such ideologies have resulted in pathological mental states. Viewers are invited to participate in a 'game' aiming to decode fact from fiction and to assess the true state of the characters' mental health, whose prolonged attachments to problematic philosophies signify that they are ultimately less likely to be sympathetic. The ambivalence of a feminist politics, or the inability to locate a coherent feminism, become potential tricks in the arsenal of the female protagonists, who communicate to us through known gendered codes and the iconicity of popular feminism. Yet while *Gone Girl* mocks the generic codes of the gothic and ultimately paints a destructive picture of a dystopian neoliberal feminism that victimises white men, *The Girl on the Train* is revealed as an authentic gothic tale complete with a heroine unwilling to acknowledge her ex-husband's controlling, violent behaviour. While both texts point to the insularity and hypocrisy of white, middle-class suburbia, it is *The Girl on the Train* that more strongly alludes to the idea that intersecting race, class and gender privileges – and the desire to maintain power conferred by one's subject position – may be potentially harmful not only to women, but also to racial and ethnic minorities. These films point to cultural anxieties relating to the neoliberal invocation of feminist discourse and seem to demonstrate uncertainty as to the best way forward in an uncertain economic climate. *Gone Girl*, which may be described by some as a type of post-recessionary 'backlash' text, succeeds in creating a highly marketable villain of the melancholic white woman who refuses to relinquish the status and opportunities that she believes neoliberal postfeminism has afforded her.

NOTES

1. In 2008, Miller notes, a report from Ernst & Young's ITEM Club labelled the UK economy a 'horror movie'; in 2009, *Time* magazine named the zombie as 'the official monster of the recession'; and that same year journalist Matt Taibbi described finance company Goldman Sachs as 'a great vampire squid wrapped around the face of humanity' (2013: 29).
2. Todd McCarthy in *The Hollywood Reporter,* for instance, writes that *The Girl on the Train* is a 'morose, grim, and intensely one-dimensional thriller', with the juxtaposition to David Fincher's *Gone Girl* unlikely to be to director Tate Taylor's benefit (2016). Clarisse Loughrey, writing for *The Independent*, states that fans filing into the cinema hoping to see the next *Gone Girl* were in for 'something of an unpleasant surprise' (2016), while Owen Gleiberman in *Variety* expresses his hope that the female movie-going audience will soon realise that 'it ultimately deserves better than decently executed female gaze victimisation pulp' (2016).

CHAPTER 5

Aristocratic Whiteness, Body Trauma and the Market Logic of Melancholia in *Black Swan*

Darren Aronofsky's *Black Swan* (2010) opens with a dream sequence in which a young ballerina dances on stage with perfect poise and precision, her disciplined body trained to perform the role of the demure, ethereal princess waiting for her handsome prince to arrive, fall hopelessly in love with her and ensure her eternal happiness. The spotlight in this dream illuminates only the dancing female body, casting the audience into darkness and obscuring the arrival of a monstrous, bestial villain from the shadows to the left of the stage. As the creature takes control of the ballerina's body, she holds her arms outstretched, gesticulating wildly for release as her movements become increasingly desperate and chaotic. The audience laments the loss of the princess heroine; the dark feathers that drift ominously in her wake signify her descent into the shadows. A sinister double then emerges, who tricks and seduces her way into the royal court, stealing the heart of the prince and threatening the stability and order of monarchical rule. *Black Swan*'s prologue recounts the famed story of *Swan Lake*, the popular Russian ballet which along with such tales as *Sleeping Beauty*, *Cinderella* and *The Nutcracker* constitutes one of the most often performed ballets by dance companies around the world today. The *Swan Lake* ballet is a story about doomed romantic love and sacrifice, but it is also essentially a tale about the aristocracy and the encroachment upon this white, civilised and privileged space by the dark, uncivilised and inhuman forces that seek to overthrow the monarchy's social power. This power is preserved largely through the maintenance of the royal blood line, a form of social control that the Black Swan directly threatens in her effort to seduce the prince. The tragic lovers, then, in choosing to throw themselves off a cliff rather than succumb to the dark corruption of their bodies, implicitly commit the ultimate sacrifice for the royal court.

Black Swan utilises this famous ballet, and its political subtext, to aid the film in creating multiple levels of character signification, with the narrative arc of the protagonist Nina Sayers (Natalie Portman) mimicking that of the 'White Swan' Princess Odette, a role she has coveted for much of her dance career. The diegetic world of the ballet, with its focus on the celebrated white woman as hyper-spectacle, object of the collective social gaze, signifies in relation to idealised constructions of neoliberal femininity with its rhetorical, mass-mediated focus on female agency, achievement and corporeal discipline. Aronofsky's film undermines key facets of neoliberal ideology and the commodification of young women with supposedly 'bright futures' in charting the psychological and bodily breakdown of a fragile ballerina who strives for perfection according to the societal dictates of those she performs for. Nina, presented as a persecuted innocent, never reaches a lasting state of cognitive awareness as to the essential futility of her own 'striving' within the parameters set by her culturally prescribed subject position, yet the film provides an intriguing examination of the interrelationship between lived experiences of mental distress and the virtual impossibility of performing 'melancholia' to a paying audience, given ballet's longstanding obsession with representing the aristocratic white woman in despair as a form of artistic beauty. *Black Swan*, however, is a deeply self-reflexive text, complicating its ideological drive, and the theatrical world of the ballet additionally operates as a thinly veiled metaphor for the commercial imperatives of the Hollywood star system. The roles played by Natalie Portman and Winona Ryder signify strongly in relation to the extra-diegetic trajectories of their filmic careers. When Nina is asked to shed the virginal, white 'princess' signifiers that she believes constitute her own identity, Portman is given the opportunity to renegotiate the terms of her own stardom for the chance of greater financial and cultural capital within the terms of the Hollywood film industry. The 'breaking down' of the signifiers of idealised white femininity allows Portman to distance herself from former facets of her childlike, virginal image through a form of performative introspection, a professional move that culminated in an Academy Award for her efforts. Important to the overarching argument of this book is not merely a consideration of the ways in which white socio-economic privilege is mobilised within the fluctuating terms of Anglo-American neoliberal feminism, and how such mobilisations function politically, although these issues will be given consideration within this chapter. It also considers the ways in which the Hollywood system, at the level of both representation and the political economy of personality, can *trade* in burdened white womanhood in a similar manner to ballet.

Originating in late nineteeth-century Russia, *Swan Lake* tells the story of Princess Odette, a gentle and kind-hearted girl who is transformed into a swan by the villainous sorcerer Von Rothbart and so seems destined to live out the remainder of her life drifting upon an enchanted lake, yearning for a return to human form. One night, Odette encounters the charismatic Prince Siegfried, who upon a birthday hunting expedition with some friends falls in love with her and vows to break the spell. During the royal celebration at which he is to choose a bride, however, Prince Siegfried is tricked into proclaiming his love for Von Rothbart's daughter Odile. Realising his terrible mistake, Prince Siegfried vows to die alongside his devastated Swan Queen rather than be bound by Von Rothbart's sorcery. The prologue of *Black Swan* does not merely tell the story of *Swan Lake*, but also foretells the tragic tale of Nina, a fragile and vulnerable dancer who is chosen to replace ageing prima ballerina Beth MacIntyre (Ryder) in the sought-after role of Odette for a New York City ballet production. Still living with her jealous and overbearing mother Erica (Barbara Hershey), Nina's development appears halted in a phase of pre-adolescent girlhood, her bedroom consisting of a colour palette of pastel pinks and whites with soft toys and dolls mounted upon the furnishings. Erica, whose dance career was cut short after becoming pregnant with Nina, exerts a form of corporeal tyranny over her daughter, insisting she clip her finger and toenails, controlling her food intake and checking her skin for signs of scratches and scars. The ballet company's director Thomas Leroy (Vincent Cassel) expresses reticence at his casting choice; believing that Nina is ideal for the role of the innocent White Swan but that she lacks the passion, sensuality and seductiveness necessary to play the Black Swan (both parts are traditionally danced by the one ballerina). Asked by Leroy to abandon her drive for technical perfection and lose herself in the role, Nina's behaviour becomes increasingly undisciplined and erratic as she imagines herself transforming into something 'darker' and less than human. Her toes form the illusion of fusing together, black feathers tear through her flesh and the sound of guttural growls and the flapping of wings comprise forms of aural persecution, seeming to emanate down twisted passageways and the darkest of corners. She becomes convinced that another ballerina, Lily (Mila Kunis), who far better embodies the qualities of the Black Swan, is conspiring to jeopardise her performance. Nina gradually descends into psychosis, believing herself to have murdered Lily during the interval of the ballet's premiere, while in fact she has stabbed herself in the abdomen with a mirror shard. Despite these injuries to the integrity of her body, and indeed *because* of them, Nina delivers a magnificent performance as the Black Swan, achieving her lifelong ambition by reaching a state of true artistic perfection.

READING NEOLIBERAL FEMININITY THROUGH THE BALLERINA BODY: CORPOREAL DISCIPLINE AND DISORDERED CONSUMPTION

Black Swan, in challenging the relationship between female empowerment, corporeal agency and neoliberalism's emphasis on individual responsibility, is a film that may be said to engage in a critical interrogation of aspects of postfeminist culture as they pertain to white, middle-class women in the West. The film explores these issues through the metaphorical vehicle of an insulated New York ballet academy – a metaphor that, due to stereotypical figurations of the female ballerina within Hollywood cinema, works successfully as ideological shorthand in conveying a number of associations between femininity and body pathology. Adrienne L. McLean, in her analysis of the historical representation of ballet on film, notes that narrative cinema continues to imagine ballet as associated paradoxically with 'agency, joy and fulfilment' on the one hand, and 'perversity, melancholy and death' on the other (2008: 14). Films such as Michael Powell and Emeric Pressburger's *The Red Shoes* (1948), she notes, popularised narratives where the ballerina's desire to dance is imbued with toxicity, so that fantasies of success and achievement become inextricably linked to tragedy and self-destruction (22). McLean points out that dance scholars hold an interest in how bodies are moulded and sculpted in relation not only to artistic technique but also the bio-political forces that constitute and regulate subjectivity. The dancing body is never only the object of the gaze, she states, but 'also a subject who participates and presents chosen aspects of her self to that gaze, willingly and consciously' (McLean 2008: 16). As the ballet film typically allows an audience to glimpse the arduous work that goes into creating a performance of glamorised spectacle, the distinction between the idealised feminine appearance of the ballet princess and the lived 'reality' of the dancer is made apparent. The lived contradiction of the female ballet dancer as both objectified and complicit in her role as spectacle through means of active corporeal manipulation thus becomes an ideal metaphor. This metaphor works to explore a pervasive mode of sociopolitical management that Foucault influentially termed 'technologies of the self' (Foucault in Martin *et al.* 1982/1988), through which citizens adopt a number of practices, skills and attitudes in order to achieve idealised states of happiness or perfection. In the specific context of gendered citizenry, the ballerinas of *Black Swan* speak to a contemporary postfeminist sensibility which, as Gill argues, presents the body as a woman's primary source of power, blurring the lines between sexual objectification and subjectification (2007: 151) and disavowing the role of political, socio-economic or cultural constraints upon the self in favour of a logic of competitive individualism (155).

As with the other female protagonists analysed in this book, Nina Sayers engages in a disciplinary monitoring of the self to achieve a societal ideal based upon the female body as spectacle. As a young woman dedicated to her career as both an artist and an object of art, Nina's perception of herself as the primary agent of her own corporeal performance is enforced through daily training where she judges the lines and contours of her body before a mirror. It is in front of a mirror that Nina performs her morning stretches as she recounts her dreams of performing the White Swan to her mother, who reassures her that she is the 'most dedicated dancer in the company'. It is in front of a mirror that Nina practices her ballet steps in unison with the other dancers in the *corps*, and in front of a mirror that she tries in vain to master the thirty-two *fouettés*, a movement danced traditionally by the Black Swan in Act Three of *Swan Lake*. It is also before a mirror that Nina applies lipstick stolen from Beth's dressing room, in the hopes that imitating the exterior of her idol will culminate in a replication not only of Beth's physical appearance, but of her fame and success also. Nina's constant surveillance over the appearance and movements of her body mark her as an active participant in a neoliberal and postfeminist media culture that Gill reminds us is produced discursively through a shift in the mechanisms of gendered power. The disciplinary gaze, Gill argues, is no longer imposed by a masculine body external to the self, but instead works to *construct* a narcissistic female subjectivity, whereby the production of the heteronormative feminine body is posited as integral to a woman's sense of identity and agency (2007: 151). The female body, Gill notes, is constantly 'evaluated, scrutinised and dissected' through various media genres and is 'always at risk of failing' (149). Feminist theorist Sandra Bartky similarly describes such forms of domination as producing in women 'an *estrangement* from her bodily being', where she is valued primarily for her corporeality and yet is encouraged to see her body as in a permanent state of deficiency (1990: 40).

The horror of *Black Swan* lies in the realisation of Nina's fear that her sense of mastery over the body is but an illusion, with Clint Mansell's eerie musical score in combination with the use of handheld camera and tight framing working to create a sense of strangeness and foreboding in these initial scenes where the protagonist gazes at her still compliant mirror image. Reflective surfaces, whether in the form of a training hall mirror or subway window, initially act as comforting reassurances to Nina as to the technical perfection of every bodily signal. Yet it is also through these reflective surfaces that she begins to catch glimpses of her unruly dark double – the mirage of her own self whose bodily movements refuse to obey the laws of reflection. As the ballet company's wardrobe director takes Nina's measurements prior to *Swan Lake*'s premiere and informs her that she has lost weight, her mirror image smiles and turns her head, prompting a panicked Nina to rapidly scan the room in fear of catching an intruder crouching amongst the costumes and mannequins. In the deserted ballet studio, Nina later attempts to engage in some last-minute rehearsing only to discover, by evidence of the floor-to-ceiling mirrors that surround her, that her arms appear to be lifting and extending independently of her will. At other points in the film, mirrors provide false visual evidence as to the appearance of dark feathers beginning to slice through her flesh. The motif of the mirror not only documents the severity of Nina's ever-deteriorating mental state, but also serves to question the validity of individual 'agency' in relation to the regulation of one's bodily appearance as exemplified through the hyperbolic femininity of the ballerina, thus beginning to indicate a violent shift in the disciplinary processes constructing Nina's subjectivity.

Long before Nina's descent into hallucinatory paranoia, the filmic audience is encouraged to read her approach to both life and art as imminently dangerous as a result of the presentation of her relationship with both herself and others as already inherently pathological. Nina embodies the intense focus on success and achievement of neoliberalism's ideal female subject on the one hand, but also the violence to the self that adherence to such stringent standards of heteronormative femininity commonly inflicts. McRobbie's argument that the pursuit of an unviable socially sanctioned femininity produces a normalisation of feminine discontents and disorders (2009: 96) applies as well to Nina Sayers as it does to the heroines of the fantasy film or the travel romance, although it presents itself in a more severe, destructive form in *Black Swan*. Nina's pathological mentality primarily manifests as the result of a struggle for control over her bodily appetites, with both her mother and dance instructor manipulating her apparent disinclination for food and sex through means conducive to serving their own ends. Female body anxiety exhibits itself within this text through the portrayal of Nina as suffering from both anorexic and bulimic tendencies, illnesses that McRobbie situates along a spectrum of female disorders associated with body image that have reached new heights over the past decade. Frequent throughout the film are extreme close-ups of Nina's jutting shoulder blades and protruding ribcage, and she is shown attempting to vomit in the bathroom following stressful rehearsals. Tension between Nina and her mother Erica, whose maternal bond with her daughter is frustrated by her inability to come to terms with her own lack of artistic success, is evident in scenes where the pair argue over Nina's food intake. In the opening minutes of the film, we learn that Erica prepares Nina only half a grapefruit for breakfast each morning and food later becomes a source of familial conflict when Nina refuses a large slice of cake offered by her mother in celebration of her new role as Swan Queen. Disordered eating, McRobbie argues, indicates a form of 'illegible rage' (2009: 94) with the societal status quo and emanates from a woman's expected adherence to 'cultural norms of female perfectibility' (97). Nina's anorexic appearance thus appears as the pathogenic potential of a contemporary cultural preoccupation with corporeal surveillance that has become so pervasive as to be normalised. The combination of Nina's hyper-vigilant attitude toward her consumption habits, her preoccupation with constant visual evidence as to ensure the correct mechanisms and workings of her dancer's body, and her predilection for self-harm establishes a set of warning signals to the audience that her mode of living is psychologically and physiologically unsustainable. Yet such a mode of living is not necessarily recognised as aberrant within the individualistic and hyper-competitive ballet environment that Nina inhabits, where the dancers exhibit a range of narcissistic, self-destructive and frequently aggressive behaviours. When we are first introduced to the ballerinas in their dressing room, they are discussing the critical financial state of the company and accordingly speculate that Thomas should endeavour to find a new star dancer 'who is not approaching menopause'. When Nina is named Swan Queen, the previously favoured candidate for the role swears at her, with Nina later discovering that someone has scrawled the word 'Whore' in red lipstick on the bathroom mirror while she has been on the phone to her mother in one of the cubicles. After the ball held to announce the new production of *Swan Lake* to the company's sponsors, Beth, having been forced into retirement, throws herself in front of a passing car after drunkenly accusing Nina of offering sexual favours in exchange for being named as her successor. The winged angel that Nina has just moments before gazed upon in the venue's forecourt, armless and with a face of melted stone, thus prefigures Beth's wilful destruction of her body. In such a precarious and hostile environment, where the wellbeing of the dancers is firmly secondary to the economic concerns of the company, Nina's vigilant and hyper-disciplinary behaviour may be construed as necessary to ensure not only success but survival according to the competitive logic of the enterprise. For in such an environment, feminine pathologies are not aberrant, but instead have become thoroughly *normalised*.

Ballet instructor Thomas Leroy holds a considerable commercial interest in imposing states of psychic distress upon his dancers in order to create great art, investing as he does in cultural discourses that have long associated melancholia and mental illness with artistic genius. As Radden summarises, within this 'unifying feature' of melancholy, from Aristotelian thinking through to the various European literary movements of the sixteenth to nineteenth centuries, the melancholic was said to be one who 'felt more deeply, saw more clearly, and came closer to the sublime than ordinary mortals' (2000: 15). It is through Thomas' relationship with Nina and his contribution to her eventual mental breakdown that the film de-romanticises the figure of the melancholy white woman, even as it refuses to challenge the popular sentiment that superior creative artistry emanates best from psychic disturbance. If the melancholy white woman may be said to be a tool through which the interrelated negotiation of neoliberalism and feminism can function as a form of political commentary, as based on how well the filmic heroine navigates various life challenges, then *Black Swan* behaves subversively in removing the possibility of self-autonomy for the film's female protagonist altogether – thus undermining a key logic of neoliberal governance. As Mark Fisher notes in his *Film Quarterly* debate with Amber Jacobs on the film, *Black Swan*'s tragic drive is startlingly unusual 'at a time when neoliberal ideology peddles the idea that we are all in control of our own fates' (2011: 59).

The melancholic state is not initially intrinsic to Nina, who while certainly exhibiting signs of psychological fragility remains naively invested in the world that governs her being, looking to others for guidance in every facet of her life and trusting that both Thomas and her mother have her best interests at heart. As Erica fondly reminisces of Nina's early days in the company while tending to one of her daughter's many ballet injuries, 'if I hadn't taken you to each and every one of your classes you would have been completely lost.' It is Thomas who first introduces the idea to Nina that true brilliance resides in emotions of despair and loss, untapped psychological and sexual repressions, and according to the psychoanalytic logic of the film, separation from the maternal body. It is he who raises the possibility to Nina that her current mode of feminine performance may not be in her best interests if she wishes to attain her goal of becoming a celebrated prima ballerina in order to dance the authoritative role of the Black Swan.[1] In proclaiming that perfection is about 'transcendence', and in declaring upon witnessing Nina's final performance that he always knew she had it in her, Thomas implies that Nina's struggle has been primarily one of discovering lost and submerged elements of self in pursuit of turning in a truly empowered performance. After Beth's suicide attempt, Thomas idealises the suffering of his former muse and reflects on the charismatic nature of the star ballerina's past performances, pointedly informing Nina that it is Beth's ability to act on her 'dark impulses' that make her so 'damn destructive' but also 'perfect' and 'thrilling to watch'. Indeed, Nina's moments of newfound agency and assertiveness are countered by an increasing number of paranoid hallucinations and delusions, while the road to her transcendence is frequently measured by Thomas in terms of how willing she is to initiate sexual advances towards him. When Nina achieves her goal of turning in a perfect performance as Odette/Odile on *Swan Lake*'s opening night, she, like Beth, has done so at great personal cost to both her body and mind. As Tarja Laine argues, the death of the protagonist in *Black Swan* lends the film an 'anti-cathartic' effect, engaging the audience in an 'affective reflection on the conflict between the vulnerability of the lived body and the instrumentalised body-as-an-object' (2015: 128), and leaving the spectator probably feeling that Nina's astounding performance was not worth her bodily sacrifices (154). The film indicates that to occupy an idealised role under neoliberalism through a resolute engagement with its core values of self-determination, resilience and achievement is both fleeting and inevitably governed by those with interests that conflict with one's own. The melancholic state does not offer any female character within this text a set of tools through which to renegotiate the relationship between neoliberalism and feminism to a lasting, positive effect upon the self – in fact, the film, in juxtaposing the bleeding body of Nina's dying swan with the cheers of

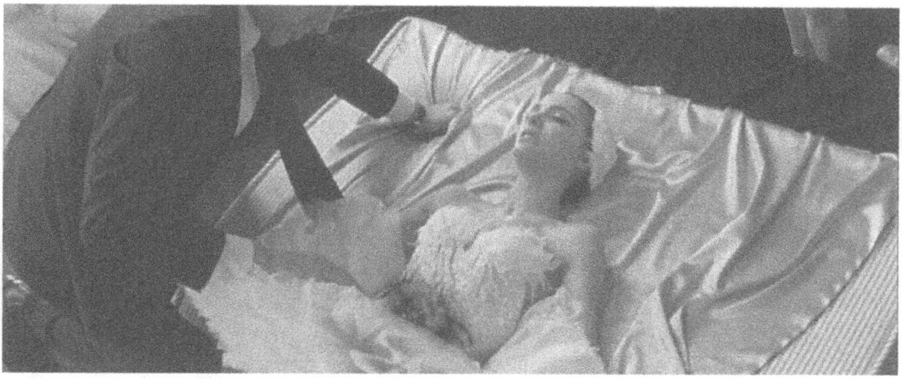

Figure 5.1 Nina's bid for perfection culminates in severe bodily injury in *Black Swan*.

an audience in rapture at having witnessed a 'sublime performance', offers an intriguing critique of such a utopian notion.

Contemporary gendered forms of power that utilise neoliberal discourse in hailing women to work on their bodies in ever more extreme ways are thus illuminated by the discordance between Nina's ecstasy in the final frames of the film and the psychological manipulation and cruelty we have witnessed her undergo. This discordance simultaneously works to de-romanticise the relationship between female agency and melancholy by presenting melancholy in part as a patriarchal tool of artistic practice rather than as a state of being that establishes the inherent specialness of the heroine, and by collapsing the precarious boundary between melancholy and mental illness. *Black Swan* utilises the death of the beautiful woman in art, the dying swan, as a cultural critique of gender relations and a critique of the place of women as performers within artistic industries, with the film able to compare the ugliness of a melancholia brought on by the failure to live up to regimented gender standards and the pleasurable melancholia provided to an audience by an art form that depends on the representation of this same female body. Ballet dancers train their entire lives in order to display themselves as beautiful melancholy objects – to provide an aesthetic image of a mood that philosopher Emil M. Cioran describes as graceful and subdued, consisting of an air of 'passivity, dreaminess and voluptuous enchantment' (quoted in Bowring 2008: 42). Elisabeth Bronfen has influentially argued that 'culture uses art to dream the deaths of beautiful women' (1992: xi), with beauty and the female art image providing an illusion of wholeness and unity that disavows lack, deficiency, the material world and indeed death itself (64). The women of *Black Swan*, who suffer from a career-induced 'time crisis' (Negra 2009: 48), desire to become art objects in a misguided belief that by doing so they will escape time, ageing and the limitations of bodily matter according to the dictates of a gendered cultural address that finds its manifestation here in a ruthless star system. It is the misguided nature of this belief, the futility of these characters' attempts in utilising melancholic emotion as a form of agency, and the self-reflexivity of the text in relation to the disposable nature of celebrity and the commercialised world of artistic production that remind us that the figure of the melancholy white woman in film must always stand in for 'something else'.

THE WHITENESS OF BALLET: ARISTOCRATIC NOSTALGIA, REPRESENTATIONS OF OTHERNESS AND THE POLITICS OF GENRE

If the ballet world works well as a metaphor for exploring the contemporary peculiarities of gendered pathology, then it also works to frame this pathology in terms of white burden due to the art form's fondness for fairy-tale narratives centring on the aristocracy, its history as a form of spectacle in the European royal courts and its longstanding cultural status as 'high art'. As Sally Banes points out, ballet has traditionally been performed in aristocratic or bourgeois venues, with the dance itself tending correspondingly to represent aristocratic or bourgeois values toward sexuality and marriage (1998: 6). *Black Swan*'s utilisation of *Swan Lake*, a story about a supernatural threat to aristocratic white power, provides the conceptual framework for a narrative that explores the ideological contradictions of white womanhood. Although there are many pleasures involved in attending classical ballet, popular performances such as *Cinderella* and *Sleeping Beauty* do indulge in a form of melancholia for an outmoded aristocratic ruling class, presented apolitically, nostalgically and idealistically through the dance as a world of endless ceremonial occasions where attendees and servants alike perform magnificent solos for an adoring king and queen. The darkness in *Swan Lake* constitutes both a threat to the white body politic *and* a threat to the integrity of the individual body of the female heroine, a forgotten princess who will allow the prince to satisfy his quest for love and also uphold his duty to family, and who symbolises the endangered aristocratic way of life. The task of the lead ballerina is to embody both the role of the pristine, virginal White Swan and her aggressive and sexualised Black counterpart through an impressive athletic endeavour that commands her to enact her own corporeal 'corruption' for the pleasure of the ballet audience. The paying audience, who consist of society's 'taste bearers', are thus entrusted with judging Nina's performative success in conveying a fairy-tale narrative centring on aristocratic whiteness and its loss.

Discussing the relationship between ballet and whiteness, McLean notes that the semiotics of the ballet have until recently been ideally white, pointing out that Theophile Gaultier in 1844 even coined the term *ballet blanc* to protest at the abundance of white tulle, tarlatan and gauze on stage (2008: 15).

She adds that classical Hollywood ballet has rarely featured a non-white body, while dance films of more recent decades tend to portray ballet as an elitist, exclusionary art form in need of acquiring vitality from 'the street', in order to remain relevant to new audiences (218).[2] In *White*, Richard Dyer utilises the figure of the Romantic ballerina in order to illustrate the ambiguity inherent in the hegemonic ideal of the angelic, white woman, whose 'non-physical, spiritual, ethereal' attributed qualities have in the past been integral to white people's claims of racial superiority and specialness (1997: 127). Yet as Dyer explains, this puritanical construct was unrealistic in its denial of sex, with white men as likely to resent the female ideal of moral elevation and sexual unavailability as to worship it (130), an idea which finds its representation in Thomas's frustration with Nina's virginity and what he perceives as her 'frigidity'. The ballerina, Dyer argues, operates as a cultural symbol of the irreconcilable contradictions of white femininity in that the dancer's ethereality and weightlessness are traditionally emphasised through costuming, lighting and pointe work, while the ballerina is always simultaneously 'a flesh and blood woman showing her legs' (1997: 130). Nina, in being asked to discard her virginal, sweet and passive persona, is being asked to dispense with a cultural image of white femininity that has only ever really existed in the realm of religious myth and artistic sign, and yet remains a key component in the ever popular ballet lexicon. The denial of corporeality that has historically been required of the bourgeois white woman and the impossibility of maintaining this ideal, especially given the sexual politics of postfeminism, finds its representation in the promotional poster for the film where Nina is portrayed as a porcelain doll, unnaturally white, wide-eyed and perfectly made up, her right cheek split by a vertical, jagged crack that belies the soft composition of flesh. Nina's physical and psychological 'fracturing' aids in literalising the struggle of neoliberal femininity as it pertains to the public's insatiable desire for both images of unobtainable corporeal perfection and spectacles of ahistorical affluent whiteness, with *Black Swan* becoming another filmic participant in envisaging the perils of neoliberal femininity in terms of white semiotics.

If Nina aspires to an illusory ideal of white womanhood, as represented by the White Swan, then the exotic and darker-skinned Lily exhibits the behavioural patterns of sexual assertiveness and voracious consumption that Nina must adopt to portray a convincing Black Swan. Lily, Beth and Erica all operate as doubles for Nina in that these characters indicate elements of the protagonist's personality that could potentially determine her future, and yet it is Lily who best embodies the protagonist's repression, with it being debatable as to whether she exists as a living human being at all or merely as a projection of Nina's fears and anxieties. Her name, an ironic reference to the phrase 'lily white' and its racialised connotations of a whiteness defined by sweetness and virtue, provides a mocking reminder of Nina's attempts to reach an unobtainable state of idealised whiteness and the futility of these attempts in her desire to attain certain professional goals. Unlike the film's fragile protagonist and the other dancers in the company, Lily appears free from both corporeal angst and the experience of time crisis, breezing in late to ballet rehearsals and freely indulging in casual sex, recreational drugs and 'extra bloody' cheeseburgers. The tattoo of dark wings that spans across her shoulder blades indicates that she is closer to the animalistic, non-cerebral ideal of the Black Swan in that she embodies the role naturally with no need of training or performance. Lily presents a threat to Nina's dreams of becoming Swan Queen in that her less disciplined, instinctive style of dance is more in keeping with the characterisation of Odile. 'Look at the way she moves.' Thomas instructs Nina from a balcony surveying the dancers below. 'Imprecise, effortless ... she's not faking it.' Nina's paranoid hallucinations often take Lily as their object, from imagining that the other ballerina is conspiring to steal her role to a fantasy of a lesbian tryst with her rival following a nightclub excursion. When Nina stumbles through the darkened ballet studio one evening, her mental distress converting the space into a makeshift house of horrors complete with fleeting shadows and the disorienting sounds of sinister growls and cackles, she witnesses Lily engaging in a sex act with Thomas, who subsequently transforms into the evil Von Rothbart, thus further confirming to Nina that Lily is in collusion with dark forces. Despite the ambiguity as to the nature of Lily's existence, it is telling that the film sees it as necessary to create a sociocultural rationale for her difference in its introduction of her as from elsewhere – as geographically Other. Lily appears happily estranged from the company's ballerinas and their atmosphere of interpersonal aggression and malicious gossip, the film proposes, as she is a newcomer 'straight off the plane from San Francisco' who never assimilates into her newfound milieu. Deflecting the racial politics of the film, Lily is cast as a bohemian left-wing counterpoint to Nina's uptight protagonist. Like *Blue Jasmine* and *Eat Pray Love*, then, *Black Swan* implicates New York and its values of upward mobility and ambition in creating a toxic atmosphere unconducive to the psychological wellbeing of white, middle-class women. Yet to read Lily's characterological differences purely as a result of geographical conditioning would be to ignore the politics of whiteness at work within classical ballet and indeed within the story of *Swan Lake* itself.

Lily, who provides a set of opposite traits to the disciplined, white female subject of neoliberalism, becomes to Nina what Sander Gilman describes as the 'bad Other' in that she operates as an externalised projection of Nina's feared loss of order and self-regulation. The externalised Other, Gilman emphasises, is always 'but the projection of the tension between control and its loss' (1985: 21), and is specific to the individual or group in socio-historical context (20). If Nina is the perfect virginal, white princess, then Lily's characteristics are inevitably enmeshed in a racialised discourse that Ruth Frankenberg notes is built upon the idea that non-white people are 'less civilised, less human, and more animal than whites' (1993: 60). Given the politics of whiteness at work in *Black Swan* and indeed more explicitly within *Swan Lake*, Nina's fears that Lily will steal her role are of course unfounded in that Lily would be fundamentally unable to occupy the 'centre' of whiteness from which the traditional ballet's meaning is made. While Lily's racial background is ambiguous, her body carries the projected *sign* of blackness in a story clearly about the perils of white femininity, with Nina's literal development of animalistic traits and tendencies corresponding directly to both her loss of whiteness and the White Swan's experience of becoming increasingly ostracised from aristocratic society. bell hooks further points out that black female sexuality has long been represented as more free and liberated and thus as licentious, accessible and available (1992: 65–6). Nina's task, as dictated by Thomas, is to gain 'freedom' from burdened white femininity, largely by becoming more sexually accessible and available to him. In keeping with a post-racial environment that rarely confronts issues of race directly, the film can tell a story specifically about white femininity and the projection of white anxiety without having to address the burden of what it may mean to be marked out as 'black' or as the 'bad Other', thus framing the postfeminist sensibility as a peculiarly white phenomenon. Lily, of course, need have no lived experience of the social injustices that continue to face non-white people, although it is notable that Mila Kunis's 'indeterminable' exoticism has been played for laughs in her comedic film roles. In Seth MacFarlane's *Ted* (2012), for example, Lori's inappropriate boss Rex (Joel McHale) daydreams about the pair's hypothetically 'spectacular' children, which would be an ideal mix of his 'top of the pyramid Caucasian genes' and Lori's 'splash of dark, beautiful, smoky Baltic? Czech?' background, while in *Bad Moms* (Jon Lucas and Scott Moore, 2016), a mother claims that she never liked Kunis's character Amy because she 'looks foreign'. In *Black Swan*, Lily's function is mainly to *perform* a mode of living that appears palatable and liberating in its operation outside the frame of idealised behaviour for young white women – behaviour that in this text is marked out as damaging and burdensome. Lily thus becomes a fantasy of what whiteness represses, or what it is not – as well as what neoliberal postfeminism represses, or what it is not – rather than a developed character in her own right.

In undermining the principles of neoliberal governmentality and its emphasis on self-autonomy, *Black Swan*'s narrative sabotages not only the white woman's command over her own body but also her relationship to space, a feat the film achieves through the utilisation of features of *mise-en-scène* as well as through the blending of tropes associated with the melodrama, *film noir* and horror genres. The film's theme of privileged white femininity under threat is thus conveyed not only through various plot points or dialogue, but also through the film's postmodern use of aesthetics and genre. *Black Swan*'s racialised play with the symbolic contrasts of black and white colour finds its emphasis in the use of chiaroscuro lighting, a technique that works to create bold shadows and strong divisions between dark and light areas of the frame. Such a visual style was utilised in the German Expressionist cinema of the 1920s and became popularised in the US through Hollywood's *film noir* cycle of the 1940s, a genre that Eric Lott describes as imbued with racial metaphor in its 'moral focus on the rotten souls of white folks' (1997: 543). *Noir* characters, Lott explains, are in danger of losing themselves in qualities that destabilise ideological constructions of the white, bourgeois self (549), with these themes of white psychosis rendered visually through shades of darkness that seem literally to encroach upon the characters' very being (546). Because these visual tropes work to convey modes of mentality and forms of action commonly renounced by the white middle class, Lott states, they comprise forms of 'artistic othering' (543). This technique is employed to similar consequence in *Black Swan*, where the heroine's increasingly distorted perception of self corresponds directly with her renegotiation of whiteness, and is conveyed not only through her relationships with the other characters but also through the movement of her body in passages of light and shadow as she finds herself in isolation within the film's *mise-en-scène*. Although Nina initially believes herself to be the architect of her own performance, the handheld camera that closely haunts her every movement and the shadows that obscure her path and threaten to envelop her in their clutches suggest victimhood. If Sara Ahmed is correct in her pronouncement that whiteness is an orientation that puts not only physical objects but 'styles, capacities, aspirations, techniques and habits' within reach (2007: 154), referring here to both the white body's command of space and within the social sphere, then Nina's fall from whiteness correlates to an increasing sense of environmental disorientation and spatial blindness. Melancholia in this film certainly carries an affective charge, allowing the protagonist to recreate the world around her in a manner that is of benefit to her artistic intentions and correspondingly of commercial benefit to the dance company. In contrast to the dreamy, wistful tones of the travel romance, where the heroine is able to retain the benefits of whiteness while incorporating elements of ethnicity in the name of discovering a new form of feminist empowerment, the sinister cinematic mood of *Black Swan* undermines the therapeutic work that purportedly allows for the renegotiation of the relationship between whiteness and neoliberal femininity as the heroine becomes overwhelmed by her introspective process. Whiteness in this film is certainly equated with pathology, yet to explore one's 'dark side' is to give oneself over to an experience that is on the one hand seductively thrilling, and on the other interminably toxic.

Nina's increasing sense of disorientation, of being 'out of place' in her world, lays the groundwork for spectacular conflicts between the distinguished and artistic world of the ballet and the far less culturally esteemed genre of horror – conflicts that primarily play out through Nina's transforming corporeality, mocking her attempts at bodily control and mimicking her struggles to embody alternate states of blackness and whiteness. In his blog post on the film, Steven Shaviro observes that *Black Swan* utilises 'body genres' (Williams 1991) such as horror, melodrama and pornography in order to create an affective atmosphere of 'psychophysical intensity', with the elements of horror in particular working to update old Hollywood's melodramatic formulae (2011). The dramatic conflict between high art and low art as inscribed upon Nina's tortured body becomes a further means by which the text works to distance Nina from her white, middle-class subject position and to critique the demands being placed upon her by members of this group, in that it challenges the boundaries of aesthetic taste by which relations of social class are in part produced. *Black Swan* is indebted to melodrama not only in its focus on familial conflict and the stifling nature of bourgeois society, but also through its overall tone, with Ben Singer arguing that the melodramatic mode is commonly characterised by intensified emotion, pathos, moral polarisation and sensationalism or spectacle (2001: 11). The characters Nina perceives as dangerous threats are typically clad in black throughout the film in reflection of the relationship between the White Swan and Von Rothbart/Odile, and thus are morally polarised in relation to the protagonist in a manner that, on the surface at least, symbolises a rigid demarcation of good and evil. Nina's conveyance of emotion is certainly overwrought, characterised by frequent bouts of panic, shame and weepiness, while her final transformation into the Black Swan is a moment of transcendent spectacle, complete with an arresting use of CGI technology that makes it appear as though Nina's arms are transforming into dark, sweeping wings as she furiously orbits the stage. Given contemporary Western culture's preoccupation with monitoring and disciplining the female body however, it is perhaps melodrama's association with a 'semiotics of the body' (Brooks 1994: 11) that is utilised to greatest effect here in conjunction with the film's instances of body horror. If Nina's rage is 'illegible' and sublimated to her desire to achieve greatness within the world of the ballet, which initially requires her to adopt feminine signifiers of innocence, passivity and sweetness, then it is also inarticulate. Nina is infantilised not only through elements of *mise-en-scène* or her mother's repeated references to her as a 'sweet girl', but also through her vocal communications, which comprise not emphatic demands or defiant protestations, but barely audible girlish whispers, leading the audience to read her speech primarily through the conflicted medium of her body.

Nina's body tells a horrific story – her fingernails peel off and then appear spontaneously to re-heal, the skin on her back shreds, bubbles and bleeds, and in one scene she experiences her legs snapping beneath her and her neck vertically stretching to inhuman proportions after racing home from hospital one day where she has visited Beth, believing that she has witnessed her idol stab herself repeatedly with a knife. Peter Brooks observes that the melodramatic body utilises gestures and actions as well as instances of excitation and irritation to give representation to repressed emotion, with melodrama striving for occasions where repression can burst through in moments of essential truth (1994: 19). Although Nina's experiences defy the human body's laws and thus qualify as delusional, these horrific and yet melodramatic scenes, overlaid by Tchaikovsky's emotively charged *Swan Lake* score, speak certain truths that Nina is incapable of verbalising. The merging of genre thus begins to form a politicised commentary of sorts, with Nina's truths speaking to the societal falsehoods that place exaggerated emphasis on corporeal mastery, and also to the powerful transcultural myth of the poetically mournful white woman, whose appearance in melancholic dance pieces forms a wistful yearning for a lost aristocratic age that classical ballet continues to sell.

MATERNAL OBSESSION AND SUFFOCATION: EXAMINING WHITE REPRESSION AND VIOLENCE THROUGH THE MOTHER–DAUGHTER DYAD

The use of the ballet world as a metaphor for bourgeois society allows *Black Swan* to mount a cultural critique centralised on the burdened white woman of neoliberalism, yet the film also provides a strong rationale for Nina's mental deterioration in presenting her as a product of an unstable and 'broken' home. Although Nina's mother Erica may herself be read as a victim of the society that has produced her, the film's heavily stereotyped depiction of her character and the lack of insight provided into her backstory allows the film to temper its social commentary through the highly familiar cinematic trope of the pathological mother–daughter relationship, and the representation of the single mother as horrific villain. Erica thus becomes a source of ambivalence regarding the gender politics of the film, as she can be read both as a by-product of a competitive neoliberal culture that denies forms of connectivity amongst women *and* as a grotesque manifestation of contemporary cultural anxieties relating to female ageing, singleness and 'inappropriate' methods of motherhood within this same context. As Anthea Taylor points out, anxieties regarding female power have long coalesced around the figure of the single woman (2011: 2) with singleness still positioned 'as an illegitimate way of being in the world' (22). Rebecca Feasey, meanwhile, states that women who do not fit the idealised image of the heterosexual, white, self-sacrificing, good mother, such as the single mother, are commonly 'judged, ranked, and found wanting within and beyond the media environment' (2012: 2).

The trope of the pathological mother–daughter dyad allows the film to stage a generational conflict that, while framed through this paradigm, speaks simultaneously to cultural ambivalence relating to the gains and failures of the second-wave feminist movement and to the contemporary intertwining of feminist rhetoric with consumer-capitalist logic. Erica's jealousy of Nina, for instance, may be partially attributed to the lack of value ascribed to parental labour as opposed to paid work (and cultural visibility) in the public sphere, a key issue that concerned white, middle-class feminist thinkers such as Betty Friedan in the 1960s. As Sadie Wearing notes, the maternal melodrama and associated rivalry between mothers and daughters is often utilised to stage conflicting attitudes toward female agency and feminism (2007: 283), the result being that complex political issues come to be represented as familial affairs. Similarly, Kathleen Rowe Karlyn argues that while variations on this theme have been intrinsic to many a familial conflict within 'the woman's film', particularly in 1940s' examples of the genre, from the early 1990s motherhood has become an 'increasingly charged' site on which to stage ideological conflicts relating to gender, class, and race (2010: 3). While the film does not explore Erica's character in depth, we do learn that she is a former ballerina who believes her career was prematurely halted because of her pregnancy. Although Nina disputes her mother's talent when she reminds her that she was twenty-eight and still in the *corps* at the time she fell pregnant, Erica is consumed with jealousy toward her daughter who goes on to experience the stardom and adoration that she always craved but felt she missed due to motherhood. The casting of Barbara Hershey in this role reverberates given that the actress's long Hollywood career – which includes two Golden Globe nominations for performances in *The Last Temptation of Christ* (Martin Scorsese, 1988) and *Portrait of a Lady* (Jane Campion, 1996) – was jeopardised due to the public attention placed on her personal life. Hershey experienced a career decline while involved in a long-term relationship with actor David Carradine, with whom she had a son, while her decision to change her last name to Seagull following the death of a bird on-set was met with derision. Erica in *Black Swan* becomes obsessed with her daughter's role as a commodity and a celebrity sign, repeatedly sketching portraits of her that are visually reminiscent of Andy Warhol's silkscreen printings of iconic American stars, yet her sketches are drawn crudely in shades of murky pink and green, with jagged edgings and black spaces where Nina's eyes should appear. The competitive and individualistic world of the ballet is thus shown as penetrating the familial environment, where Erica is unable to reconcile her maternal role with Nina's newfound status as idealised commodity. Her artwork, which represents Nina as a blinded image, a cultural construction bound for

Figure 5.2 Erica's obsessive artwork in *Black Swan.*

endless repetition, mimics Nina's paranoid experience of losing her sense of subjectivity.

This representation of familial violence between women as threatening to obscure wider structures of cultural violence threatens to play into longstanding myths that segregate the idealised 'angelic' mother from what E. Ann Kaplan describes as her 'evil witch' counterpart (1992: 9). Although there is some indication of the external forces that have shaped Erica's behaviour, she comes to embody these larger cultural conflicts and to administer their harmful outcomes in a manner that serves to deflect attention periodically away from the more subversive themes evident in the film. In an Anglo-American context that hypes individual empowerment while encouraging neo-conservative choices in relation to marriage and family (McRobbie 2009: 255), Erica appears as a horrific societal aberration, a failure of the neoliberal feminist dream – not entirely unsympathetic, yet also an ideal female villain for the postfeminist era. As an ageing woman, Erica (like Beth) is deemed to be of less cultural value than Nina, and so chooses to exert a form of corporeal policing over her daughter to maintain a certain investment in the allure of a commercial culture that predominantly trades in fetishistic images of youth, beauty and whiteness, and bestows temporary success on those who serve to embody these images. Erica appears uncomfortably committed to the idea of career and independence from the family unit, a dream that she herself never achieved but for which her daughter is currently striving, and so Erica becomes pathologically invested in her maternal role to compensate for her own past failings. Erica's mental instability and threatening presence towards Nina in the family home means that she resembles more closely a stock horror villain akin to the infamous Margaret White of Brian de Palma's *Carrie* (1976) rather than the self-abnegating (yet more nuanced) character of maternal melodrama such as *Stella Dallas* (King Vidor, 1937). Erica is immediately introduced as a threatening force in her daughter's life at the beginning of the film after Nina awakens from a nightmare in which she has danced the prologue to *Swan Lake* and experienced Von Rothbart taking control of her body. Dressed in black while Nina appears in virginal white, Erica is paralleled with the sinister antagonist of the ballet as she proceeds to invade Nina's personal space by admonishing her daughter for what she perceives to be her inappropriate bodily habits. Erica's obsessive interest in Nina's body takes the form of controlling her meals, checking her skin for bruises and scars, removing her clothing, tucking her in at bedtime and interrogating her as to whether Thomas has made any unwanted sexual advances. When Thomas orders Nina to get in touch with her sexuality through masturbation, Nina is unable to orgasm after imagining that her mother is asleep in the corner of her bedroom. Erica is thus implicated directly in Nina's inability to perform the role required of adult female sexuality, with the film utilising psychoanalytic discourses in order to link Nina's mental health problems to her upbringing within an atypical familial unit.

In the psychoanalytic terms outlined by Karen Horney, Erica qualifies as a 'masculine mother' in that she has rejected her feminine role and adopted masculine tendencies that allow her to engage in domineering behaviour towards the girl child by prying into her affairs and sabotaging her relationships with men (Kaplan 1992: 109). Famously, Julia Kristeva has described the desire of the mother to preserve the pre-Oedipal bond as symptomatic of a specific female melancholia (1989). Such representations have a long history within the Hollywood film industry, which has struggled over the decades to negotiate changing power dynamics and gender roles within American society. Writing on similar representations of the mother in the classic Hollywood films *Now, Voyager* (Irving Rapper, 1942) and *Marnie* (Alfred Hitchcock, 1964), Kaplan hypothesises that 'pop-Freudian stereotypes' were a key means of exploring the increasing threat of women within the public sphere in the post-war era, with such theories comprising a convenient avenue for expressing deeper forms of societal discomfort with transforming gender roles (110). In *Black Swan*, the pathological mother–daughter relationship suggests the harmful ruptures inherent in neoliberal feminist ideology and the cultural invisibility of the ageing female body. Yet as in the films Kaplan analyses, this mother figure also expresses deeper social anxieties relating to the extreme potentialities of 'off-script' feminine behaviour within this restrictive, patriarchal environment.

Such behaviour, in a film that in its tragic drive does not consider a progressive or indeed political use of female agency outside the terms of the confining postfeminist sensibility, is envisaged as terrifying and likely to be replicated within future mother–daughter relationships that circulate in a similar social environment. Erica and Beth, after all, represent doubles for Nina in that they exhibit behavioural tendencies that have resulted inevitably from a patriarchal societal structure that declares women irrelevant and invisible at a relatively young age. Beth, unlike Erica, was a highly successful dancer and thus serves as an indicator that even if Nina achieves her goal of becoming a celebrated prima ballerina, the same fate of madness and inner rage awaits her as it does all the dancers within the company. The dancers therefore are enmeshed in a generational cycle of pathology and inner violence that appears difficult to break; while 'the mother' is represented as playing a key role in socialising her daughter into the ways of a world that she knows will disadvantage her. As Hollywood film engages with the complexities of neoliberal feminism and renegotiates its terms in accordance with wider ideological shifts, new cinematic female villains come to be born who embody its more deleterious elements and are implicated in perpetuating a cycle of gendered violence, even though they themselves are not favoured by its terms.

Importantly, the mother–daughter dyad is not merely a means through which postfeminist ambivalence is framed through generational conflict, but is also a primary trope through which narratives of female repression and the renegotiation of the white, bourgeois self take place. Wider discourses that examine the sicknesses inherent in an affluent, white society are therefore encapsulated in gendered stories that narrate the difficulties involved in locating an empowered female subjectivity. Variations on this theme have appeared in popular contemporary films such as *Titanic* (James Cameron, 1997) and *Alice in Wonderland* – texts that, like *Black Swan*, utilise melodramatic tropes but ultimately celebrate the will of the individual to create a new destiny by breaking away from the white hegemonic power structures that disadvantage women, as symbolised by a mother who is both oppressed and oppressive. Burton's *Alice in Wonderland* borrows from *Titanic*'s highly successful narrative formula in representing Alice's mother's behaviour as contributing strongly to her melancholic state. In this film, Alice's dissatisfaction with the limitations placed upon her body are conveyed initially through a stilted conversation she has with her mother alluding to the sexism of feminine dress conventions as the pair travel in a carriage while seated in suffocating proximity to one another. Underland, by comparison, becomes a space where Alice can impose her own rules and revel in her newfound corporeal freedom away from the scrutinising maternal gaze. In these texts, as the protagonist distances herself from the oppressive mother figure, she simultaneously disassociates from a form of hegemonic whiteness that is unable to accommodate her differences in behaviour and attitude, or that she perceives not to be in the best interests of her future wellbeing and personal happiness. The mother in this context therefore becomes a symbol of cyclical gendered repression, or indeed a symbol of failure, in that she has been fundamentally unable to renegotiate the terms of her subject position in a manner that will allow her greater individual freedoms. Yet the utilisation of the mother–daughter dyad in relation to existential suffocation is also found in more foreboding auteur pieces like Von Trier's *Melancholia* and Michael Haneke's *The Piano Teacher* (2001), which present the female individual as enmeshed hopelessly in power dynamics beyond her control. The intricacies of how the mother–daughter bond unfolds narratively differs from film to film in accordance with a number of factors, including genre, the auteur's signature, the intricacies of the text and certainly in Haneke's case the specificities of national context. Yet the conceptualisation of the mother whose feelings of over-attachment towards her daughter culminates in abusive behaviours bears marked similarities in all these seemingly disparate films. In framing stories of white, bourgeois repression and violence through the metaphor of the maternal body, these films can represent such familial and societal arrangements as cyclical – or indeed as ominously *reproductive*.

Black Swan's mother–daughter relationship, in its violent and inescapably self-destructive conclusion, bears a particularly marked resemblance to Haneke's *The Piano Teacher*, a film also set within the exclusive and hierarchical ranks of a high art institution. In an article that chronicles Natalie Portman's preparation for the role, journalist Jenelle Riley quotes the actress as stating that *The Piano Teacher* was the only film Aronofsky suggested she watch to get a sense of the type of mother–daughter relationship the director wished to portray (2011). *Black Swan*, like other films analysed within this book, represents heteronormative desire as untenable for the melancholic white woman. Yet unlike fantasy texts such as *Alice in Wonderland* and *Pirates of the Caribbean*, the film cannot envisage a world where queer identity is embraced to positive effect upon the self. Instead, the possibility of lesbian or even incestuous desire is implicated not only in Nina's psychological breakdown but also in the cyclical structure of bourgeois, white violence. Similar to *Black Swan* in theme and narrative drive, Haneke's film also centres upon a repressed white woman, Erika Kohut (Isabelle Huppert), who struggles to maintain cultural legitimacy as a piano player and teacher while living in a claustrophobic apartment in which she sleeps beside her domineering mother (Annie Girardot) night after night. Like Nina, Erika engages in self-mutilation practices, but unlike the *Black Swan* protagonist she is also intensely voyeuristic and deeply masochistic in her sexual behaviours. Haneke's cinema demonstrates a preoccupation with the violence of patriarchal, middle-class social arrangements, a theme he has explored in critically lauded films such as *Funny Games* (1997) and *The White Ribbon* (2009), with Catherine Wheatley pointing out that *The Piano Teacher* utilises melodramatic iconography, settings and tropes to engage with the ideological origins of the genre as an allegory for class tensions (2006: 118). Akin to the presence of Tchaikovsky's compositions for *Swan Lake* in Aronofsky's film, the repeated appearance of Schubert's 'Winterreise' in *The Piano Teacher* connects Erika to her chosen means of artistic expression and comprises a distinct mode of language that disconnects her from society (Wheatley 2006: 120).

Like Nina, Erika is infantilised by her mother, who in this text remains nameless, existing only as maternal symbol, and whom Wheatley suggests the protagonist both loves and fears due to her dependence on the maternal body and misapprehension of it as part of herself (121). Jean Wyatt mounts a convincing argument in her discussion of maternal '*jouissance*' within the film, in stating that the text exhibits the ghosted fragments of Vienna's Nazi past with fascist, authoritarian modes of social control transposed both onto the mother–daughter relationship and Erika's subsequent interaction with her students. Erika, Wyatt notes, engages in excessively controlling and dehumanising behaviour toward her pupils in the form of shaming and humiliating them sexually – behaviour that recalls 'the hallmarks of Nazi discipline' and replicates the dynamics of the maternal dyad in the family home (2005: 474). Erika's relationship with her mother is mirrored through the mother–daughter relationship of her star pupil Anna (Anna Segalevitch), a student for whom she demonstrates intense jealousy, and whose piano skills she decides to sabotage by hiding broken glass in her jacket pocket. *The Piano Teacher*, with its bleak social analysis and lack of clarifying denouement, bears little resemblance to popular Hollywood narratives that contain utopian drives and socially idealistic conclusions. Yet the mother–daughter relationship as a trope for analysing the violence of white, bourgeois society is a point of similarity that has its roots in longstanding Western mythologies of femininity and in filmic melodrama. *Black Swan*, though indebted to Haneke's film, lacks specific historical allusions in relation to racial violence, choosing instead to parallel Nina's story to that of the 'White Swan', a mythical and ahistorical ideal of aristocratic femininity, and thus is less able (and less willing) to sustain a broader critique of the processes of control and exclusion at the heart of American social hierarchies. Yet while 'the mother' may symbolise compliance with forms of gendered repression that disadvantage daughters, this figure also embodies the sicknesses of white hegemonic power structures that have victimised the mother and have always threatened to exclude her. The mother's capacity as a reproductive figure allows her to be utilised as a frightening transnational metaphor for exploring how such violence proliferates, with the role of 'mother' represented as doubling with that of societal caretaker.

EXTRA-TEXTUAL STAR DISCOURSE: THE MARKET LOGIC OF MELANCHOLY

To perform the role of the monstrous mother or the mentally distressed daughter in a film like *Black Swan* of course may confer significant benefits on the actress who plays her as she navigates the Hollywood labour market. To concentrate analysis solely on the ideological workings of this film at the level of narrative would be to miss key aspects of how this text creates meaning, particularly given its pronounced self-reflexivity in relation to the production and marketing of celebrities. Barbara Hershey's portrayal of Erica, for example, recalls the performances of other Hollywood icons who have played the part of 'female grotesque' to lasting critical acclaim, allowing for renewed visibility in the cultural sphere through the renegotiation of star image. Writing of memorable star turns by Bette Davis in *All About Eve* (Joseph L. Mankiewicz, 1950) and *What Ever Happened to Baby Jane?* (Robert Aldrich, 1962) as well as that of Gloria Swanson in *Sunset Boulevard* (Billy Wilder, 1950), Ann Morey argues that such performances, often played out through the trope of the maternal melodrama, are able to confer professional power upon the ageing actress in that they function as 'an acknowledgement of an actress's artistic effort and ability to perform at the margins of conventional femininity'(2011: 104). If the actress's stardom has declined over recent decades, her career may be reinvigorated through an association with a successful auteur, or she may be able to showcase a new range of performance skills absent from her previous body of work as a result of the different strategies involved in the commodification and marketing of her image. Films that engage self-reflexively with the burden of past celebrity success and its loss, the detritus of fame and its impact on interpersonal relations, and the emptiness of a commercial industry that perceives the body as a disposable commodity are not uncommon in recent popular cinema. The 2014 Academy Award for Best Picture was after all awarded to Alejandro González Iñárritu's *Birdman*, a film starring Michael Keaton as a washed-up actor notorious for his role in a superhero franchise decades gone by, who attempts to revive his career by directing, writing and starring in a Broadway production. Keaton's role as Riggan Thomson parallels his own star trajectory, with the actor best known for his performances in Tim Burton's highly successful *Batman* films of the late 1980s and early 1990s. In chronicling the destructive desire for cultural adoration at all costs as well as the commercial and individual stakes involved in the naming of a work as 'great art', the film deals in similar themes to *Black Swan*, with Thomson eventually receiving critical praise for his 'super-realist' method performance when he shoots himself on stage, a moment akin to the audience's rapture at witnessing Nina's dying swan as she bleeds profusely from the abdomen.

The critique of industry inherent in these films, however, and the introspective performances of actors struggling with their place in relation to the corporate machine is *in itself* a commercial strategy that offers actors like Portman and Keaton a chance to renegotiate the terms of how they are marketed as Hollywood commodities. Graeme Turner states that the aim of celebrity is to develop the public persona as a financial asset (2004: 34) and to engage in a range of strategies that increase the value of that commodity to the industry (35). Portman's role in *Black Swan* allows her to reference the virginal, white, girlish identity previously used to market her films and simultaneously to create distance from this same image through a method performance designed both to acknowledge and to shed the restrictive elements of its defining terms. Following her role in *Black Swan*, Portman's star text has been notably globalised, with a move to Paris, an association with the luxury Dior fashion and make-up brand and a greater involvement with non-Hollywood productions, such as her 2015 directorial feature debut *A Tale of Love and Darkness*, based on the novel by Israeli author Amos Oz. This mode of star text regeneration had already been trialled by Aronofsky in the 2008 film *The Wrestler*, which stars 1980s' leading man Mickey Rourke as an ageing professional athlete endeavouring to relive his glory days while also struggling to make ends meet and repair his personal relationships. Emotional soliloquies within the film invite the audience to compare the star trajectory of protagonist Randy 'the Ram' Robinson to that of Rourke himself (who turned his back on Hollywood for a boxing career in the 1990s after developing a reputation as being difficult to work with), and to share in both his pain and desire for a professional comeback. One of the film's promotional posters quotes *Newsweek* in commanding viewers to 'Witness the Resurrection of Mickey Rourke', while the actor, like Portman and Keaton, was nominated for numerous accolades on the awards circuit. Aronofsky therefore utilises *The Wrestler* and *Black Swan* to stage spectacles of celebrity revelation that simultaneously repair and/or reinvent the celebrity image and promote the star as marketable product.[3] If celebrity power has a 'liquid' nature, which David P. Marshall argues is not dissimilar to that of stock market commodities (1997: 6), then the relationship between Aronofsky and his stars becomes one of commercial interdependency, with the success of the films ideally culminating in both increased professional power for his stars and the enhancement of his status as a contemporary cinematic auteur with considerable industrial influence.

Natalie Portman's performance in *Black Swan* is an attempt to reach a category of stardom in which the actor's talent and skill is foregrounded over a typecast persona or the performer's celebrity status. While the careers of Hollywood actresses such as Meryl Streep and Cate Blanchett may be categorised within the privileged category of 'star as performer', Geraghty notes the presence of a gendered hierarchy of stardom with women more likely to be cast as celebrities and therefore subject to intense scrutiny and gossip about their private lives (2000: 187–9). It is therefore common for female performers, especially those who are successful yet limited by wage disparity, ageism and typecasting, to attempt temporarily to disrupt the markers of privilege and capital, including youth, beauty, whiteness and heteronormativity that their career has to that point profited from. This is an attempt to garner acclaim for a superior level of acting skill and to obtain a greater degree of control over their careers. Kevin Esch argues that method acting commonly comprises self-imposed bodily transformation, most typically in the form of extreme weight loss or gain, to ensure greater fidelity of performance (2006: 96). Though they are controversial, Esch points out that method performances attract a significant amount of publicity and critical acclaim, and have become synonymous with popular understandings of what constitutes dedication to the craft, or 'serious acting' (98). Portman's performance in *Black Swan* needs to be read also in relation to this industrial trend. For example, Charlize Theron, previously known for her roles as the 'beautiful girlfriend' in films such as *The Cider House Rules* (Lasse Hallström, 1999) and *The Legend of Bagger Vance* (Robert Redford, 2000), reinvigorated her career through her performance in the independent film *Monster* (Patty Jenkins, 2003), in which she played mentally ill real-life serial killer Aileen Wuornos, a socially rejected victim of abuse who turns to prostitution and a life of crime while struggling to support her female lover. Theron received widespread acclaim not only for her performance but also her willingness to alter her physicality and thus her association with glamour and beauty, gaining fourteen kilos and wearing make-up designed to age and deglamorise her for the role.

Successful performances such as Theron's may result in greater mobility and choice for the actress in terms of the selection of roles she is offered, and further chances for fictional transgressions that challenge dominant ideologies at the level of the text but at the same time are contained by the notion that it is a socially idealised, normative body that is only temporarily transgressing. Performing melancholia and dissatisfaction with the status quo, as Nicole Kidman does as Virginia Woolf in *The Hours* (Stephen Daldry, 2002), or the mental distress and social deviance that Theron conveys as Aileen Wuornos, comprise prime forms of career opportunity for the female actress disadvantaged in the industry by her gender and yet privileged by her adherence to the white, bourgeois codes of physical beauty and social respectability that grant her a significant degree of performative power in the cultural sphere. White women in Hollywood, as represented by *Black Swan*'s ballerinas, occupy the performative centre while non-white women or those marked by working-class signifiers are still rarely cast as leads in major productions and do not have the same capacity for industrial mobility when it comes to a choice of major film roles. While there have been some exceptions to this rule, Halle Berry's performance in *Monster's Ball* (Marc Forster, 2001) being perhaps one of these, it continues to be notably more difficult for a non-white woman to attract significant critical acclaim and positive media attention for a brave 'transgressive' film performance given that the centralised presence of her body would *already* constitute such a transgression.

In *Black Swan*, the textual critique of late capitalism's intersection with popular Anglo-American ideas as to what constitutes female agency allows Natalie Portman an opportunity to redefine the terms of her stardom amidst these cultural fluctuations in relation to understandings of neoliberal feminism. Portman, who was born in Israel and identifies as Jewish, has largely been sold as an idealised white star. In keeping with a long Hollywood tradition of anglicising actors' surnames, she dropped her birth name Hershlag in a move not dissimilar to that of Winona Horowitz, who later became known as Winona Ryder.[4] The professional standing of Nina and Beth within *Black Swan*'s ballet company parallels that of the two stars in relation to the Hollywood industry, with Portman presenting as a younger, more bankable alternative to the older star. Ryder's appearance in *Black Swan*, not unlike Rourke's performance in *The Wrestler*, represents both an acknowledgement of her past 'failings' as a public figure and her willingness to re-enter the world of artistic production as a repackaged commodity.[5] Portman, on the other hand, was a commercially successful actress at the time of filming *Black Swan*, yet had been struggling to shed aspects of her teenage image in making the transition to adult roles. Coming to prominence as the street-wise and coquettish twelve-year-old Mathilda who plays an assassin's apprentice to Jean Reno's jaded hitman in *Léon: The Professional* (Luc Besson, 1994), Portman subsequently appeared in films including the *Star Wars* trilogy (George Lucas 1999, 2002, 2005), *Garden State* (Zach Braff, 2004) and *Where the Heart Is* (Matt Williams, 2000). These performances highlighted her characters' bravery and unique world view, but also amplified her vulnerability, innocence and childlike nature. Even in the 2004 film *Closer* (Mike Nichols) in which the actress played an erotic dancer, the character was still marked conspicuously by a naivety and waifish innocence, while Portman worked publicly to lampoon her clean-cut image, most notably through a *Saturday Night Live* rap skit in which she swore and drank, and joked about drug-taking and cheating on her university exams. Portman, whose star text emphasises her upper middle-class upbringing and Harvard education, describes herself as a feminist who wishes for a greater variety of complex roles for women.[6] *Black Swan* provided such a vehicle for her in that the strategic self-reflexivity of the film highlighted the problematic infantilising of her image into adulthood, and also allowed for an introspective method performance in requiring the actress to enact the simultaneous breakdown and *breakthrough* of this career-limiting constructed image of virginal, childlike whiteness.

In a 2010 *Vanity Fair* interview tellingly titled 'Natalie Portman on *Black Swan:* I'm only acting, dammit!', journalist John Lopez muses that the role feels 'tailor-made' to surpass Portman's reputation as 'the Audrey Hepburn of her generation', with her performances to that point comprising a 'mere chrysalis stage to something larger'. Portman's much-publicised extreme weight

Figure 5.3 Portman's performance in *Black Swan* is a staged escape from childlike roles.

loss and intensive daily ballet training for the role helped promote her as an actress immensely dedicated to her craft, not dissimilar to Nina in the film, while her emotive performance comprised a form of method acting that, Dyer notes, tends to privilege expressions of 'disturbance, repression and anguish' as moments of supposed authentic revelations of the repressed self (1998: 141). Marshall adds pertinently that the introspective method performances of stars like Marlon Brando and James Dean involved the audience in the search for their authentic selves as this style of acting allowed for 'the permutation that the internal expression of a character can also be a playing out of the psychological dimensions of the star his or herself' (1997: 89). Portman's performance thus involves the audience in her introspective search for the truth of her being, and associated campaign for a renegotiation of her image in line with these newly conveyed authentic aspects of her inner life. The method-style of performance is a bid to be associated with a prestige category of acting typically affiliated with acclaimed male actors such as Brando and more recently Daniel Day Lewis, the latter known for his prolonged, intense periods of inhabiting characters off-set. Yet it is a bid that is certainly not without its gendered pitfalls. Rosemary Malague points to the existence of a manipulative teacher/student model when it comes to female method acting, with the male teacher often able to take credit for a female student's performance due to his professed ability to extract authentic emotion from her, thus conferring artistic prestige upon himself in a manner that devalues the actress's responsibility for her own performance (2012: 18). It may certainly be said that such an artistic interdependency is held to exist between Aronofsky and Portman, Von Trier and Dunst, or indeed any number of male auteurs and gifted female stars, and it is an artistic interdependency that is represented in the film through Nina's relationship with Thomas. Nevertheless, the female star's melancholic relationship with her own image construction and the strategic deployment of this introspective process on screen points to the existence of a political economy of melancholy by which actresses can enact forms of white burden in order to accrue greater levels of capital within the Hollywood industry. This capital is of course still bound by the patriarchal power structures inherent within the enterprise, yet the presence of such a commercial strategy as aligned with *Black Swan* complicates the text's critique of neoliberal feminism. If Natalie Portman herself may be said to form yet another double for the protagonist Nina, then her own career strategies form a parallel trajectory where extreme discipline and bodily punishment are rewarded with more autonomy in relation to film production and role choice as well as a renegotiated form of stardom that may allow for further longevity in the industry. If the hierarchical nature of film stardom calls for intense competition between actresses, given that few substantial roles are available to women, with even fewer available to non-white women, then Portman's performance in *Black Swan* certainly comprises a beneficial move in a tight market.

CONCLUSION

The deployment of melancholic emotion within *Black Swan* thus becomes complicated, with the film's extra-textual narrative operating in a manner that partially parallels and yet ultimately softens the film's critique of the destructive relationship that exists between neoliberal governmentality and white, middle-class women. *Black Swan*, like the other films within this book, is about female burden as related to the failings of neoliberal feminism, with the semiotics of the ballet framing this burden in relation to an insular form of whiteness, which is critiqued only in relation to those who are allowed to benefit from its privileges. The film explores neoliberalism's gendered politics primarily through the bourgeois, white woman whose capacity for upward mobility has been highlighted in its rhetoric. *Black Swan*, also like other texts analysed within this book, posits the question as to whether forms of female agency can be discovered by searching beyond the parameters of the white, middle-class signifiers of the self, and ultimately indicates that it cannot, therefore undermining the contemporary Western obsession for therapeutic self-reinvention. Yet the ideological work of *Black Swan* is troubled (though not necessarily negated) through its self-reflexivity in relation to the commercial imperatives of Hollywood stardom, and its introduction of a female star as appearing to enact her own feelings of burden in an industry that both celebrates and limits her. Portman *is* in fact empowered by her 'bravery' in challenging the codes of virginal whiteness that her star image is built upon, and so the film's extra-textual discourse presents a counter narrative of white female introspection and emancipation that is introduced here as a valuable career strategy for gaining greater mobility within a patriarchal industry.

NOTES

1. As dance scholar Sally Banes observes of the Black Swan character in *Swan Lake*, she is independent, assertive and 'dazzlingly vertical' in her movements, in contrast to Odette's 'soft, feathery steps, lyricism, swooning backbends and lowered gaze', with Odile's complicated *fouetté* turn sequence all the more impressive for not requiring male support (1998: 61).
2. McLean notes, for instance, that in *Flashdance* (Adrian Lyne, 1983), ballet experts express disdain for the heroine owing to her working class and racial status, while in *Save the Last Dance* (Thomas Carter, 2001), the ballet is represented as uptight and snobbish in comparison to the hip-hop and club dancing favoured by the African-American characters.
3. Barry King argues in his 2008 *Social Semiotics* article 'Stardom, celebrity and the para-confession' that televised celebrity confessionals on shows such as *Oprah* perform a similar function in protecting the integrity of the star as marketable commodity (2008: 122).
4. For an extended discussion of Jewish identity and racialisation in the American context see Karen Brodkin's *How Jews Became White Folks & What That Says about Race in America* (2004).
5. A sought-after actress in the 1990s, Ryder starred in popular vehicles including *Edward Scissorhands* (Tim Burton, 1990), *The Age of Innocence* (Martin Scorsese, 1993) and *Little Women* (Gillian Armstrong, 1994), before suffering a significant decline in professional status after a highly publicised arrest for shoplifting in 2001.
6. As quoted in 'Role reversal', an interview with the actress conducted by fellow actor Tom Hiddleston for *Elle* magazine in November 2013.

CHAPTER 6

Sofia Coppola's Melancholic Aesthetic: Vanishing Femininity in an Object-oriented World

Director Sofia Coppola's feature film *Somewhere* (2010) opens with a prolonged sequence in which the audience, positioned as witnesses by a stationary camera placed at the side of a desert road, observes a car repeatedly driving past the same location in a desolate landscape. This car, belonging to the male protagonist Johnny Marco (Stephen Dorff), a Hollywood actor disenchanted by the artificial celebrity trappings of his LA lifestyle, operates as a metaphor for a key existential theme in Coppola's oeuvre – that of the futility and pointlessness of white, upper-class existence in the late capitalist era. Johnny is unable to reach a destination that can promise human interconnection and fulfilment, and so is condemned to journey in continual circles, passing the same landmarks in an eternal mode of transition. *Somewhere*, while engaging in a treatment of similar themes to Coppola's other features *The Virgin Suicides*, *Lost in Translation*, *Marie Antoinette* and *The Bling Ring* (2013), differs from the director's typical fare in its exploration of middle-aged masculinity and fractured father–daughter relationships. Yet what this opening scene exemplifies is not only the presence of themes relating to white alienation and aimlessness, but also a commercialised melancholic aesthetic integral to Coppola's brand of authorship. Coppola's 'beautiful and tragic world' (Lane and Richter 2011: 200) involves both an immersion in and an ironic distancing from the image-saturated, consumer-capitalist regime that governs the lives of her protagonists, who are unencumbered by work, devoid of a sense of personal agency and lacking in meaningful avenues through which to contribute to society. It is, however, precisely this impossibility of leading a fulfilling life under neoliberal capitalism that is Coppola's main selling point, with the cinematic mood of dreamy, wistful yearning that permeates her texts capable of being packaged and sold as an appealing state of dissociative 'romantic ennui' (Yunuen Lewis 2011: 179). Perhaps most distinct in Coppola's first three features, a group of texts that R. Barton Palmer has termed the director's

Young Girls trilogy (2012: 35), the figure of the melancholic white woman is integral to this auteur's bid for artistic cultural capital in the male-dominated Hollywood industry.

Coppola's cinema trades in the expression of a state of melancholic burden, a type of painful yet pleasurable neurasthenia, experienced only by the white and privileged, that the protagonists are unable to alleviate. These heroines are heralded for their attractiveness, educational achievements, economic and career opportunities (or capacity to achieve political change, in the case of Marie Antoinette), as well as being recognised as important targets on the consumer market. There is a potent recognition in Coppola's work, however, that the white, upwardly mobile woman of neoliberal capitalism – in her hyper-visibility – operates as a mere icon of politicised discourse. She is a constructed image, and as such is subject to the whims, fantasies and vilifications of the crowd that has placed her on a pedestal. No matter how hard the heroine tries, she is unable to craft a sense of self when she must also act as a projection of signs. The Lisbon girls in *The Virgin Suicides*, for instance, are the objects of neighbourhood gossip and local media speculation, with one suburban mother commenting after the death of the first sister Cecilia (Hanna R. Hall) that while the other girls evidently have 'bright futures' ahead of them, the youngest 'was just going to end up a kook'. Death, in this film, is the only way to escape unwanted surveillance and the societal expectation of the 'bright future', which this text insinuates may in fact be nothing more than bourgeois fantasy. Coppola protagonists are typically young, female, blonde, almost translucently pale (the ideal heroine is embodied by the director's favoured lead performer Hollywood actress Kirsten Dunst, who plays both Marie Antoinette and Lux Lisbon), and exist in a state of melancholic reflection and disconnection. Unlike the protagonists of the travel romance or the fantasy film, the Coppola protagonist is unable to alleviate her melancholic state by experimenting beyond the borders of white, upper-class identity, and nor is this importantly ever posed as a viable option, as it is in *Blue Jasmine* and *Black Swan*. The Tokyo environment in *Lost in Translation* must remain unknowable and impenetrable to Charlotte (Scarlett Johansson), who can voice her hopes and fears only to fellow traveller Bob Harris (Bill Murray), a middle-aged American celebrity who is increasingly disenchanted by both his career and his marriage and as such is someone who can 'speak her language'. Similarly, the broader political context of economic mismanagement and wealth inequality leading to the French Revolution and Marie Antoinette's demise must be largely eradicated from Coppola's film on the subject, which instead chooses to focus far more intently on Marie's inner personal pain and unhappiness at the political and social expectations placed upon her at the Court of Versailles. It is an integral feature of Coppola's cinema that protagonists who are racialised as white and socio-economically empowered are incapable of decentring their experience to see, hear or otherwise relate to subjects racialised as non-white – especially in so far as these subjects are positioned below them in status and class hierarchies. This is true not only of the characters, but also of the ideological drive of the texts themselves.

The Coppola heroine is almost painfully visible as she lives out her day-to-day existence under an intense public scrutiny that affords her no capacity to engage in any form of political agency, while her boredom and melancholic introspection allow for her to view expected modes of social performance from a certain dissatisfied distance. In fact, the more the heroine's private life is exposed to public view and composed via public discourse, the less assured her sense of self seems to be as she heads toward her inevitable disappearance, or indeed demise. The audience is made aware of the heroine's act of 'vanishing', and as such the protagonist's hyper-visibility comes to be infused with a sense of pathos that may allow for a feminist interpretation of the heroine's interpellation within recognisable postfeminist and neoliberal ideologies. We know that, no matter how often Charlotte listens to audio tapes promising spiritual guidance or attempts to develop a sense of self through the consumption of Japanese culture, she will remain uncertain about the most appropriate way to navigate her life and find fulfilment in her marriage and career. We also know that Marie Antoinette's attempts to re-brand her image and discover a sense of identity by adorning herself in elaborate costumes and throwing lavish parties overflowing with champagne will fail to conceal her role as a political pawn that will eventually see her discarded in favour of new regimes promising new futures.

There is an acknowledgement within these films that while white women can consume or rise up the political/corporate ladder, they cannot act in meaningful ways in order to transform what Aileen Moreton-Robinson calls the 'possessive logic of white, patriarchal sovereignty' (2015: xi). These heroines display a sense of knowing as to their prescribed political and cultural roles, and appear almost bored with the infinite amount of leisure time that stretches before them. As Wolf Lepenies points out, 'melancholy and boredom belong together' with 'the melancholic, in the midst of his everyday boredom, having no choice but to get caught up in himself' (1992: 87). This comment is indeed a pertinent one, as Coppola's interpretation of female melancholia as both an aspect of a filmic character's disposition and of a text's aesthetic mood thus becomes an integral expression of the contemporary political climate that while able to act as an insightful commentary can also at times appear sublimely self-indulgent. Coppola's cinema speaks to a female audience knowledgeable of the trappings of postfeminist commodity culture and the role of middle-class women within a neoliberal economy. Yet her cinema also capitalises on the association of melancholia with specialness in offering poetic, romanticised portraits of protagonists confined not only by their society but by their own propensity for introspective processes that prove both pleasurable and pointlessly apathetic. It is precisely through their melancholy and the act of fading away, a depoliticised immersion in the white, privileged self, that these young women immortalise themselves in the memories of others and ironically become retrospectively bestowed with a degree of importance.

SOFIA COPPOLA AS CELEBRITY AUTEUR BRAND

Sofia Coppola, daughter of famed Hollywood director Francis Ford Coppola, is a recognisable auteur strongly associated with what Timothy Corrigan calls a 'brand-name vision whose aesthetic meanings and values have already been determined' (1998: 40). As such, Coppola's name functions as a marketing tool, with Karen Hollinger pointing out that modern-day auteurs have 'taken on commercial significance as superstar personalities and cult figures' (2012: 232). The auteur image is constructed by public appearances, press releases and interviews in a manner that influences the reception of their films (Hollinger 2012: 232) and functions in accordance with the industrial mechanics of Hollywood stardom. Coppola has been able to capitalise on her auteur brand by commercial endeavours extending beyond the film industry, for instance collaborating with Marc Jacobs on perfumes and handbags and starting her own Japanese-based clothing line Milk Fed. Lane and Richter suggest that Coppola's regular appearances as a 'style impresario' in fashion publications such as *Vogue* and *Vanity Fair* aid in empowering her through a 'logic of consumerism', in which she is able to achieve 'modes of self-representation within the realm of material objects and spectacle' (2011: 193). The degree to which a director can be seen as the sole architect of a piece of work has of course been a matter of some debate within film scholarship. Theories of cinematic authorship, originally pioneered by the young French film filmmakers and critics writing for the magazine *Cahiers du Cinéma* in the 1960s, arose out of dissatisfaction with what these theorists perceived to be the banal tradition of a French cinema overly dependent on literary adaptation at the expense of creative expression. Alexandre Astruc's famous treatise on the *camera-stylo*, or camera pen, explored the emergence of forms of cinematic language that would allow certain directors to express their thoughts and preoccupations through film in a manner akin to the novelist or painter (Astruc 1948/1968: 18–19). Andrew Sarris, a proponent of these theories within the American context, suggested three criteria by which a director may be elevated to the status of auteur within the critical canon – technical competence, a distinguishable 'signature' as evidenced through recurrent stylistic characteristics (1962/2009: 452), and an interior meaning to be extrapolated from the tension existing between the director's material and his or her personality, or what Sarris termed an '*élan* of the soul' (453).

Advocates of cinematic authorship were not without their dissenters. Pauline Kael's rebuttal article to Sarris, published by *Film Quarterly* in 1963, notoriously accused him of indulging in masculinist bias, while other critics noted the collaborative and intertextual nature of film production and other forms of mass media. Poststructuralist thinkers dispensed with the notion of the author as the source behind a text, with Roland Barthes arguing that a writer can never engage in truly original expression, but rather can only quote from a range of cultural signs from a 'ready-formed dictionary' (1967/1981: 211). Michel Foucault, meanwhile, spoke of the author as 'a function of discourse' (1969/1981: 284) as opposed to a creator who endows texts with meaning, and called not for the abandonment of the subject but rather for an analysis of the conditions and forms through which authors are produced (290). Although these views have gained credence within authorship studies with scholarship indeed exhibiting a more complex approach to the discussion of the cinematic auteur, the author as romanticised figure still retains a high degree of cultural currency both in the world of commerce and in the world of theory. In fact, as Janet Staiger states, the idea of the author continues to occupy a role of especial importance for those who do not occupy positions of dominance within society, 'in which asserting even a partial agency may seem to be important for day-to-day survival or where locating moments of alternative practice takes away the naturalised privileges of normativity' (2003: 27). The auteur has thus occupied an area of interest for feminist film critics who have sought to reinvestigate the work of female directors including Dorothy Arzner, Maya Deren, Chantal Akerman and Sally Potter amongst others, for their subversive treatment of classical Hollywood filmmaking and the gender politics that mainstream cinema relies upon to tell its stories.[1]

As one of the few high-profile female directors working in Hollywood today, Coppola's cinema would seem a prime candidate for a feminist analysis of the gender politics inherent within her work, yet it is not until relatively recently that her output has received any kind of sustained critical attention. In general, feminist scholars have preferred to focus on the few contemporary female filmmakers who have achieved a degree of critical acclaim on the international festival circuit, perhaps most notably Jane Campion, rather than a director such as Coppola whose investment in typically postfeminist pleasures ensures that her films attract as much scorn for their alleged shallowness as they do acclaim.[2] As Tasker points out, female filmmakers such as Penny Marshall and Nancy Meyers can be found wanting in their capacity to innovate or provoke, given that popular culture is typically only deemed critically acceptable when considered to be politically transgressive or aesthetically challenging (2010: 216). According to Amy Woodworth, one of the first to engage in a feminist analysis of Coppola's oeuvre, this critical oversight may be partially attributed to the political ambiguity inherent within the films' aesthetics, with the director often framing and lighting her female protagonists in ways that appear complicit with patriarchal systems of representation (2008: 145). In addition, Woodworth notes the reluctance of feminist scholars to engage in analyses of female directors working in Hollywood, who favour instead arthouse and independent products by directors including the aforementioned Campion, Akerman and Potter with a more explicit feminist agenda and remarkable use of form (141). Woodworth sees this critical tendency as limiting given mainstream cinema's increasing adoption of avant-garde techniques and the capacity of popular Hollywood films to 'best function as cultural barometers' (142). This oversight, however, may also be explained by Coppola's apparent investment in a postfeminist sensibility, given the emphasis within her films on excessive consumption, the frivolity of celebrity culture and elaborate spectacle, and her own accordant cultivation of a girlish and apolitical persona. Coppola is a notoriously evasive interviewee, with journalists frequently commenting on her softly spoken demeanour and vague responses to questions. In a promotional piece for *The Bling Ring* published in *The Guardian*, interviewer Ryan Gilbey describes himself as feeling as though he is 'trapped on the outside trying to get in' as Coppola 'politely draws the blinds' (2013). In a more explicit refusal to politically engage with the thematic material of her texts, Coppola, when asked of her position on feminism by SBS journalist Helen Barlow, stated that she does not 'want to be political and make political statements. I don't talk about political things' (Barlow, 2013). Coppola lacks the willingness to engage in a more objective discussion regarding a potentially feminist agenda behind her work and her characters are almost uniformly unable to pinpoint a broader rationale behind their melancholic state. Yet it is possible for the critic or viewer to read a commentary on the relationship of the filmic, melancholic white woman with her political context through the ironic and detached attitude that Coppola's films exhibit towards postfeminist commodity culture, and also through notable attributes of the films' *mise-en-scène* and cinematography.

Coppola is affiliated with the emergence of 'smart cinema' – a mode of film-making that Jeffrey Sconce argues is characterised by a tonal 'predilection for irony, black humour and fatalism' (2002: 350), and which is marketed (and critically appraised) in opposition to mainstream, mass-produced Hollywood fare (351). As Caitlin Yunuen Lewis explains, Coppola's auteur brand exhibits a 'cool postfeminist' sensibility born not only from contemporary conceptualisations of postfeminism but also whiteness and counterculturalism (2011: 176). The director may therefore be understood as an 'heir to Francis Ford's mildly countercultural legacy', with Yunuen Lewis pointing out that both father and daughter are considered simultaneously to be part of mainstream Hollywood and yet somewhat artistically distinct (175). Sconce clarifies that smart cinema operates at the intersection of Hollywood cinema, art cinema and

Figure 6.1 Lux Lisbon's knowing wink in *The Virgin Suicides.*

independent production, and suggests that this form of filmmaking typically employs classical narrative and formal conventions, yet provides a critique of middle-class taste and culture through tonal experimentation (2002: 352).

The Virgin Suicides, for instance, demonstrates characteristics associated with what Claire Perkins has termed the 'suburban smart film' (2012: 133) in its utilisation of teen cinema's 'liminal terms' as a means of critiquing utopian ideals (155), the film's treatment of taboo themes (136), and the evocation of small-town America as a landscape of 'blankly drawn and forgettable spaces' (134). In this manner, Coppola can be marketed as an auteur uniquely able to understand the frustrations of her postfeminist audience, whom she can address through her films with a knowing wink. The film's opening credit sequence, in fact, illuminates female protagonist Lux Lisbon's diaphanous visage as she appears to float amongst the clouds against the pale blue sky before addressing the spectator directly with a secretive smile and just such a knowing wink. Lux is knowledgeable of the key role that she plays in commercial fantasies of heavenly whiteness and youthful femininity. Her ironic address is here indicative of the text's commentary on the seductive allure of the female image within commodity culture, as evidenced through the film's numerous fantasy sequences and the parallels that the text draws between the Lisbon sisters and artistic products of male fantasy, including Vladimir Nabokov's Lolita and William Shakespeare's Ophelia. In addition, the flat, monotonous narration of this film appears detached from the potentially shocking subject matter of the text, and instead reflects the mundanity of the cultural repetition of such female images. As Sconce argues of the intention behind an ironic address, the point is to divide the audience into those who understand the material and those who do not – 'to ally oneself with sympathetic peers and to distance oneself from the vast "other" audience' (2002: 352).

Coppola's characters are unable to articulate their sadness or dissatisfaction precisely because the power dynamics within which they are caught up are invariably complex and beyond the female subject's comprehension. Yet Coppola's framing of these characters works to emphasise their disconnection and alienation, privileging their subjectivity and working to encourage viewer empathy, while her use of stylistic excesses captures the temporary allure of commodity fetishism and its false promises to deliver alleviation from boredom or melancholy.

CRUEL POSTFEMINISM: THE PARADOX OF THE COMMODIFIED CONSUMER

In an article attempting to capture Sofia Coppola's key themes and preoccupations, Belinda Smaill describes the director's work as both enmeshed in and critical of the postfeminist sensibility, arguing that these characters display a knowingness about the rules and regulations of postfeminist neoliberalism and yet cannot find a sense of personal satisfaction in abiding by its terms. The emphasis that postfeminist and neoliberal discourses place upon the 'active, freely choosing, self-reinventing' female subject (Gill and Scharff 2011: 7) becomes burdensome to the Coppola heroine, who while demonstrating a strong investment in material objects is also 'plagued by a lack of life direction as well as moral and existential uncertainty' (Smaill 2013: 158). The protagonist's feelings of detachment and isolation, she argues, are a crisis pertaining to 'the absence of a desired object when desire becomes almost an imperative' (158). When Marie Antoinette engages in frivolous consumption as a means of escaping the political pressure to ensure an alliance between Austria and France by consummating her marriage and bearing a child, Coppola employs rock music soundtracks and montage editing – most notably in the 'I Want Candy' sequence – depicting Marie and her friends indulging excessively in champagne and cake while mulling over the latest fabric materials, dresses and shoes. Marie's will to indulge is also encoded as a form of rebellion by the opening shot of the film, which depicts the French queen surrounded by pink and white cakes while reclining on a *chaise longue* as a maid slips a pair of heels onto her feet, with Marie pausing only to offer a defiant stare at the filmic viewer who may potentially judge her for her consumption habits. Yet as Lane and Richter argue of this scene, Marie here also 'co-creates herself as a material object' (2011: 189) – her self-objectification becomes her only route for achieving personal expression and self-understanding (190). This is a world where the female subject is endowed with the capacity for individual agency and the power to manifest social change only at the level of rhetoric, and so Marie falls for the allure of the commodity as a key means through which to aid in cultivating a personalised life world. The postfeminist 'utopia' that Marie creates for herself allows her to temporarily forget the politicised forces that circulate an image of her which she cannot control, and her efforts here to a degree mirror the relationship of affluent, white women with both the neoliberal discourses that celebrate them and the postfeminist commodity culture that calls on them to achieve empowerment through shopping. The film's anachronistic referencing of contemporary moods and sensibilities is represented by the text not only through the contemporary pop music soundtrack, but also in the presence of popular modern fashion brands such as Manolo Blahnik.

While *Marie Antoinette* is a film that certainly revels in the elaborate spectacle afforded by the queen's lavish Versailles lifestyle, it is also a film that pauses to reflect on the politics of its immersion in feminine commodity culture, primarily through its emphasis on Marie's melancholic subjectivity. This interpretation is given credence by scenes that juxtapose Marie's excessive spending habits with those where we see the protagonist alone, gazing from a carriage window while contemplating her fractured marriage or the latest letter from her mother reminding her of her insecure position at Versailles. Both Marie and her husband Louis (Jason Schwartzman) are depicted as childlike in nature, and thus ill-equipped for their roles as political figureheads, with Louis introduced through a scene that depicts him sword-fighting with his friends, while Marie at her Austrian home is shown to be somewhat oblivious to the plans being made for her future, preferring instead to play with her dog Mops and race down the palace corridors. When Marie arrives at Versailles, a handheld camera captures not only the queen's trepidation as she wanders slowly through the crowds, but also the blank, stern faces of those required by royal custom to welcome her. The formal protocol of Versailles provides no real space for human warmth and interconnection, with the temporary joy offered by the commodity becoming one of the few avenues Marie has to escape political pressure and the malicious gossip of those in the royal court. This joy is always short-lived and transient, with *Marie Antoinette*'s director fully cognisant of the laws of consumer-capitalist ideology, which Jean Baudrillard characterises as a form of 'magical thinking' (1998: 31), promising a satisfaction and happiness that it can never fully deliver (69). Baudrillard additionally argues that the 'invitation to self-indulgence' is primarily directed at women, who strive to fashion themselves after a mythical female model, and whose relation to themselves thus becomes 'objectivised and fuelled by signs' in a manner tantamount to a form of self-consumption (95). Marie's investment in a postfeminist sensibility, which as Tasker and Negra remind us 'elevates consumption as a strategy' for healing social ills and dissatisfactions (2007: 2), and her status as both disempowered subject and decorative object, prefigure the queen's eventual fate as consumable object of the political machine and indeed her contemporary status as a consumable 'pop' icon of consumption.

In *The Virgin Suicides*, too, the young neighbourhood boys attempt to understand the Lisbon sisters through attempts at decoding their perceived emotional attachments to material objects, only to discover that the girls seem almost to become less decipherable as more and more items are collected about them. Upon discovering Cecilia's diary, the boys learn about the everyday lives of the sisters and yet this is not enough to satisfy their deep-seated curiosity about these young women, whom they perceive to be more like mythical creatures than flesh-and-blood human beings. They thus resort to inventing fantasy scenarios as they read Cecilia's words, picturing the girls wandering dreamily through sunlit fields in the company of a white unicorn, while the male narrator (Giovanni Ribisi) admits that the boys' job was 'merely to create the noise that seemed to fascinate them. We knew that they knew everything about us and we couldn't fathom them at all.' Similarly, when Mr Lisbon (James Woods) invites one of his male pupils, Peter (Chris Hale) over to dinner at the house as a reward for assisting with a classroom solar system installation, the boy becomes transfixed by the various feminine accoutrements and religious iconography in Lux's bedroom before Lux herself knocks on the door, interrupting both Peter's fantasy and the suspenseful extra-diegetic musical score that marks his immersion in the mystical, feminine space. Like Marie Antoinette however, the Lisbon girls are co-created as objects of consumption themselves. First, the sisters are introduced to the audience through pre-existing visual and literary metaphors of girlhood that aid the film in signifying on an intertextual level, and allow Coppola to engage in a meta-cinematic commentary on the consumable female image. As Masafumi Monden notes in his discussion of the film's aesthetic imagination of girlhood, Lux's characterisation as coquettish yet innocent is reminiscent of Lolita, as are scenes that register with cinematic depictions of Nabokov's heroine, such as those in which Lux sucks on candy apples or sunbathes in a bikini while the knife sharpener gives her a 'fifteen-minute demonstration for free' (Monden 2013: 146). The girls' fragility and their ultimate acts of suicide of course draw parallels with Ophelia – the tragic Shakespearean heroine whom psychologist Mary Pipher famously drew upon in her 1994 best-selling book *Reviving Ophelia: Saving the Selves of Adolescent Girls* – which professes a deep concern about contemporary societal pressures facing teenagers (1994). *The Virgin Suicides* takes a tongue-in-cheek view of the perils of female adolescence, utilising these popular tropes of girlhood to explore the impossibility of female agency in a world where white, middle-class girls are objects of alternating despair, admiration, concern or lust, and yet very rarely are deemed capable of giving voice to such emotions themselves.

Our introduction to the interior of the Lisbons' home consists of a close-up of the bathroom shelf, in which various feminine items including nail polish, perfume bottles and a fan are bathed in a cold, blue light accompanied by the sound of a tap steadily dripping and ambulance sirens approaching from the distance. As the narrator informs us that 'Cecilia was the first to go', the scene cuts to a shot of Cecilia lying in the shallow waters of the bathtub after her first suicide attempt, her skin exhibiting the same cold, blue pallor while her eyes stare blankly at the ceiling. A visual analogy is thus drawn between the lifeless material objects that Cecilia owns and her own lifeless body in the tub, constructed as an object of gossip and fascination within the community. Similarly, while the boys in their idealised memories of the Lisbon sisters profess to care about the girls, wondering for instance if they could have been more attentive to signs of mental illness, their encounters with them indicate the more encompassing desire to render the girls sexualised objects in their adolescent fantasies. When the Lisbons' neighbours ask local high school boys about their interactions with the sisters, the narrator informs us that their interviewees 'were always the stupidest boys and made terrible sources of information', as they were unable to shed light on the girls' personalities and preferred instead to brag about their supposed sexual encounters with them. Yet when Lux rebels from her mother's strict rules and regulations by having sex with random men on the roof of the family home, these same neighbourhood boys partake in the opportunity to view Lux's naked body through a telescope, munching on popcorn as an accompaniment to these evenings of unexpected, illicit entertainment. Lux is here likened to a cinematic image *within* the diegesis – her body existing as a form of idealised wish fulfilment for these boys, who are prevented their desired access to her subjectivity in part because of their concurrent urge to possess her as an object. As in *Marie Antoinette*, Coppola troubles the subject/object distinction that postfeminist empowerment rhetoric relies upon, and explores femininity as an essentially unknowable concept that can only be interpreted superficially through a range of commodity signs. Even in death, the Lisbon sisters cannot escape the societal discourses that attempt to assign meaning to their lives – their images remain in cultural circulation, to be appropriated by those looking for objects that will provide the fleeting happiness that the idealised commodity always promises. It is in death that these women become agents of a different kind of social action – the regretful commemoration of their memories assigns their existence a cultural meaning and gravitas that they never could have achieved though daily lived reality.

NARRATING FEMALE EXPERIENCE THROUGH DISCOURSES OF CELEBRITY AND SCANDAL

It is in fact in death that 'the Lisbon sisters' as cultural symbols become more powerful, in part due to the narrative of scandal that their rebellious acts of suicide generate amongst the suburban community. As Adrienne L. McLean and David A. Cook explain, 'scandal is a commodity with proven market value' (2001: 3), with the private life of a publicised individual able to be sold by a mass media able to 'set the limits for what is good, bad, transgressive, acceptable' (4). The hyper-visibility of the melancholic white woman, then, becomes a means by which the diegetic public can judge the failures of these individuals adequately to embody the promises of the politicised discourses that elevate them. If Coppola is intrigued by the ideological mechanisms of neoliberal postfeminism, then she also expresses interest in how discourses of celebrity may be utilised to draw analogies to the role of young white women within an intensified image economy. Coppola's heroines are unable to escape the crowd's glare, and thus strive to create private spaces for themselves where they can exercise forms of agency. Yet these private spaces also become subject to the crowd's 'right to know' – these young women's attempts at defining a sense of self are frequently hijacked by individuals and groups who harbour conflicting agendas, as evidenced by the boys' accumulation and re-signification of Cecilia's diary in *The Virgin Suicides*. The teen deaths become a hot local news event, eagerly reported on by Channel Two journalist Lydia Perl (Suki Kaiser), who struggles to interview the reclusive Mrs Lisbon (Kathleen Turner) by clamouring over stacks of unclaimed newspapers that lie outside the front door – a sign that the family continues to reject the media-driven narratives that circulate about their lives. Adolescent angst is treated as a televised special topic of investigation, with a young woman named Rannie (Leah Straatsma) interviewed regarding her role in the accidental manslaughter of her grandmother after she baked a pie full of rat poison in an apparent attempt to mimic Madame Bovary's suicide. These media-driven narratives that the Lisbon deaths generate are treated in Coppola's typically ironic and detached manner and do not afford the residents any real glimpse into the impetus behind the actions of the sisters. The suicide awareness campaign at the local high school, for instance, becomes a failed institutionalised attempt to make sense of the sisters' feelings – the rationale behind the act of suicide is reduced to a set of bullet points providing information on depression, while banal debate as to whether the awareness pamphlet to be handed out to students should be green or red is of prime importance to the teaching faculty.

The opening credits to *Marie Antoinette* spell out the title sequence in lettering reminiscent of tabloid magazine font, which foreshadows the queen's eventual downfall as a result of the politicised gossip that comes to define

Figure 6.2 Marie Antoinette as 'Queen of Debt'.

her character. Later in the film, the camera trains upon a portrait of Marie clutching a rose and wearing a dark blue dress – a costume that almost resembles mourning wear given its contrast to the pretty pastel colours the queen typically favours – as news headlines including 'Queen of Debt', 'Beware of Deficit' and 'Spending France into Ruin' are plastered across the bottom of the screen. The queen's simulated image, whether celebrated or decried, contains far more political and social power than the flesh-and-blood Marie will ever be able to wield, with her inanimate portrait and marked shifts in her image construction conjoining to replace and redefine her reality and indeed foreshadow her tragic fate. It is telling that the most famous line attributed to Marie Antoinette, the notorious 'Let them eat cake', is here relegated to a fantasy sequence – a snippet of gossip that Marie assures her friends is 'nonsense' and a mere 'ridiculous story'.

It is only as spectres or social ghosts that Coppola's melancholic white women can take up places of importance within history – not for any actions or words that they have spoken, but in actions and words they are *deemed* to have spoken. Even the Lisbon sisters are granted a kind of omniscient power in death and the ability to foreshadow socio-economic shifts, with the narrator informing us that local residents 'dated the demise of our neighbourhood from the suicides of the Lisbon girls. People saw their clairvoyance in the wiped-out elms, the harsh sunlight and the continuing decline of our auto industry.' Through gossip and scandal, Marie Antoinette and the Lisbon sisters come to occupy a role of political and social importance, with their role in a mediatised culture serving to collapse the individual into a public persona that can then be utilised to elevate individuals or to ostracise and cast them out in the name of political transformation. The increasing visibility of the heroines in both texts correlates directly with the likelihood of impending corporeal disappearance through death, with Coppola's cinema exploring the interplay that she sees as occurring in both fetishistic excess and existential absence.

Even when the Coppola protagonist is not herself an object of excessive attention, the publicity-driven world of the commodified image nevertheless threatens to impinge upon her interpersonal relationships and her life's direction. Charlotte in *Lost in Translation* is not discussed or debated publicly in the same manner as Marie Antoinette or Lux Lisbon, and yet we are to understand that it is her immersion within the global city of Tokyo, with its constant barrage of neon lights, karaoke music and entertainment advertising, and her own husband's evident worshipping of celebrity culture, that are contributing to the intensification of her current existential crisis. Female characters in Coppola films may perhaps be divided into two disparate groups – vapid, celebrity-obsessed girls and women such as the teenagers in *The Bling Ring*[3] and the actress Kelly (Anna Faris) in *Lost in Translation*, who care only about the mass circulation of their images and how they may profit from it, and more poetic, introspective types such as the Lisbon sisters, Marie Antoinette and Charlotte, who demonstrate a melancholic, despondent attitude to the image-obsessed worlds within which they reside and with whom the audience is encouraged to empathise. Charlotte, a Yale philosophy graduate, is an intellectual who feels unable to transform her interests in writing and photography into a meaningful career path that will also generate income, and so therefore feels 'stuck' in life. When Charlotte informs Hollywood celebrity Bob that she has attempted writing but hates what she writes and that 'every girl goes through a photography phase, you know like horses', she is lamenting the fact that her creative output may not be deemed special enough by the public to allow for her to engage in it fulltime as a living. Her choice to prioritise her own interest in philosophical enquiry over a university qualification that is more likely to guarantee financial security is commented on by Bob in the hotel bar, when he notes sarcastically that there is a 'real buck' to be made in the philosophy racket. Yet Bob also harbours a concealed admiration for Charlotte, whom he sees as somewhat of a kindred spirit given that he would much rather be performing in stage plays than earning two million dollars for starring in a Japanese whisky commercial. Bob's attraction to Charlotte thus has its basis in regret over his decision to take a job purely for the financial rewards and disenchantment with the global circulation of his monetised image.

Charlotte's own sense of alienation is fuelled in large part by her strained marriage to photographer husband John (Giovanni Ribisi), who has travelled to Japan to shoot rock music bands and subsequently becomes infatuated with the aura of celebrity and glamour that he encounters amongst the other foreign travellers to the country. As a result, Charlotte is left alone in her hotel room idly passing the time by reclining on the bed in her underwear, knitting scarves and applying make-up in the mirror, or curling up on the balcony and gazing at the sprawling metropolis several floors below. When John attempts to engage her in discussion about the relationship between costume and the saleable rock 'n' roll image, Charlotte is unable to feign interest and attempts to change the subject by asking him if her knitted scarf appears finished. Her investment in feminine pleasures such as knitting and the application of make-up become a means of distracting herself from her loneliness and inability to connect with John, who, she learns gradually, harbours superficial values built upon materialism and artifice that differ greatly from her own. Similarly, John's keen interest in the exuberant actress Kelly, who flatters him by gushing that he is her 'favourite photographer', comes with an attendant dismissal of Charlotte and her intellectual pursuits. When Kelly informs the pair that she has been doing 'millions of interviews a day' and has attempted to preserve anonymity by checking into the hotel under the pseudonym Evelyn Waugh, Charlotte sniggers and points out that Kelly has made a fundamental error given that Evelyn Waugh was male. John, however, expresses displeasure with Charlotte's comment in noting that 'not everyone went to Yale' and that she doesn't always have to point out how stupid people are. Through her interactions with John and Kelly, Charlotte comes to realise that her own interests and values constitute anomalies in a world that is essentially commodity-driven and status-obsessed, with any actions that she may choose to take likely to prove fruitless to her goals of self-realisation. The only human bond Charlotte is capable of forming is with Bob, an older, married man, who experiences similar feelings of alienation and inertia, and this bond too can only ever be temporary, built as it is upon the transient role each will play as tourists in Japan's capital and indeed as tourists in each other's lives. Perhaps Bob and Charlotte's unique connection is best encapsulated by a scene in which the pair spend time together late one evening in Bob's hotel room and reminisce about their first impressions of one another. As they share these memories, *La Dolce Vita* plays on the television in the original Italian language with Japanese subtitles. Fellini's film about the search for a meaningful existence in a society characterised by wealth, excess and the adoration of celebrity provides a parallel to the obstacles that Bob and Charlotte face in their own search for existential meaning. The juxtaposition of the audible Italian language and the visual presentation of the Japanese subtitles provides a dual layer of incomprehensibility to these native English speakers, who experience Tokyo as an overwhelming collection of impenetrable signs.

THE IMPOSSIBILITY OF RACE FANTASY IN ALLEVIATING WHITE BURDEN

The characters' inability to overcome the melancholic state is nevertheless integral to the commercial appeal of Coppola's cinema, given that her films are characterised by a mood of aimless drifting and romantic ennui that would be ruined by overt emotion precipitating constructive action. While the presence of spaces of alterity may encourage the protagonist's attempts at alleviating her melancholic boredom, she always remains cognisant of the fact that such endeavours will lead inevitably to failure and the exacerbation of her feelings of emptiness. Not unlike the films' knowing treatment of postfeminist philosophies, the texts also demonstrate a keen awareness of the cultural preoccupation with international travel and the appropriation of ethnic dress and custom as a means of alleviating the tedium of white experience. In some respects, *Lost in Translation* operates in marked contrast to the popular romance *Eat Pray Love* in its refusal to invest in the supposedly restorative powers and spiritually regenerative potential of tourism. Charlotte often appears perplexed within her newfound urban environment, struggling to navigate the Tokyo subway system and unable to read her city map. When she encounters a Buddhist prayer ceremony and hears the monks chanting in harmony, Charlotte becomes distressed by her inability to feel moved by the experience in comparison with John's enthusiastic embrace of Japanese culture, which culminates in a teary confession while on the phone to a friend back home that she does not know who she married. Charlotte's tourist excursion fosters a prolonged period of introspection, yet *Lost in Translation* does not allow for the symbiotic fusion of person and place that the typical travel romance does, nor does it propose that the consumer-capitalist logic of neoliberal feminism can be 'transcended' spiritually. The idea of the foreign locale as existing in a distinct capacity from the influences of global capitalism is here highlighted as a ludicrous Western fantasy given Tokyo's excessive parade of commercialised images and the penchant of the Japanese people for American celebrities and popular culture. Yet despite this refusal to invest in commercial touristic discourse, the film's heavily stereotyped depiction of its Japanese characters ensures that the emphasis of the text is centred upon the soul searching of the white American characters. The 'unknowability' of the Tokyo environment aids in perpetuating a cinematic mood characterised by sustained periods of white melancholia.

Todd McGowan, in his article 'There is nothing *Lost in Translation*', argues that Coppola's film explores the absence at the heart of global capitalism's excesses, with Bob and Charlotte the only Western characters able to recognise the 'duplicity of plenitude' in the failure of global capitalism to provide the enjoyment that it promises (2007: 54). Pointing out that the film invites the

Figure 6.3 Charlotte is unable to alleviate her melancholy through travel in *Lost in Translation*.

spectator to associate the Japanese culture and language with a certain 'mysterious enjoyment' that ultimately turns out to be mythical (58), McGowan states that for Coppola the Japanese Other 'does not house a wealth of strange or even exotic content –it is not a mystery to be solved – but is simply a void' (59). Homay King, in her discussion of the role of Asian 'objects, riddles and metaphors' as standing in for the larger unknowns that defy Western cognitive processes within the lineage of Hollywood cinema (2010: 3), states that *Lost in Translation* is largely consistent with predictable visual tropes that have come to signify East Asia and its diasporas. Describing these visual tropes as including crowds of foreigners who move chaotically 'without regard for the rules of continuity', a disorienting use of space that 'collapses foreground and background', and a cluttered *mise-en-scène* of hanging objects and neon signage, King argues that these cinematic worlds become 'dumping grounds for dead letters, overdetermined icons, and mutterings that belong to no dialect in particular' (3). Yet King notes that unlike the male hero of the *film noir*, the female protagonist of *Lost in Translation* does not experience a sense of mastery in these unfamiliar spaces and frequently exhibits a lack of control and loss of bearings. She cannot discover any secrets about the foreign locale, but only about herself (163). King does not suggest that *Lost in Translation* refuses to speak on behalf of the 'Orient', but rather that it does so in a unique manner (167). Her comment here is pertinent, as although Tokyo within this film is unable to provide Charlotte with what she so desperately seeks – answers as to how she may find happiness and fulfilment in life – it does provide her with the means by which she comes to realise her own chronic dissatisfaction and so to recognise the fundamental failures at the heart of neoliberalism's emphasis on 'can-do' femininity. Charlotte's vacation – on which she does not have to work, care for others or carry out routine chores – provides her with the space through which to engage in a prolonged period of melancholic reflection on her own alienation. Such an extended opportunity for soul searching may indeed appear profoundly attractive to audience members used to the daily demands of work, bills, childcare and various other economic and social pressures, and it is worth noting that tourism bodies capitalised on the film in order to promote Tokyo as an ideal holiday destination. Koichi Iwabuchi points out that the Japanese National Tourist Organisation created a campaign centring on *Lost in Translation* packages, which invited tourists to come and enjoy the sites depicted in the film, while the luxurious hotel in Shinjuku where Bob and Charlotte stay has become increasingly popular with US celebrities (2008: 551). While the film does provide a great showcase for various locations within Tokyo that may certainly appeal to viewers despite the protagonist's inability to feel awed by them, the representation of Tokyo as a colourful and chaotic backdrop that, in its impenetrability, provides the ideal impetus for a form of white introspection is also likely to hold considerable appeal.

The Lisbon sisters in *The Virgin Suicides* are unable to travel to foreign locations, spending much of their time cloistered within the four walls of their suburban home as a means of appeasing their religious mother, yet the film takes a similar approach to *Lost in Translation* in its treatment of themes relating to the white burden and the regenerative potential of cultural appropriation. Following Cecilia's first suicide attempt, her therapist Dr Horniker (Danny DeVito) conducts the Rorschach test by holding up a series of inkblot images that the teenager must interpret to allow the doctor to gain an insight into her mental state. Cecilia's deadpan responses include naming the obscure shapes as a banana, a swamp and an afro respectively, leading the therapist to inform Mr and Mrs Lisbon that Cecilia's suicide attempt was a frustrated cry for help and that she would benefit from social outlets where she could interact with boys of her own age. Cecilia's fantasies associated with tropical locations like the Caribbean thus allow the therapist to draw linkages between her desire for travel and the social limitations of virginal, white femininity. In the sisters' final weeks, we are told that their only contact with the outside world consisted of the brochures that they ordered selling high-end fashions and exotic vacations. These images of the Great Wall of China and 'gold-tipped Siamese temples' not only allow the Lisbon girls to indulge in fantasies of escape from the blankness that constitutes white feminine identity, but also aid in informing the romanticised, nostalgic narratives that the neighbourhood boys construct in order to perpetuate the belief that they bonded with the sisters and understood their characters. As the voiceover narration informs us as photographic images of the smiling sisters on tour with their male counterparts appear on the screen, these 'impossible excursions' encourage the boys to take pleasure in scenarios that could never have come to pass, but also to participate in a denial of the fading of memory that inevitably accompanies another's corporeal death. 'We hiked through dusty passes with the girls,' the narrator tells us, 'stopping every now and then to help them with their backpacks, placing our hands on their warm, moist shoulders and gazing off into papaya sunsets ... Cecilia hadn't died; she was a bride in Calcutta.' Yet as the narrator then goes on to lament, 'the colour of their eyes was fading along with the exact location of moles and dimples. From five they had become four and they were all, the living and the dead, becoming shadows.'

As in *Lost in Translation*, the allure of the exotic Other occupies a source of transient fantasy that remains in the realm of wishful thinking, never promising a lasting transcendence over the melancholic state and yet also importantly working to preserve the text's primary interest in the mysterious nature and nostalgic idealisation of white feminine identity. As Michele Aaron notes in her discussion of the film's commentary on Western culture's 'necromantic obsession' with white women, Lux's 'dishwashing detergent' name alludes to Coppola's tendency to cleanse the film of the novel's racial politics, pointing out that the filmic adaptation of Jeffrey Eugenides' written work conveniently eradicates the latter's treatment of racial unrest (2014: 82). Within the novel, for instance, the local Chamber of Commerce expresses concern that the suicides will lead to its predominantly white residents choosing to shop elsewhere, with the narrator wondering whether certain 'improvements' were made to the town centre to scare off black people – 'the ghost in the window of the costume shop', he states, 'had an awful, pointed, hooded head' (Eugenides 1993: 99). Additionally, the suburban residents express paranoia at the prospect of invasion, with the Lisbons having built a bomb shelter near their recreation room and Mrs Lisbon harbouring an 'abundant supply' of fresh water and canned goods in case of a nuclear attack (163). While we are told briefly in Coppola's film that a popular theory behind the suicides held 'the immigrant kid' Dominic Palazzolo to blame because of his decision to jump off his parent's roof following his schoolyard love interest's departure for Switzerland, this intriguing attribution of blame to those deemed outsiders in the white, middle-class, suburban milieu is raised fleetingly, only to be left unexplored.

Interestingly, while *The Virgin Suicides* seems ideologically and aesthetically reliant upon the cultural construction and mythological ideation of white, middle-class Catholic femininity, 2015 saw the release of Deniz Gamze Ergüven's *Mustang*, a thematically very similar feminist film set within a conservative Turkish village. A French, German and Turkish co-production, *Mustang* tells the story of five sisters who are put under house arrest by their uncle and grandmother after they are spotted playing 'inappropriately' in the ocean with local schoolboys. Accused of pleasuring themselves by 'rubbing their parts' on the boys' shoulders and subsequently deemed 'whores', the girls' computers and phones are confiscated and they are forced to wear brown, shapeless smocks so as not to draw attention to their burgeoning sexuality. Spending their days washing windows and learning how to improve the nutritional value of soup, the girls' family attempts to socialise them into their future roles as Muslim wives and mothers, before marrying them off in order of age. Like *The Virgin Suicides*, *Mustang* explores the difficulties of navigating adolescent female sexuality within a prescriptive patriarchal and religious environment. The youngest sister Lale (Güneş Şensoy) pads her sister's bra, running about the house wearing it, and lusts after footballers despite not being allowed to attend games alongside male spectators. Her siblings Sonay (İlayda Akdoğan) and Ece (Elit İşcan) engage in sexual encounters outside the home, managing on occasion to escape near-constant surveillance and defy rules that prohibit sexual intercourse prior to marriage. An internationally successful film nominated for multiple Cannes and César Awards, *Mustang* demonstrates the potential transnational appeal and adaptability of texts that explore forms of melancholic burden in a neoliberal, postfeminist era. Yet this film reimagines and reconceptualises this thematic material in important ways that highlight fundamental differences in race and gender politics within the respective contexts.

Ergüven, unlike Coppola, is an avowedly political filmmaker who is highly critical of Turkish president Recep Tayyip Erdoğan and what she sees as an increasingly conservative attitude towards women in Turkish society. Stating in a 2016 interview with *The Guardian* that Erdoğan is 'polarising' and 'corrupt', Ergüven notes his belief that women are fit only to be wives and mothers, and criticises his perception of them as merely sexual beings. Arguing that these attitudes are reminiscent of the 'middle ages', Ergüven states that such views are dangerous and work to sanction violence against women (Cooke 2016). While *The Virgin Suicides* has all its sisters eventually kill themselves, allowing for their memory to be preserved through dreamlike, poetic sequences that reify their youth and idealised whiteness, only one sister in *Mustang* chooses to do so. During a family dinner, Ece attempts to make her sisters laugh as her Uncle listens intently to former Deputy Prime Minister Bülent Arınç's speech that laments the days when women blushed upon being looked at by men, and calls for them not to act provocatively or laugh in public. After being asked to leave the table, Ece shoots herself – her despair and oppression here linked directly with the conservative views held by the country's top politicians. The sisters in *Mustang*, as indicated by the wild and free-roaming animal that the title evokes, are more active and resistant in opposing their treatment than the melancholic Lisbon sisters. Such characterisations may work to challenge perceptions of conservative Muslim femininity held by many in Western Europe and the US, where this film met with critical praise. Nur (Doğa Doğuşlu) burns a chair in protest at being of accused of behaving inappropriately with the boys, while she and Lale by the film's conclusion have managed to escape to Istanbul – a cosmopolitan urban space imagined as allowing greater possibilities for them. The politics of travel here are notably distinct from Coppola's, reflecting Ergüven's perception of Turkey as a country caught between Eastern and Western traditions – as she stated to SBS journalist Helen Barlow in a May 2016 interview held to accompany the release of the film in Australia – and her own upbringing and education in France. The positive reception of the film in countries like France and the US probably corresponds to a creeping distrust of Islam – especially given the symbolic resonance of Istanbul here as comparatively modernising force in contrast to the village, and the framing of the village as 'backward', and there is undoubtedly more to be said here about the politics of transnational financing and filmmaking in representing the lives of Muslim women. Nevertheless, while Coppola's aesthetic emphasises the ethereality of her heroines – images that are echoed through her fashion and perfume campaigns – Ergüven's film engages in a sustained, political critique of invasive corporeal surveillance and discipline, most notably in her treatment of the practice of virginity testing.

THE WHITENESS OF THE MELANCHOLIC AESTHETIC AND THE COMMERCIAL APPEAL OF CINEMATIC MOOD

It is in fact the combination of the melancholic state with images of white, feminine idealisation that typifies the aesthetics of mood within Coppola's cinema – a defining feature of her work and an integral component to the saleability of her particular brand of authorship. As Woodworth explains, the director's first three features are driven not by plot but rather by 'moods, associations, and resonant images', with nonverbal techniques including music, lighting and bodily movement utilised to illuminate the characters' emotional interiority (2008: 139). Coppola's films are not driven by action or dramatic moments. We do not witness a great deal of the impact of the French Revolution on Marie Antoinette or her eventual death, for instance, with the film preferring to foreshadow the fate of the royal family by concluding with a shot of the king and queen's vandalised bedroom. To place too much emphasis on political or social happenings within the characters' environment, or the actions, deeds and thought processes of those other than the protagonist would be to cause significant ruptures within the films' distinctive cinematic mood, which is dependent on the heroine's sustained experience of melancholic emotion and the cinematic medium's privileged access to her subjectivity. In Coppola's work, there is a key interrelationship between the protagonist's emotional state and the aesthetic and narrative means by which cinematic moods are evoked.

The heroine's transcendence of the melancholic state would thus be to break with the key immersive features that typify Coppola's brand and encourage her audience's pleasurable investment in the creative work. In '*Stimmung*: exploring the aesthetics of mood', Robert Sinnerbrink explains that cinematic mood describes how distinctive fictional worlds are created via 'a shared affective attunement' that works to orient the spectator within that world (2012: 148). He argues that these mood cues are significant not merely in that they serve as triggers through which to elicit audience emotion, as mood is encountered as a meaningful and 'emotionally orienting' semi-independent, immersive feature that overrides conventional narrative (161). Emotion is not only communicated or evoked cognitively, but also aesthetically through sensibility, reflection and feeling (Sinnerbrink 2012: 152). Sinnerbrink explores the role of gesture, silence and landscape in *Brokeback Mountain* (Ang Lee, 2005) in creating a mood of 'toughness and isolation coupled with lyricism and melancholy' (156), as well as the uncanny treatment of sound and silence in *Mulholland Drive*'s (David Lynch, 2001) Club Silencio sequence in order to convey the theoretical importance of a consideration of cinematic mood.

Coppola's Young Girls trilogy is driven by the subjective experiences of her heroines, who spend much of their time staring out windows, reclining on beds, wandering alone aimlessly through imposing architectural spaces, or spending lazy days in expansive gardens with friends. Her cinema is characterised by long takes indicating the monotonous interminability of time, the use of shallow focus emphasising the protagonist's isolation within her environment, and diffuse lighting that aesthetically idealises the heroine while simultaneously chronicling her act of corporeal fading. Coppola's use of cinematic mood, which amalgamates a melancholic aesthetic characterised by dreaming, wistfulness and nostalgia with classic Hollywood codes reifying whiteness, signifies with regard to the political present in that it carves out an appealing space of quiet reflection in relation to the seemingly determinist discourses of postfeminism and neoliberalism. Yet these appealing spaces, advertised so powerfully through her films, also set a powerful fashion agenda of their own. Coppola, after all, notably recreated this distinctive mood in the campaign for popular Marc Jacobs perfume *Daisy*, which centres upon a pair of fair-skinned models in white smock dresses lying in a sunlit daisy field as they clutch oversized bottles of the perfume in a state of transient bliss. Coppola's cinema thus occupies a dual position in relation to neoliberal postfeminism. Her work critiques the excesses of global capitalism and the commodification of young white women within a commercial culture, yet it also profits from the creation of these fantasy spaces of reflection and solitude that can be sold to these same women through campaigns like *Daisy*. This campaign may appeal to the weary postfeminist subject, yet ultimately circulates within the same consumer-capitalist logic.

Coppola's cinema, in its artistic representation of the melancholic state, takes its place within a lineage of artistic works aiming to depict this ambiguous emotion visually, perhaps most notably originating with Albrecht Dürer's 1514 engraving *Melencolia I*. Melancholy, as Emily Brady and Arto Haapala point out, is an aestheticised emotion that plays a significant role in both encounters with artworks and in the human response to the natural environment (2003). It is indeed in natural spaces that the Coppola heroine appears to take the most pleasure in her periods of melancholic reflection and the sensation of her body is at one with the earth's elements. It is also in these natural spaces that she may indulge her artistic and philosophical sensibilities, with Marie Antoinette regaling her friends with quotes from Jean-Jacques Rousseau, whose work inspired leaders of the French Revolution. Cecilia in *The Virgin Suicides*, meanwhile, partakes in painting and poetry while musing that 'the trees are like lungs filling with air'. Arguing that melancholia as a 'mature' and 'refined' emotion differs from sadness, depression and despair, Brady and Haapala state that melancholia holds an element of pleasure in that it requires solitude as well as periods of 'reflection and contemplation of things we love and long for, so that the hope of having them adds a touch of sweetness that makes melancholy bearable'. Melancholia, like the sublime, may be inspired by an encounter with nature, with the authors noting that the 'desolate moor' or 'vast, gloomy ocean' provides an ideal solitary setting to evoke this particular mood. In *Marie Antoinette*, Marie seems most at peace while staying with her female friends and daughter Marie Therese (Lauriane Mascaro) within the gardens of her private abode *Le Petit Trianon*. This scene is notably marked by its combination of silence and the ambient sounds of birdsong and breeze rustling through the hedges, in contrast to the pop music soundtracks that provide the extra-diegetic accompaniment to Marie's excessive consumption at Versailles. At *Le Petit Trianon*, Marie is shown in a white lacy dress basking in the sunlight, picking flowers (including daisies) with Marie Therese, fetching eggs from the henhouse and chatting amiably with her female companions while enjoying porcelain jugs full of fresh milk. Visual representations of Marie in harmony with the natural environment are paralleled with images of animals similarly enjoying the lush greenery, including a goat chewing on grassy blades, a swan drifting upon a tranquil lake and a lamb frolicking in the fields, which the queen later encourages her daughter to feed. Marie Antoinette's private abode comprises a mood of feminine homosociality, innocence and simple pleasures, a far cry from the manufactured opulence, political regimentation and malicious gossip of Versailles.

The Lisbon girls, like Marie, are aligned similarly with this metaphor of natural, innocent beauty endangered by humanity's civilising processes, in part owing to the parallels drawn between their deaths and dying plant life. The neighbourhood boys learn upon reading Cecilia's diary that she has an

Figure 6.4 Coppola's melancholic aesthetic is evoked through images of 'natural' and timeless white femininity in *The Virgin Suicides*.

obsession with dying trees, while Mr and Mrs Lisbon refuse to believe that a tree in their own yard is sick after the girls are chastised for attempting to prevent it from being cut down – an obvious parallel, of course, to the parents' reluctance to admit to the precarious mental state of their daughters. Yet there are also fantasy sequences that depict the girls dancing, picking dandelions and playing with sparklers amongst idyllic golden fields in a celebration of their eternal memory. It is this mood that Coppola replicated for the *Daisy* campaign, which in its pleasurable melancholic tone sells a fantasy of idealised white womanhood in its 'natural' and 'timeless' state – free from the pressures of compulsory heteronormativity, upward mobility and, ironically, the temptation to consume. This mood is understood as fleeting and bittersweet, with Marie quoting Rousseau's philosophical musings to her friends. 'If man has been corrupted by artificial civilisation, what is the natural state?' she asks. 'The state of nature from which he has been removed? Imagine wandering up and down the forest, without industry, without speech, and without home.' These philosophical musings on an uncorrupted state of being are also what young women are invited to imagine when they consume the perfume, which packages 'refined' melancholic emotion as a fleeting state of feminine bliss, while capitalising on the consumer's investment in Coppola's ironic take on neoliberal postfeminist culture and her fetishising of youthful white femininity.

The mood of melancholia and loss that permeates Coppola's cinema is not to be gleaned only in these moments of transient oneness with nature, but also by the very fact that these female characters may themselves be engaged in a slow process of fading away from public visibility – of corporeal vanishing. In *Vanishing Women: Magic, Film, and Feminism*, Karen Beckman argues that the woman in process of vanishing is linked with the birth of cinema by early filmic representations of the vaudeville magic act, where a magician would appear to cause the mysterious disappearance of his female assistant. The Victorian fascination with the vanishing woman of stage magic, she points out, coincided with national census figures in the UK that indicated a vastly growing female population, leaving men in the minority (2003: 19). The cultural fascination with disappearing women resulted from a perceived *hyper-visibility* or excess of femininity, an issue that Beckman explores in relation to Queen Victoria's mourning period following the death of Prince Albert when she states that British republicanism emerged 'not in response to the Queen's absence alone but to the combination of this absence with both her excessive consumption and her excess of mourning' (18).[4] The act of female vanishing can indeed exhibit discomfort with feminine political and social power, yet Beckman argues that tropes of female vanishing within artistic representation may also provide strategies of resistance to 'problematic paradigms of female visibility' in that vanishing, unlike the violence of eradication, is always in process and occupies a position between absence and presence (19), as well as female agency and vulnerability (191). Coppola's cinema utilises such strategies of female vanishing in her critique of the role of young women within late capitalism's culture of the commodified image and her examination of neoliberal postfeminism's failure to provide these women with a voice and sense of direction. Marie Antoinette and the Lisbon sisters are indeed very publicly visible, with Marie in particular seen to also engage in excessive consumption practices, and yet these melancholic white women also experience burgeoning feelings of depression that allow them to feel as though they are not socially connected or indeed entirely present. When Marie and her friends play a game entitled 'Who am I?' in which each player has a card containing the name of a notable figure attached to their forehead, Marie's question in order to ascertain her ascribed identity is to ask if she is present in the room, to which everybody replies that she is not. When her irreverent friend the Duchesse de Polignac (Rose Byrne) asks the same question however, the response is a resounding 'yes!' The duchess, unlike Marie, does not ascribe to social etiquette. She gets drunk, is excessively loud and demonstrates irreverence for space by running screaming down the halls. While Marie has fun with the duchess, her friend is not bound by the same political pressures and therefore exhibits an overdetermined social *presence* and pronounced joy for life that the melancholic and reflective Marie does not. It is, however, precisely through the aesthetically beautiful moments of pensive melancholy that Marie experiences, conveyed through artistic codes associated with white idealisation, that Coppola can create a tension between postfeminist visibility and excess on one hand and feminine political absence and voicelessness on the other. This tension produces a commentary that may be construed as feminist in that it allows these women essentially to live a second life whereby others' memories of them can be mined to produce new understandings of their socially prescribed subject positions. Yet this tension also utilises the discomfort that white ideology exhibits in relation to the female body in order to produce images of tragic, poetic femininity that become appealing in their representation as eternal, immortal and ultimately *special*.

In *Marie Antoinette* and *The Virgin Suicides*, the audience is made aware that these filmic heroines *will* die, and as such a sense of melancholia accompanies their very appearance on the cinematic screen. It is through these nostalgic imaginings of the heroines, who often appear semi-translucent and as though they are made up of heavenly light, that Coppola's Young Girls trilogy most clearly participates in its overt idealisation of angelic whiteness. In *White*, Dyer explores the historical association of white women with virtue, pointing to the poet Coventry Patmore's Victorian idealisation of the 'angel in the house', which held that white middle-class women should be passive, domesticated and integral to the spiritual wellbeing of their husbands and families (1997: 126). The angelic white woman, Dyer explains, became the personification of the 'claim that what made whites special as a race was their non-physical, spiritual, indeed ethereal qualities' (127) – a claim that finds its aesthetic representation in women that appear as though they 'are bathed in and permeated by light' (122). White women glow rather than shine, as shine evokes connotations of sweat, bodily emissions and 'unladylike labour' (122), and yet to be ideally white in its pursuit of corporeal denial and spiritual perfection, Dyer states, is in fact unobtainable, as to occupy this racial position would equate to 'absence: to be really, absolutely white is to be nothing' (78). Yunuen Lewis, applying Dyer's arguments to Coppola's cinema, notes that these female protagonists are indeed defined by lack and appear only to thrive when bathed in light, which enhances their pallor, fair hair and delicate femininity (2011: 190).[5] In fact, the Lisbon sisters seem literally only able to communicate *by* light, for instance when they send coded messages to their neighbours by flashing their bedroom lamps. When the local boys fantasise about taking the sisters on a car journey, sunlight permeates their facial features so that they appear as if composed of the sun's rays. The girls within this dreamlike sequence are shown to be happy and radiant, pleased to be in the company of their neighbours and taking part in a leisurely activity away from the confinement of their suburban abode. Yet the youthful laughter that provides an accompaniment to this scene does not appear to emanate from the girls themselves, betraying an eerie lack of fidelity to the image and reminding the audience that the visuals they are witnessing are merely illusory. When the boys imagine taking the girls on an international travel excursion, the narrator laments the fading of his memories of the sisters as the photographs dissipate to a blank, white canvas. The cinematographic technique of the fade is utilised here to indicate not only the fading of memory or the ebbing away of the sisters' lives, but also the irreconcilability of such fantasies with the idealisation of ethereal white womanhood, which is defined by its absence and lack.

While the Lisbon sisters are memorialised in terms consistent with such ideals of heavenly whiteness, the scenes that depict their everyday lived realities allude to an incongruous tension between religious ideals of abstinence and purity and the cultural dictates that call on adolescent girls to connote an air of sexual availability and to manage their femininity through conspicuous consumption. Both Lux's bedroom and the sisters' bathroom vanity are cluttered with an assortment of feminine items intertwined with religious iconography, such as rosary beads draped around perfume bottles and statues of the Virgin Mary that appear as if lit from within. After Cecilia's suicide attempt, a blood-spattered picture of the Virgin falls from her hand as emergency services carry her from the bathroom. Mrs Lisbon demonstrates the desire to monitor the girls' sexuality, keeping them confined to their rooms and burning Lux's rock 'n' roll records after she breaks curfew. As a result, the sisters become despondent and depressed with the understanding that they are to emulate the impossible standards of white femininity as personified by the Virgin Mary, and yet their attempts at cultivating a sexually alluring, youthful femininity also culminate in failure and hurt. It is, after all, Lux's sexual encounter with her high school crush Trip Fontaine (Josh Hartnett), who abandons her on the high school football field with no means of transport home, that results in her breaking curfew. Lux's anguish at the loss of her records, a 'real' event within the diegesis, contrasts sharply with the air of pensive melancholia that characterises the film's nostalgic fantasy sequences. Similarly, Marie Antoinette's despair at her inability to produce a male heir, which results in her bursting into tears and collapsing on the floor, is contrasted to the pleasurable melancholia she and her friends indulge in while at *Le Petit Trianon*. In exploring the contrasts that occur between the protagonists' experience of gendered powerlessness and ephemeral moments of pensive bliss, both *Marie Antoinette* and *The Virgin Suicides* display a knowingness about the discourses that circulate in relation to both melancholy and the ideological and aesthetic codes relating to hegemonic whiteness. Yet the successful signification of Coppola's films is dependent upon a dual position that can simultaneously provide a political and cultural commentary on postfeminism and white femininity, and benefit from an immersion within these same discourses. A consideration of the texts' cinematic mood is thus integral to a critique of Coppola's cinema, given that it is this mood that *leaks* beyond the diegetic material of the films and plays a crucial role in the saleability of Coppola's fashion endeavours, the appeal of the director as a celebrated personality, and indeed in how the text is likely to be remembered over the years and decades following its release. *The Virgin Suicides*, it may be argued, is certainly not unlike Peter Weir's *Picnic at Hanging Rock*, the 1975 Australian film about a group of private schoolgirls who mysteriously disappear while on a class picnic. This film, while also inviting commentary on the gendered restrictions facing adolescent girls, is remembered largely for its haunting and melancholic tone, which raises far more questions than it answers in relation to the girls' fate. It is precisely the film's use of mysterious and ethereal white femininity, which is initially present before becoming distressingly absent amongst the harsh and foreboding Australian terrain, that keeps these feminine symbols of tragic whiteness culturally relevant in the minds of audiences, while importantly also lending the text its iconic status. This figure remains a textually powerful symbol of female disenfranchisement in art across the decades, from the era of first-wave feminism that *Picnic at Hanging Rock* references, to the second-wave era in which it was written and produced, to the updating and re-circulation of these images within Coppola's postfeminist-oriented cinema.

CONCLUSION

It is Sofia Coppola's association with the smart cinema movement that allows her body of work to speak at the intersection between Hollywood mainstream and independent production, providing the director with a space in which to capitalise on the ideological pervasiveness of postfeminist and neoliberal discourses while simultaneously critiquing the limited forms of agency that such ideologies afford young, affluent white women. Coppola as an auteur brand circulates within what Cook describes as an intensified promotional culture where the auteur plays a crucial role in commodity production. While this does not necessarily divest the director's creative work of elements of subversive potential, Cook points to 'the fact that critical or personal elements of style are motivated by business interests in response to consumer demands inevitably inflects the counter-cultural status of the new auteurism' (2014: 215). Despite a degree of critical scorn having been levelled at Coppola's cinema for its alleged over-investment in a shallow postfeminist sensibility, it is apparent that the films' exploration of the feminine role within commodity culture, the political and socio-economic currency of scandal and the emphasis placed upon the protagonist's experience of melancholic despondency, does provide scope for a fruitful feminist analysis of the director's work. Coppola's films, like the other texts analysed within this book, do however explore the failures of postfeminism and neoliberalism in terms of white burden. It is this burdened, melancholic whiteness, sold not only through the texts but also through Coppola's celebrity auteur persona and her fashionable collaborations with other icons of countercultural American 'cool' such as Marc Jacobs, which comprises the pleasurable romantic ennui that informs the sensibility and aesthetic mood of her work. Coppola's films are not explicitly political, precisely because an examination of the heroine's role within her broader cultural context or a rupture of the melancholic state would jeopardise the commercial appeal of her brand, which is built upon a fantasy aesthetic that idealises tragic, white femininity in all its ethereal glory, and depends upon the investment of its affluent young consumers. It is precisely in the disappointments and fluctuations of postfeminist and neoliberal discourses that Coppola has been able to capitalise on a cultural sensibility of female melancholia and inertia and present this mood in a romanticised and poetic manner. In so doing, she has been able to carve out a unique space for herself as a high-profile and influential female auteur.

NOTES

1. See for instance Judith Mayne's *Directed by Dorothy Arzner* (1994), Gwendolyn Audrey Foster's *Identity and Memory: The Films of Chantal Akerman* (1999) and Catherine Fowler's *Sally Potter* (2009).
2. This ambivalent attitude towards Sofia Coppola's signature themes and style is perhaps illustrated through the divisive response to *Marie Antoinette* from Australian film critics Margaret Pomeranz and David Stratton in their weekly ABC television show *At the Movies*. While Stratton declared the film to be apolitical and 'superficial', stating it to be like '*Mean Girls* go to Versailles', Pomeranz disagreed, praising Coppola's attempt to portray the 'naïve and vulnerable' Marie's subjective experience, and describing the film as 'terribly moving' (2015).
3. The teenage girls in *The Bling Ring* obsess about celebrity culture and see it as the key means through which to make sense of their own lives, which culminates in their decision to burgle the homes of Hollywood actresses, models and socialites including Lindsay Lohan, Audrina Partridge and Paris Hilton. In committing these crimes, the girls are in fact rewarded with their greatest desire by having celebrity notoriety bestowed upon them by the press and as such are never seen to express regret over their actions. While none of the female characters in this film exhibit melancholic tendencies, the lone male participant in the crimes Marc Hall (Israel Broussard) engages in a broader commentary on the wider cultural preoccupations that may have resulted in his newfound Facebook stardom. Marc points to the American fascination with Bonnie and Clyde-style antiheroes, and implicates his feelings of social alienation and low self-esteem in his decision to participate in The Bling Ring.
4. Adrienne Munich argues in 'Good and plenty: Queen Victoria figures the imperial body' that the monarch's excessive appetite for food made of her a transgressive spectacle (2003: 47).
5. Yunuen Lewis also points to Sofia Coppola's cultivation of her own public persona in accordance with the codes of 'classic' white femininity associated with American icons such as Audrey Hepburn and Jackie Kennedy, as opposed to the codes of glamorous Italian femininity embodied by stars like Sophia Loren, in noting that she is 'dressed, positioned and constructed to connote elegance, managed sexuality, demureness, self-control, emotional etiquette, and an ethereal denial of the abject, the bodily and the earthly' (2011: 187).

Conclusion: Melancholic White Femininity, Cultural Resonance and the Shifting Politics of Representation

This book has illustrated some of the key ways in which contemporary Hollywood cinema has negotiated melancholic, white femininity in relation to the discursive fluctuations of neoliberal postfeminism within the US context. It has argued that the melancholic white heroine of popular Hollywood cinema functions as a vehicle for exploring the excesses of American capitalism and the ideological fracturing inherent within postfeminist popular commentary. From the turn of the new millennium, the middle- and upper-class white woman has appeared in several popular cinematic offerings as troubled by her role within a neoliberal postfeminist society – the terms of which have previously been held to celebrate her rather than impose limitations. This female character is burdened by social expectations relating to upward mobility and career advancement, by a materialist culture that both lauds her participation in consumer capitalism and simultaneously commodifies her, and by the cultural emphasis placed upon corporeal discipline and the appropriate performance of hegemonic femininity. What is intriguing about this body of films, however, are not only the commentaries they express in relation to contemporary forms of gendered power in the West, but the way in which they implicate the protagonist's race and class position in her pathological state. Postfeminist popular commentary has privileged the white, middle-class subject, and as such it is the heroine's race and class identity, as well as her ongoing experience of gender inequality, that is held to contribute to her melancholia. Whiteness and affluence within these texts is linked to unhappiness and existential inertia – a failure to achieve the contentment and successes that neoliberal postfeminism promises, or the lack of a will to *desire* such rewards. However, encounters with those not privileged by the logic of these discourses are often depicted as holding the key to new forms of femininity, and accordingly a modified relationship to white privilege. Neoliberal postfeminism within these films is usually a negative influence – a bad investment that the heroine *should* wish to detach herself from – and the degree to which the protagonist still adheres to these philosophies by the film's conclusion plays a fundamental role in how sympathetic she may appear to audiences. As articulated in the introduction, the heroine's process of renegotiating her investment in such recognisable discourses is a matter of importance not only to her own personal happiness, but also to the various social environments that she comes to interact with. These stories of melancholic femininity, then, tend to individualise the failures of neoliberal postfeminism, or to attribute the 'working through' of its problems to a specific social group. These textual fantasies stand in for a more nuanced analysis as to the ongoing systemic inequalities produced and sanctioned by these dominant cultural philosophies in favour of a sustained, and at times fetishistic, emphasis on white pain.

The female protagonist of these popular Hollywood texts typically suffers from a culturally induced malaise or sickness that bears recognisable similarities across a range of films, and signifies in relation to dominant postfeminist tropes. The melancholic state becomes a point of mental and social dislocation that the protagonist must work through to renegotiate her relationship with socially normative definitions of gender empowerment that she has come to find debilitating. These texts resonate with what McRobbie describes as postfeminist melancholia, whereby a feminist politics is perceived to have become an object of loss, and indeed in the more utopian genres where the white woman can overcome her melancholic state, this achievement often coincides with the discovery of alternative forms of female agency. I have also argued, however, that as adherence to neoliberal postfeminism requires faith in governmental power structures, the capitalist system and belief in the veracity of (and capacity to achieve) the American dream, these films also often signify in accordance with shifts in the United States' global image and the image the country has of itself. The melancholic white woman, then, even as she speaks to a female audience who may be disenchanted by postfeminist ideologies, has acted as a manifestation of brewing cultural anxieties. Her narrative trajectory provides a commentary on the power of the image in its commodity form and/or as a political tool, the perilous reliance on nuclear family formation as a route to personal contentment and social stability, and the social over-investment in capital. The melancholic state, while often held to be a marker of privilege and creative giftedness, is nevertheless problematised when one considers the historical gendering of emotion and neuroses. The treatment of female melancholia within these films is politically precarious and conditional, with the idealisation of the heroine dependent on several factors, including how willing she is to recognise her investment in neoliberal postfeminism as a failing one, and the degree to which she has or has not become an agent in perpetuating some of its more harmful philosophies.

This book contributes to the study of postfeminist media culture in its exploration of how the dominant discursive tropes associated with this gendered cultural sensibility inevitably fluctuate and evolve given its interrelationship with neoliberalism as an also continuing project. In charting some of the ways in which postfeminist popular commentary does this through an analysis of white female melancholia as a popular cinematic trope, the importance of race and class privilege to the construction of the idealised postfeminist subject comes into clearer visibility. This analysis as to how whiteness and class privilege are characterised as sources of female melancholia, alongside the experience of gendered disempowerment, is a contribution to a field of work that has called for further analysis of postfeminism's racial politics. Melancholia operates as a means of segregating the female protagonist emotionally from her social milieu and the white, patriarchal power structures that disadvantage her, with the working through of the melancholic state typically involving the heroine's fantasy of dispensing or realigning her relationship with race and class privilege. While these texts have cinematic precursors that relate to political and social movements in the US national past – the sexual revolution or the civil rights movement for example – these narratives exhibit themes that require contemporary contextualisation. These films frame white women as the primary bearers of burden in a neoliberal postfeminist culture, and over-determine the importance of their relationship to these paradigms in a manner that has varying implications for those less favoured by the logic of these ideologies. It is additionally imperative to remain cognisant of Hollywood as a system designed to make money, with performances of melancholia and mental distress able to confer industry prestige upon white, middle-class, female directors and performers who hold advantages based on their race and class but are disadvantaged by their gender. This occurs through a process of cultural sense making that doubles as star labour and image renegotiation, and can also occur regardless of the specific politics of the text. This is important to consider given the ongoing debates in relation to the comparative lack of opportunity afforded to non-white personnel in Hollywood, and how this coincides with the different relationship that non-white and working-class women have with neoliberal postfeminist culture.

HOLLYWOOD AND THE POLITICS OF REPRESENTATION IN THE TRUMP ERA

It must be noted that following last year's award ceremony controversies, noted in the introduction to this book, the eighty-ninth Academy Awards, and associated industry prize galas including the Golden Globes, Emmys and Screen Actors Guild Awards, have this year demonstrated a renewed commitment to honouring the work of African-American industry professionals in particular. Late 2016 and early 2017 have thus far been notable for the critical successes of films such as *Hidden Figures* (Theodore Melfi, 2016) – a drama about the racial discrimination faced by black female mathematicians at NASA during the Space Race of the 1960s – and *Moonlight* (2016), the Barry Jenkins feature about a young black man who struggles with his sexuality and bullying at school while growing up with a drug-addicted mother in the Miami projects. Of the twenty available nominations for acting, seven went to non-white performers, including accolades for Denzel Washington and Viola Davis for the cinematic adaptation of the August Wilson play *Fences* (Denzel Washington, 2016), and a nomination for Ethiopian-Irish actress Ruth Negga in *Loving* (Jeff Nichols, 2016), a film about Richard and Mildred Loving's 1967 Supreme Court bid to overturn state laws prohibiting interracial marriage. Given that this book's emphasis has been on the ubiquity of white postfeminist melancholia, it is significant that both *Fences* and *Moonlight* tell stories of disenfranchised black masculinity, and feature lead characters who exhibit a melancholic longing for the lives they could have led. In *Fences*, Denzel Washington plays Troy Maxson, a rubbish collector in the 1950s who dreamed of playing professional baseball but was passed over for the major leagues – a decision that Troy believes was made based on race. Troy takes out his anger on his family, including sabotaging his son Cory's chances of playing college football. In *Moonlight*, Chiron (Trevante Rhodes) is as an adolescent unable to pursue his feelings for Kevin (André Holland), due to homophobia within his community and the expectation of adherence to a heteronormative, hard-bodied, black masculinity. His reunion with Kevin in adulthood is thus tinged with melancholia for a life and love that might have been. *Fences* and *Moonlight* are significant films, not least because they present modes of melancholic emotion that are specific to the experience of African-American characters in differing historical and social contexts, and which operate as a point of contrast with the predominantly white forms of melancholia typically favoured by Hollywood cinema. The point of mentioning these films, however, is not to congratulate Hollywood for achieving aimed-for 'diversity' quotas or to suggest in any way that black history and culture are now achieving representational equivalence with white representation in US cinema. The citation here of prizes and accolades afforded to films such as *Moonlight* indicate how organisations like the Academy of Motion Picture Arts and Sciences – which still has an overwhelmingly white membership and aims to classify films based on 'quality' and 'good taste' – are instrumental in sanctioning the distribution of independent films with predominantly non-white casts. *Moonlight*, for example, was initially rolled out to only two cinemas in my home country of New Zealand, indicative of the distributor Roadshow's ambivalence as to whether the film would prove popular enough with audiences. Furthermore, it would be remiss not to point to the hyperbolic critical reception of fellow award frontrunner *La La Land* (Damien Chazelle, 2016) – a film about young, aspiring white entertainers who exhibit a melancholic attachment to code-era Hollywood – as indicative of a certain racial tension in the Academy's bid for inclusiveness within 'quality' categories, to the point where *La La Land* was even falsely read out as the Best Picture winner. Nevertheless, the appearance of these films has contributed to creating a cinematic landscape that is undoubtedly not as 'whitewashed' as it was in 2013, when I first embarked upon research for this book. Furthermore, given that there has been a resurgence in far-right nationalism and racial divisiveness within the United States, it is inevitable that representational politics will shift and interact with the current political climate in new and complex ways.

A film like *Hidden Figures*, with its uplifting Hollywood storyline, triumphant soundtrack (including the song 'I See a Victory' by Pharrell Williams and Kim Burrell) and depicted re-education of white bosses and supervisors at NASA, may invite a reading of the story as indicative of past injustices that have been overcome. Yet in the context of the Black Lives Matter campaign, the Trump administration's renewed pursuit of undocumented immigrants, as well as a controversial ban on refugees and travellers to the US from seven Muslim-majority countries, it may also be more difficult to read the film in accordance with 'post-racial' ideologies. In fact, the film was marketed as particularly relevant to the contemporary political climate. In a 2017 interview with *Elle* magazine entitled 'The *Hidden Figures* cast on why their film is so necessary right now', actress Taraji P. Henson (who plays Katherine Johnson) states to Antonia Blyth that the film was made in 2016, as opposed to five or ten years ago, because 'the universe needed it now' and declares that it almost feels as if 'it is 1962 again'. Fellow cast member Janelle Monáe, meanwhile, cites the film's segregation-era storyline as an example of how difficult times in the present can also be overcome, and discusses the importance of representing those who 'are oftentimes uncelebrated'(Blyth 2017). At the twenty-third annual Screen Actors Guild Awards, where the cast won for Outstanding Performance, Henson noted that the film is 'about unity' and what happens 'when we come together as a human race' (Crucchiola 2017). In fact, in predominantly liberal Hollywood, the 2017 award season was notable for the number of politicised victory speeches, to the point where not making a statement on the Trump presidency was making the most political statement of all. The shifting politics of cinematic representation into the Trump era thus raises intriguing issues in relation to industry trends and celebrity activism. To conflate the message of *Hidden Figures*, and the specificities of the oppression of black Americans, with contemporary policies targeting Muslims, is to conflate forms of racial and religious violence that have differing genealogies and stakes, and thus arguably works to flatten the specificity of experience in favour of a Hollywood-sanctioned liberal humanism. Meryl Streep's claim in her Golden Globes speech that Hollywood belongs to the most vilified category of society, along with foreigners and the press (Weaver 2017), seems remiss in equating right-wing criticism of Hollywood satire or activism with the persecution experienced by illegal immigrants and refugees. It also risks advocating for an industry victimhood, and a privileging of celebrity activism over other forms. Furthermore, the reception of such speeches is likely to also be complicated, given the wealth of the individuals involved and the rising economic inequality within the United States that in part fuelled Trump's campaign.[1] The volatile political climate thus raises interesting avenues of enquiry for media scholars and will undoubtedly be explored in detail over the coming years.

NOTES FOR FURTHER RESEARCH

What the above observations indicate is that this book analyses female melancholia specifically in relation to neoliberal postfeminist discourses, and in a cultural context where these ideologies are undergoing processes of renegotiation. As such, my argument has some limitations in relation to the temporal parameters of the project, the United States as chosen national context, and the selection of films. It is therefore necessary to draw attention to the fact that these variants of contemporary female melancholia and the tropes that I have identified are but the work of a specific moment and do not comprise an exhaustive list of the ways in which female mental distress exhibits itself on screen. There may additionally be other films not discussed within these pages that complicate, or indeed enrich, the analysis of the ways in which postfeminist melancholia manifests itself within popular Hollywood cinema and the importance of race and class privilege to these representations. To concentrate on Hollywood product was a strategic choice given that popular American cinema dominates at the multiplex in other primarily English-speaking countries, such as the UK, Australia and New Zealand. It is within these nations that I believe the themes discussed within this book would have the highest degree of cultural convergence given the similarities in socio-economic systems that privilege whiteness, a comparable history of feminism, past and present political alliances with the US, and the sheer pervasiveness and influence of American popular culture. Nevertheless, analyses of melancholic femininity in relation to neoliberal postfeminism could be carried out in relation to local cinema production within nationally specific contexts – a task that has been beyond the scope of this study, yet may provide a more nuanced discussion as to the specificities of race relations within different countries. Australia and New Zealand, as white settler nations, have a cinematic history of tales involving melancholic white femininity in films such as *Picnic at Hanging Rock*, *The Piano* (Jane Campion, 1993), *Holy Smoke!* (Jane Campion, 1999) and more recently *Strangerland* (Kim Farrant, 2015). This melancholia is experienced in terms of an estrangement from a landscape perceived as foreign, alienating and harsh. It would therefore be interesting to assess as to whether recent manifestations of female melancholia within Australia and New Zealand cinema exhibit any relationship with neoliberal postfeminist ideologies, or whether the success of these narratives depends more frequently upon the protagonist's temporal, cultural and urban dislocation. These films are characterised by the female character's sense of homelessness and the conflict her presence bears to indigenous histories and counterclaims to country, even though this conflict may not be made explicit within the text.

It would, in fact, be theoretically possible to carry out an analysis of female melancholia as related to neoliberal postfeminist discourse within the local cinemas of many different countries. Beyond Anglo-American and Western European cinema, there are likely to be fewer parallels with my findings given that the construction of melancholic white femininity in Hollywood fare typically signifies in relation to a 'Western' lineage of feminism and depends upon assumed entitlements to social and economic comforts that may not be quite so taken for granted in other countries. Nevertheless, the adoption of neoliberal policies in countries undergoing shifts in the political economic order, for instance in the context of post-war nation building, could generate a wealth of studies exploring the interrelationship between neoliberal governmentality, gender and race relations through the figure of the melancholic woman in cinema, who in these contexts may not necessarily be marked by white privilege. Such studies, however, would not challenge the findings outlined within this book or the investment of Anglo-American audiences in the popular characters that I have discussed here. I have argued for a culturally contextualised reading of white female melancholia in contemporary Hollywood cinema as related to neoliberal postfeminist ideologies, while acknowledging the cinematic lineage of these characters and narratives. If the melancholic white woman has a past, then reason suggests that she must also have a future. The relationship between feminism, whiteness and governmental rhetoric is always in a process of fluctuation and, as such, the melancholic white woman will continue to operate as a figure through which to negotiate attendant cultural anxieties. Future forms of cinematic female burden may not align entirely with the themes discussed here, yet this character is likely to recirculate within the popular sphere in new ways, with a whole new set of reasons to be melancholy.

NOTES

1. See Erik Sherman's 2016 *Forbes* article 'What a Trump administration might mean for income inequality' for a discussion of this issue.

Bibliography

AAP (2010), 'Aussie Alice savaged by movie critic', *Sydney Morning Herald*, 1 March, <www.smh.com.au/news/entertainment/film/aussie-alice-savaged-by-movie-critic/2010/02/28/1267291817486.html> (accessed 5 May 2014).

ABC News (Australia) (2014), *Cate Blanchett Thanks Gough Whitlam for Free Education* [online video]. 4 November. Available from: <https://www.youtube.com/watch?v=6uNhvvR6XKI> [accessed 9 May 2017].

Aaron, Michele (2014), 'Cinema and suicide: necromanticism, dead-already-ness, and the logic of the vanishing point', *Cinema Journal*, 53:2, 71–92.

Ahmed, Sara (2004), *The Cultural Politics of Emotion*, Edinburgh: Edinburgh University Press.

Ahmed, Sara (2007), 'A phenomenology of whiteness', *Feminist Theory*, 8:2, 149–68.

Alexander, Ella (2013), 'Cate Blanchett's help for Woody Allen', *Vogue UK*, 24 September, <www.vogue.co.uk/article/cate-blanchett-blue-jasmine-interview-woody-allen-film> (accessed 18 April 2015).

Amos, Valerie and Pratibha Parmar (1984), 'Challenging imperial feminism', *Feminist Review*, 17, 3–19.

Ang, Ien (1995), 'I'm a feminist but … "other" women and postnational feminism', in Barbara Caine and Rosemary Pringle (eds), *Transitions: New Australian Feminisms*, St Leonards: Allen & Unwin, pp. 57–74.

Anker, Elisabeth R. (2014), *Orgies of Feeling: Melodrama and the Politics of Freedom*, Durham: Duke University Press.

Armitt, Lucie (2007), 'Dark departures: contemporary women's writing after the gothic', in Benjamin A. Brabon and Stéphanie Genz (eds), *Postfeminist Gothic: Critical Interventions in Contemporary Culture*, New York: Palgrave Macmillan, pp. 16–30.

Ascheid, Antje (2006), 'Safe rebellions: romantic emancipation in the women's heritage film', *Scope: An Online Journal of Film and Television Studies*, 4.

Astruc, Alexandre [1948] (1968), 'The birth of a new avant-garde: *La caméra-stylo*', in Peter Graham (ed.), *The New Wave: Critical Landmarks*, London: BFI, pp. 17–23.

Banes, Sally (1998), *Dancing Women: Female Bodies on Stage*, London: Routledge.

Barlow, Helen (2013), '*The Bling Ring*: Sofia Coppola interview', *SBS*, 6 August, <www.sbs.com.au/movies/article/2013/08/06/bling-ring-sofia-coppola-interview> (accessed 5 October 2015).

Barlow, Helen (2016), '*Mustang* director talks empathy, freedom, and powerful female characters', *SBS*, 13 May, <www.sbs.com.au/movies/article/2016/05/12/mustang-deniz-gamze-erguven-interview> (accessed 3 February 2017).

Barthes, Roland [1967] (1981), 'The death of the author', in John Caughie (ed.), *Theories of Authorship*, London: Routledge, pp. 208–14.

Bartky, Sandra Lee (1990), *Femininity and Domination: Studies in the Phenomenology of Oppression*, New York: Routledge.

Baudrillard, Jean (1998), *The Consumer Society: Myths and Structures*, London: SAGE Publications.

Beckman, Karen (2003), *Vanishing Women: Magic, Film, and Feminism*, Durham: Duke University Press.

Berlant, Lauren (2011), *Cruel Optimism*, Durham: Duke University Press.

Bernardi, Daniel (ed.) (1996), *The Birth of Whiteness: Race and the Emergence of US Cinema*, New Brunswick, NJ: Rutgers University Press.

Bernardi, Daniel (ed.) (2001), *Classic Hollywood, Classic Whiteness*, Minneapolis: University of Minnesota Press.

Bernardi, Daniel (ed.) (2008), *The Persistence of Whiteness: Race and Contemporary Hollywood Cinema*, Abingdon: Routledge.

Blyth, Antonia (2017), 'The *Hidden Figures* cast on why their film is so necessary right now', *Elle*, 30 January, <www.elle.com/culture/movies-tv/news/a42530/hidden-figures-sag-awards-interview/> (accessed 23 February 2017).

Bogle, Donald (1973), *Toms, Coons, Mulattoes, Mammies, and Bucks: An Interpretive History of Blacks in American Films*, New York: Viking Press.

Bonilla-Silva, Eduardo (2006), *Racism without Racists: Colour-Blind Racism and the Persistence of Racial Inequality in the United States* (2nd edn), Oxford: Rowman & Littlefield Publishers.

Bonnett, Alastair (2000), *White Identities: Historical and International Perspectives*, Harlow: Prentice Hall.

Boone, John (2016), 'A comprehensive list of celebrities who have spoken out about the lack of diversity at the Oscars', *Entertainment Tonight*, 25 January, <www.etonline.com/news/180489_actors_who_have_spoken_out_on_oscars_lack_of_diversity/> (accessed 22 February 2016).

Bourdieu, Pierre [1984] (2010), *Distinction: A Social Critique on the Judgement of Taste*, Abingdon: Routledge Classics.

Bowring, Jacky (2008), *A Field Guide to Melancholy*, Harpenden: Oldcastle Books.

Boyle, Kirk and Daniel Mrozowski (eds) (2013), *The Great Recession in Fiction, Film, and Television: Twenty-First-Century Bust Culture*, Lanham: Lexington Books.

Brabon, Benjamin and Stéphanie Genz (eds) (2007), *Postfeminist Gothic: Critical Interventions in Contemporary Culture*, New York: Palgrave Macmillan.

Brady, Anita (2016), 'Taking time between G-string changes to educate ourselves: Sinéad O'Connor, Miley Cyrus, and celebrity feminism', *Feminist Media Studies*, 16:3, 429–44.

Brady, Emily and Arto Haapala (2003), 'Melancholy as an aesthetic emotion', *Contemporary Aesthetics*, 1.

Brashares, Ann (2001), *The Sisterhood of the Travelling Pants*, New York: Delacorte Press.

Brodkin, Karen (2004), *How Jews Became White Folks & What That Says about Race in America*, New Brunswick, NJ: Rutgers University Press.

Bronfen, Elisabeth (1992), *Over her Dead Body: Death, Femininity and the Aesthetic*, Manchester: Manchester University Press.

Brooks, Peter (1994), 'Melodrama, body, revolution', in Jacky Bratton, Jim Cook and Christine Gledhill (eds), *Melodrama: Stage, Picture, Screen*, London: BFI, pp. 11–25.

Brown, Wendy (2005), *Edgework: Critical Essays on Knowledge and Politics*, Princeton: Princeton University Press.

Burgin, Victor, James Donald and Cora Kaplan (eds) (1986), *Formations of Fantasy*, London: Methuen.

Butler, David (2009), *Fantasy Cinema: Impossible Worlds on Screen*, New York: Wallflower.

Butler, Jess (2013), 'For white girls only? Postfeminism and the politics of inclusion', *Feminist Formations*, 25:1, 35–58.

Butler, Judith (1993), *Bodies That Matter: On the Discursive Limits of Sex*, New York: Routledge.

Butler, Judith (1997), 'Performative acts and gender constitution: an essay in phenomenology and feminist theory', in Katie Conboy, Nadia Medina and Sarah Stanbury (eds), *Writing on the Body: Female Embodiment and Feminist Theory*, New York: Columbia University Press, pp. 401–19.

Carroll, Rebecca (2015), '*Suffragette*'s publicity campaign and the politics of erasure', *The Guardian*, 6 October, <https://www.theguardian.com/film/2015/oct/05/suffragette-film-publicity-campaign-erasure-feminism> (accessed 10 March 2016).

Chomsky, Noam (2005), *Imperial Ambitions: Conversations with Noam Chomsky on the Post 9/11 World*, London: Hamish Hamilton.

Chomsky, Noam (2010), *Hopes and Prospects*, Chicago: Haymarket Books.

Chopra-Gant, Mike (2006), *Hollywood Genres and Postwar America: Masculinity, Family and Nation in Popular Movies and Film Noir*, London: I. B. Tauris.

Church Gibson, Pamela (2013), *Fashion and Celebrity Culture*, London: Bloomsbury Academic.

Cobb, Shelley (2015), 'Is this what a feminist looks like? Male celebrity feminists and the postfeminist politics of equality', *Celebrity Studies*, 6:1, 136–9.

Cohen, William B. (1970), 'The colonised as child: British and French colonial rule', *African Historical Studies*, 3:2, 427–31.

Cook, Pam (1996), *Fashioning the Nation: Costume and Identity in British Cinema*, London: BFI.

Cook, Pam (2014), 'History in the making: Sofia Coppola's *Marie Antoinette* and the new auteurism', in Tom Brown and Belén Vidal (eds), *The Biopic in Contemporary Film Culture*, New York: Routledge, pp. 212–27.

Cooke, Rachel (2016), 'Deniz Gamze Ergüven: For women in Turkey it's like the Middle Ages', *The Guardian*, 15 May, <https://www.theguardian.com/film/2016/may/15/deniz-gamze-erguven-mustang-turkey-interview-rachel-cooke> (accessed 3 February 2017).

Coon, David R. (2014), *Look Closer: Suburban Values and American Values in Film and Television*, New Brunswick, NJ: Rutgers University Press.

Corrigan, Timothy (1998), 'Auteurs and the new Hollywood', in Jon Lewis (ed), *New American Cinema*, Durham: Duke University Press, pp. 38–63.

Crandell, George W. (1997), 'Misrepresentation and miscegenation: Reading the racialised discourse of Tennessee Williams's *A Streetcar Named Desire*', *Modern Drama*, 40:3, 337–46.

Crucchiola, Jordan (2017), 'See Taraji P. Henson's beautiful Screen Actors Guild Awards speech on behalf of *Hidden Figures*', 30 January, <www.vulture.com/2017/01/taraji-p-hensons-sag-speech-for-hidden-figures.html> (accessed 13 August 2017).

Cvetkovich, Ann (2012), *Depression: A Public Feeling*, Durham: Duke University Press.

Davies, William (2014), *The Limits of Neoliberalism: Authority, Sovereignty and the Logic of Capitalism*, London: SAGE Publications.

Deaton, Angus (2013), *The Great Escape: Health, Wealth, and the Origins of Inequality*, Princeton: Princeton University Press.

Dejmanee, Tisha (2016), 'Consumption in the city: the turn to interiority in contemporary postfeminist television', *European Journal of Cultural Studies*, 19:2, 119–33.

Devine, Fiona and Mike Savage (2000), 'Conclusion: renewing class analysis', in Rosemary Crompton, Fiona Devine, Mike Savage and John Scott (eds), *Renewing Class Analysis*, Oxford: Blackwell Publishing, pp. 184–99.

Doane, Mary Ann (1985), 'The clinical eye: medical discourses in the "woman's film" of the 1940s', *Poetics Today*, 6: (1–2), 205–27.

Doane, Mary Ann (1987), *The Desire to Desire: The Woman's Film of the 1940s*, Bloomington: Indiana University Press.

Donald, James (ed.) (1989), *Fantasy and the Cinema*, London: BFI.

Duvall, Spring-Serenity (2009), 'Dying for our sins: Christian salvation rhetoric in celebrity colonialism', in Robert Clarke (ed.), *Celebrity Colonialism: Fame, Power and Representation in Colonial and Postcolonial Cultures*, Newcastle: Cambridge Scholars Publishing, pp. 91–107.

Dyer, Richard (1997), *White*, London: Routledge.

Dyer, Richard (1998), *Stars* (2nd edn), London: BFI.

Ehrenreich, Barbara (2009), *Bright-Sided: How Positive Thinking is Undermining America*, New York: Picador.

Eisenstein, Zillah R. (2004), *Against Empire: Feminisms, Racism, and the West*, London: Zed Books.

Elsaesser, Thomas [1987] (2012), 'Tales of sound and fury: observations on the family melodrama', in Barry Keith Grant (ed.), *The Film Genre Reader IV*, Austin: University of Texas Press, pp. 433–63.

Elsaesser, Thomas (2015), 'Black suns and a bright planet: Lars von Trier's *Melancholia* as thought experiment', *Theory and Event*, 18:2, http://muse.jhu.edu/article/578627 (accessed 1 December 2017).

Emmet Jones, Robert (1961), 'Tennessee Williams' early heroines', in John D. Hurrell (ed.), *Two Modern American Tragedies: Reviews and Criticism of 'Death of a Salesman' and 'A Streetcar Named Desire'*, New York: Charles Scribner, pp. 111–17.

Esch, Kevin (2006), 'I don't see any method at all: the problem of actorly transformation', *Journal of Film and Video*, 58:1, pp. 95–107.

Eugenides, Jeffrey (1993), *The Virgin Suicides*, London: Bloomsbury.

Faludi, Susan (1991), *Backlash: The Undeclared War Against Women*, New York: Crown.

Fanon, Frantz [1967] (2008), *Black Skin, White Masks*, London: Pluto Press.

Feasey, Rebecca (2012), *From Happy Homemaker to Desperate Housewives: Motherhood and Popular Television*, London: Anthem Press.

Feay, Suzi (2015), '*The Girl on the Train* by Paula Hawkins Review – a skilful memory loss thriller', *The Guardian*, 8 January, <https://www.theguardian.com/books/2015/jan/08/the-girl-on-the-train-paula-hawkins-review-novel> (accessed 13 March 2017).

Felski, Rita (ed.) (2008), *Rethinking Tragedy*, Baltimore: Johns Hopkins University Press.

Ferraro, Thomas J. (2005), *Feeling Italian: The Art of Ethnicity in America*, New York: New York University Press.

Figlerowicz, Marta (2012), 'Comedy of abandon: Lars von Trier's *Melancholia*', *Film Quarterly*, 65:4, 21–6.

Fisher, Mark and Amber Jacobs (2011), 'Debating *Black Swan:* gender and horror', *Film Quarterly*, 65:1, 58–62.

Fisher, N. R. E (1992), *Hybris: A Study in the Values of Honour and Shame in Ancient Greece*, Warminster: Aris & Phillips.

Fishman, Robert (1987), *Bourgeois Utopias: The Rise and Fall of Suburbia*, New York: Basic Books.

Flatley, Jonathan (2008), *Affective Mapping: Melancholia and the Politics of Modernism*, Cambridge, MA: Harvard University Press.

Flew, Terry (2014), 'Six theories of neoliberalism', *Thesis Eleven*, 122:1, 49–71.

Flood, Alison (2012), '*Gone Girl* by Gillian Flynn – review', *The Guardian*, 20 May, <https://www.theguardian.com/books/2012/may/20/gillian-flynn-gone-girl-review> (accessed 9 March 2017).

Flynn, Gillian (2012), *Gone Girl*, New York: Crown.

Foster, Gwendolyn Audrey (1999), *Identity and Memory: The Films of Chantal Akerman*, Wiltshire: Flicks Books.

Foster, Gwendolyn Audrey (2003), *Performing Whiteness: Postmodern Re/Constructions in the Cinema*, New York: SUNY Press.

Foster, Gwendolyn Audrey (2005), *Class Passing: Social Mobility in Film and Popular Culture*, Carbondale: Southern Illinois University Press.

Foucault, Michel [1969] (1981), 'What is an author?' in John Caughie (ed.), *Theories of Authorship*, London: Routledge, pp. 282–92.

Fowkes, Katherine A. (2010), *The Fantasy Film*, Oxford: Wiley-Blackwell.

Fowler, Catherine (2009), *Sally Potter*, Urbana: University of Illinois Press.

Fradley, Martin (2011), '"Why doesn't your compass work?" *Pirates of the Caribbean*, fantasy blockbusters and contemporary queer theory', in Karen Ross (ed.), *The Handbook of Gender, Sex and Media*, London: Wiley-Blackwell, pp. 294–312.

Frankenberg, Ruth (1993), *White Women, Race Matters: The Social Construction of Whiteness*, Minneapolis: University of Minnesota Press.

Freud, Sigmund [1917] (2000), 'Mourning and melancholia', in Jennifer Radden (ed.), *The Nature of Melancholy: From Aristotle to Kristeva*, Oxford: Oxford University Press.

Fuller, Sean and Catherine Driscoll (2015), 'HBO's *Girls*: gender, generation, and quality television', *Continuum: Journal of Media and Cultural Studies*, 29:2, 253–62.

Gabbard, Glen O. and Krin Gabbard (1999), *Psychiatry and the Cinema* (2nd edn), Washington: American Psychiatric Press.

Garber, Marjorie (1992), *Vested Interests: Cross-Dressing and Cultural Anxiety*, New York: Routledge.

Garrett, Roberta (2007), *Postmodern Chick Flicks: The Return of the Woman's Film*, Basingstoke: Palgrave Macmillan.

Gay, Roxane (2014), 'Emma Watson? Jennifer Lawrence? These aren't the feminists you're looking for', *The Guardian*, 11 October, <https://www.theguardian.com/commentisfree/2014/oct/10/-sp-jennifer-lawrence-emma-watson-feminists-celebrity> (accessed 5 March 2016).

Genz, Stéphanie and Benjamin A. Brabon (2009), *Postfeminism: Cultural Texts and Theories*, Edinburgh: Edinburgh University Press.

Geraghty, Christine (2000), 'Re-examining stardom: questions of texts, bodies and performance', in Christine Gledhill and Linda Williams (ed.), *Reinventing Film Studies*, London: Arnold, pp. 183–201.

Gilbert, Elizabeth (2006), *Eat, Pray, Love: One Woman's Search for Everything across Italy, India and Indonesia*, New York: Penguin.

Gilbey, Ryan (2013), 'Sofia Coppola on *The Bling Ring:* what these kids did really took ingenuity', *The Guardian*, 5 July, <https://www.theguardian.com/film/2013/jul/04/sofia-coppola-the-bling-ring-interview> (accessed 2 October 2015).

Gill, Rosalind (2007), 'Postfeminist media culture: elements of a sensibility', *European Journal of Cultural Studies*, 10:2, 147–66.

Gill, Rosalind and Christina Scharff (eds) (2011), *New Femininities: Postfeminism, Neoliberalism and Subjectivity*, Basingstoke: Palgrave Macmillan.

Gilman, Sander L (1985), *Difference and Pathology: Stereotypes of Sexuality, Race and Madness*, New York: Cornell University Press.

Girgus, Sam B. (2002), *The Films of Woody Allen*, Cambridge: Cambridge University Press.

Gleiberman, Owen (2016), 'Film review: *The Girl on the Train*', *Variety*, 3 October, <http://variety.com/2016/film/reviews/the-girl-on-the-train-review-emily-blunt-1201872781/> (accessed 15 April 2017).

Goldberg, David Theo (2009), *The Threat of Race: Reflections on Racial Neoliberalism*, Malden: Blackwell Publishing.

Grosz, Elizabeth (1994), *Volatile Bodies: Towards a Corporeal Feminism*, St Leonards: Allen & Unwin.

Guerrero, Ed (1993), *Framing Blackness: The African American Image in Film*, Philadelphia: Temple University Press.

Guglielmo, Jennifer (2003), 'White lies, dark truths', in Jennifer Guglielmo and Salvatore Salerno (eds), *Are Italians White? How Race is Made in America*, London: Routledge, pp. 9–11.

Hage, Ghassan (2003), *Against Paranoid Nationalism: Searching for Hope in a Shrinking Society*, Annandale: Pluto Press.

Hamad, Hannah (2014), *Postfeminism and Paternity in US Film: Framing Fatherhood*, New York: Routledge.

Hamad, Hannah and Anthea Taylor (2015), 'Introduction: feminism and contemporary celebrity culture', *Celebrity Studies*, 6:1, 124–7.

Hanson, Helen (2007), *Hollywood Heroines: Women in Film Noir and the Female Gothic Film*, London: I. B. Tauris.

Harris, Anita (2004), *Future Girl: Young Women in the 21st Century*, New York: Routledge.

Harris, Cheryl I. (1993), 'Whiteness as property', *Harvard Law Review*, 106:8, 1707–91.

Harvey, David (2005), *A Brief History of Neoliberalism*, Oxford: Oxford University Press.

Hawkins, Paula (2015), *The Girl on the Train*, London: Doubleday.

Hiddleston, Tom (2013), 'Role reversal: interview with Natalie Portman', *Elle Australia*, November 2013, pp. 80–7.

Hollinger, Karen (2012), *Feminist Film Studies*, Abingdon: Routledge.

Hollows, Joanne and Rachel Moseley (eds) (2006), *Feminism and Popular Culture*, New York: Berg.

hooks, bell (1992), *Black Looks: Race and Representation*, Boston: South End.

Hyler, Steven E, Glen O. Gabbard and Irving Schneider (1991), 'Homicidal maniacs and narcissistic parasites: stigmatisation of mentally ill persons in the movies', *Hospital and Community Psychiatry*, 42:10, 1044–48.

Iwabuchi, Koichi (2008), 'Lost in TransNation: Tokyo and the urban imaginary in the era of globalisation', *Inter-Asia Cultural Studies*, 9:4, 543–56.

Jermyn, Deborah (2009), 'I heart NY: the rom-com's love affair with New York city', in Stacey Abbott and Deborah Jermyn (eds), *Falling in Love Again: Romantic Comedy in Contemporary Cinema*, London: I. B. Tauris, 9–25.

Johansen, Emily (2016), 'The neoliberal gothic: *Gone Girl*, *Broken Harbour* and the terror of everyday life', *Contemporary Literature*, 57:1, 30–55.

Jurca, Catherine (2011), *White Diaspora: The Suburb and the Twentieth-Century American Novel*, Princeton: Princeton University Press.

Kael, Pauline (1963), 'Circles and squares', *Film Quarterly*, 16:3, 12–26.

Kaplan, E. Ann (1992), *Motherhood and Representation: The Mother in Popular Culture and Melodrama*, London: Routledge.

Karlyn, Kathleen Rowe (2010), *Unruly Girls, Unrepentant Mothers: Redefining Feminism on Screen*, Austin: University of Texas Press.

Keating, AnaLouise (2012), *Transformation Now! Toward a Post-Oppositional Politics of Change*, Champaign: University of Illinois Press.

Kellner, Douglas (2009), *Cinema Wars: Hollywood Film and Politics in the Bush–Cheney Era*, Oxford: Wiley-Blackwell.

Kennedy, Tanya Ann (2017), *Historicising Post-Discourses: Postfeminism and Postracialism in United States Culture*, Albany: State University of New York Press.

Kim, Sue (2004), 'Beyond black and white: race and postmodernism in *The Lord of the Rings* films', *Modern Fiction Studies*, 50:4, 875–907.

King, Barry (2008), 'Stardom, celebrity and the para-confession', *Social Semiotics*, 18:2, 115–32.

King, Homay (2010), *Lost in Translation: Orientalism, Cinema, and the Enigmatic Signifier*, Durham: Duke University Press.

Kolin, Philip C. (2000), *Williams: A Streetcar Named Desire*, Cambridge: Cambridge University Press.

Kristeva, Julia (1989), *Black Sun: Depression and Melancholia*, New York: Columbia University Press.

Laine, Tarja (2015), *Bodies in Pain: Emotion and the Cinema of Darren Aronofsky*, New York: Berghahn Books.

Lane, Christina and Nicole Richter (2011), 'The feminist poetics of Sofia Coppola: Spectacle and self-consciousness in *Marie Antoinette*', in Hilary Radner and Rebecca Stringer (eds), *Feminism at the Movies: Understanding Gender in Contemporary Hollywood Cinema*, New York: Routledge, pp. 189–203.

Lawrence, Jennifer (2016), 'Why do I make less than my male co-stars?' *Lenny*, 13 October, <www.lennyletter.com/work/a147/jennifer-lawrence-why-do-i-make-less-than-my-male-costars> (accessed 5 March 2016).

Lee, Michael J. and Leigh Moscowitz (2013), 'The rich bitch: class and gender on the *Real Housewives of New York City*', *Feminist Media Studies*, 13:1, 64–82.

Lepenies, Wolf (1992), *Melancholy and Society*, Jeremy Gaines and Doris Jones (trans.), Cambridge, MA: Harvard University Press.

Lopez, John (2010), 'Natalie Portman on *Black Swan:* I'm only acting, dammit!' *Vanity Fair*, 14 September, <https://www.vanityfair.com/hollywood/2010/09/natalie-portman-on-black-swan-im-only-acting-dammit> (accessed 9 September 2014).

Lott, Eric (1997), 'The whiteness of film noir', *American Literary History*, 9:3, 542–66.

Loughrey, Clarisse (2016), '*The Girl on the Train* film is driving book fans off the rails', *The Independent*, 10 October, <www.independent.co.uk/arts-entertainment/films/news/the-girl-on-the-train-film-book-reviews-emily-blunt-a7353836.html> (accessed 15 April 2017).

Lumby, Catharine (1999), *Gotcha: Life in a Tabloid World*, St Leonards: Allen & Unwin.

Lusk, Darian (2014), 'Trent Reznor on the sonic world he created for *Gone Girl*', CBS News, 4 October, <www.cbsnews.com/news/trent-reznor-on-the-sonic-world-he-created-for-gone-girl> (accessed 5 May 2017).

Macpherson, Pat (1997), 'The revolution of little girls', in Michelle Fine, Lois Weis, Linda C. Powell and L. Mun Wong (eds), *Off White: Readings on Race, Power, and Society*, London: Routledge, pp. 283–97.

Malague, Rosemary (2012), *An Actress Prepares: Women and The Method*, Abingdon: Routledge.

Marchetti, Gina (1993), *Romance and the 'Yellow Peril': Race, Sex, and Discursive Strategies in Hollywood Fiction*, Berkeley: University of California Press.

Marshall, David P. (1997), *Celebrity and Power: Fame in Contemporary Culture*, Minneapolis: Minnesota University Press.

Martin, Luther H., Huck Gutman and Patrick H. Hutton (eds) (1988), *Technologies of the Self: A Seminar with Michel Foucault*, Boston: Massachusetts University Press.

Maslin, Janet (2012), 'The lies that buoy, then break a marriage: *Gone Girl*, by Gillian Flynn', *New York Times*, 29 May, <www.nytimes.com/2012/05/30/books/gone-girl-by-gillian-flynn.html?mcubz=1> (accessed 15 March 2017).

Mayne, Judith (1994), *Directed by Dorothy Arzner*, Bloomington: Indiana University Press.

McCarthy, Todd (2016), '*The Girl on the Train*: film review', *Hollywood Reporter*, 3 October, <www.hollywoodreporter.com/review/girl-train-review-934350> (accessed 10 April 2017).

McClintock, Anne (1995), *Imperial Leather: Race, Gender and Sexuality in the Colonial Contest*, London: Routledge.

McDonnell, Andrea (2014), *Reading Celebrity Gossip Magazines*, Cambridge: Polity Press.

McGowan, Todd (2007), 'There is nothing *Lost in Translation*', *Quarterly Review of Film and Video*, 24:1, 53–63.

McHugh, Kathleen A. (2015), 'Giving credit to paratexts and parafeminism in *Top of the Lake* and *Orange is the New Black*', *Film Quarterly*, 68:3.

McLean, Adrienne L. (2008), *Dying Swans and Madmen: Ballet, the Body and Narrative Cinema*, New Brunswick, NJ: Rutgers University Press.

McLean, Adrienne L. and David A. Cook (eds) (2001), *Headline Hollywood: A Century of Film Scandal*, New Brunswick, NJ: Rutgers University Press.

McRobbie, Angela (2009), *The Aftermath of Feminism: Gender, Culture and Social Change*, London: SAGE Publications.

Meyers, Marian (1997), *News Coverage of Violence against Women: Engendering Blame*, Newbury Park: SAGE Publications.

Miller, April (2013), 'Real-to-reel recessionary horrors in *Drag Me to Hell* and *Contagion*', in Kirk Boyle and Daniel Mrozowski (eds), *The Great Recession in Fiction, Film, and Television: Twenty-First-Century Bust Culture*, Lanham: Lexington Books, pp. 29–51.

Mohanty, Chandra Talpade (1988), 'Under Western eyes: feminist scholarship and colonial discourses', *Feminist Review*, 30, 61–88.

Mohanty, Chandra Talpade (2003), *Feminism without Borders: Decolonising Theory, Practicing Solidarity*, Durham: Duke University Press.

Monden, Masafumi (2013), 'Contemplating in a dream-like room: *The Virgin Suicides* and the aesthetic imagination of girlhood', *Film, Fashion & Consumption*, 2:2, 139–58.

Moreton-Robinson, Aileen (2015), *The White Possessive: Property, Power, and Indigenous Sovereignty*, Minneapolis: University of Minnesota Press.

Morey, Ann (2011), 'Grotesquerie as marker of success in aging female stars', in Su Holmes and Diane Negra (eds), *In the Limelight and Under the Microscope: Forms and Functions of Female Celebrity*, New York: Continuum, pp. 103–25.

Mulvey, Laura (1975), 'Visual pleasure and narrative cinema', *Screen*, 16:3, 6–18.

Munich, Adrienne (2003), 'Good and plenty: Queen Victoria figures the imperial body', in Tamar Heller and Patricia Moran (eds), *Scenes of the Apple: Food and the Female Body in Nineteenth and Twentieth-Century Women's Writing*, Albany: State University of New York Press, pp. 45–64.

Murphy, Brenda (1992), *Tennessee Williams and Elia Kazan: A Collaboration in the Theatre*, Cambridge: Cambridge University Press.

Nash, Charlie (2016), 'Milo: feminism and Islam both "set on destroying the American way of life"', *Breitbart*, 12 October, <www.breitbart.com/milo/2016/10/12/milo-feminism-islam-set-destroying-american-way-life/> (accessed 14 May 2017).

Negra, Diane (2001), 'Romance and/as tourism: Heritage whiteness and the inter(national) imaginary in the new woman's film', in Matthew Tinkcom and Amy Villarejo (eds), *Keyframes: Popular Cinema and Cultural Studies*, London: Routledge, pp. 82–98.

Negra, Diane (2009), *What a Girl Wants? Fantasising the Reclamation of Self in Postfeminism*, New York: Routledge.

Negra, Diane and Yvonne Tasker (2013), 'Neoliberal frames and genres of inequality: recession-era chick flicks and male-centred melodramas', *European Journal of Cultural Studies*, 16:3, 344–61.

Negra, Diane and Yvonne Tasker (eds) (2014), *Gendering the Recession: Media and Culture in an Age of Austerity*, Durham: Duke University Press.

Newsday staff (2016), 'Donald Trump speech, debates and campaign quotes', *Newsday*, 9 November, www.newsday.com/news/nation/donald-trump-speech-debates-and-campaign-quotes-1.11206532 (accessed 24 January 2017).

Nicholls, Mark (2004), *Scorsese's Men: Melancholia and the Mob*, Melbourne: Pluto Press.

Nolte, John (2017), 'Culture war backfire: polls show left losing gender debate to more traditional millennials', *Daily Wire*, 3 April, <www.dailywire.com/news/15042/culture-war-backfire-polls-show-left-losing-gender-john-nolte> (accessed 23 May 2017).

Overbeek, Henk and Bastiaan van Apeldoorn (eds) (2012), *Neoliberalism in Crisis*, New York: Palgrave Macmillan.

Palmer, R. Barton (2012), 'Some thoughts on new Hollywood multiplicity: Sofia Coppola's Young Girls trilogy', in Claire Perkins and Constantine Verevis (eds), *Film Trilogies: New Critical Approaches*, Basingstoke: Palgrave Macmillan, pp. 35–55.

Peihani, Maziar (2012), 'The global financial crisis of 2008: an analysis of contributing trends, policies and failures', *Banking & Finance Law Review*, 27:3, pp. 465–93.

Perkins, Claire (2012), *American Smart Cinema*, Edinburgh: Edinburgh University Press.

Pheasant-Kelly, Francis (2013), *Fantasy Film Post 9/11*, New York: Palgrave Macmillan.

Pipher, Mary (1994), *Reviving Ophelia: Saving the Selves of Adolescent Girls*, New York: Penguin Books.

Pitlor, Heidi (2015), '*The Girl on the Train* by Paula Hawkins', *Boston Globe*, 3 January, <https://www.bostonglobe.com/arts/books/2015/01/03/book-review-the-girl-train-paula-hawkins/s1VAJ2tsJ5HAGyxHLGrbUI/story.html> (accessed 16 March 2017).

Pomeranz, Margaret and David Stratton (2015), 'Review of *Marie Antoinette*', *At the Movies with Margaret & David*, 10 October, <www.abc.net.au/atthemovies/txt/s1801757.htm> (accessed 13 August 2017).

Prestigiacomo, Amanda (2015), 'Top ten batsh*t-crazy feminist fails of 2015', *Daily Wire*, 28 December, <www.dailywire.com/news/2164/top-ten-batsht-crazy-feminist-fails-2015-amanda-prestigiacomo> (accessed 27 May 2017).

Primorac, Antonija (2012), 'Corsets, cages and embowered women in contemporary Victoriana on film', *Film, Fashion & Consumption*, 1:1, 39–55.

Projansky, Sarah (2001), *Watching Rape: Film and Television in Postfeminist Culture*, New York: New York University Press.

Projansky, Sarah and Kent A. Ono (1999), 'Strategic whiteness as cinematic racial politics', in Thomas K. Nakayama and Judith N. Martin (eds), *Whiteness: The Communication of Social Identity*, London: SAGE Publications, 149–77.

Quart, Leonard (2006), 'Woody Allen's New York', in Charles L. P. Silet (ed.), *The Films of Woody Allen: Critical Essays*, Oxford: Scarecrow Press, pp. 13–20.

Radden, Jennifer (ed.) (2000), *The Nature of Melancholy: From Aristotle to Kristeva*, Oxford: Oxford University Press.

Radner, Hilary (1993), 'Pretty is as pretty does: free enterprise and the marriage plot', in Jim Collins, Hilary Radner and Ava Preacher Collins (eds), *Film Theory Goes to the Movies*, New York: Routledge, pp. 56–76.

Radner, Hilary (2011), *Neo-Feminist Cinema: Girly Films, Chick Flicks, and Consumer Culture*, New York: Routledge.

Redmond, Sean (2007), 'The whiteness of stars: looking at Kate Winslet's unruly white body', in Sean Redmond and Su Holmes (eds), *Stardom and Celebrity: A Reader*, London: SAGE Publications.

Riesman, David (1950), *The Lonely Crowd: A Study of the Changing American Character*, New Haven: Yale University Press.

Riley, Jenelle (2011), 'Natalie Portman finally "reconciled" with career', *Reuters*, 7 February, <www.reuters.com/article/us-portman-idUSTRE7160U920110207> (accessed 3 September 2014).

Robinson, David J. (2003), *Reel Psychiatry: Movie Portrayals of Psychiatric Conditions*, Port Huron: Rapid Psychler Press.

Rodino-Colocino, Michelle (2014), 'The great he-cession: why feminists should rally for the end of white supremacist capitalist patriarchy', *Feminist Media Studies*, 14:2, 343–7.

Roediger, David (2007), *The Wages of Whiteness: Race and the Making of the American Working Class*, London: Verso.

Rojek, Chris (2007), 'Celebrity and religion', in Sean Redmond and Su Holmes (eds), *Stardom and Celebrity: A Reader*, London: SAGE Publications, pp. 171–81.

Rosaldo, Renato (1989), 'Imperialist nostalgia', *Representations*, 26, 107–22.

Rottenberg, Catherine (2014), 'The rise of neoliberal feminism', *Cultural Studies*, 28:3, 418–37.

Sandberg, Sheryl (2013), *Lean In: Women, Work, and the Will to Lead*, New York: Alfred A. Knopf.

Sandhu, Sukhdev (2011), '*Melancholia*, review', *The Telegraph*, 29 September www.telegraph.co.uk/culture/film/filmreviews/8797335/Melancholia-review.html (accessed 22 February 2016).

Sarotte, Georges-Michel (1995), 'Fluidity and difference in three plays by Tennessee Williams: *The Glass Menagerie, A Streetcar Named Desire* and *Cat on a Hot Tin Roof*', in Marc Maufort (ed.), *Staging Difference: Cultural Pluralism in American Theatre and Drama*, New York: Peter Lang Publishing, pp. 141–57.

Sarris, Andrew [1962] (2009), 'Notes on the auteur theory in 1962', in Leo Braudy and Marshall Cohen (eds), *Film Theory and Criticism* (7th edn), Oxford: Oxford University Press, 451–55.

Schapiro, Barbara (1986), 'Woody Allen's search for self', *Journal of Popular Culture*, 19:4, 47–62.

Schiesari, Juliana (1992), *The Gendering of Melancholia: Feminism, Psychoanalysis, and the Symbolics of Loss in Renaissance Literature*, New York: Cornell University Press.

Schwarzbaum, Lisa (2011), 'Cannes Film Festival: Lars von Trier's stunning *Melancholia* – The end of the world (and a challenge to *The Tree of Life*)', *Entertainment Weekly*, 18 May, <http://ew.com/article/2011/05/18/cannes-film-festival-lars-von-trier-melancholia-terrence-malick/> (accessed 22 February 2016).

Sconce, Jeffrey (2002), 'Irony, nihilism and the new American "smart" film', *Screen*, 43:4, 349–69.

Shaviro, Steven (2011), 'Black swan', *The Pinocchio Theory*, 5 January, <www.shaviro.com/Blog/?p=975> (accessed 14 August 2017).

Sherman, Erik (2016), 'What a Trump administration might mean for income inequality', *Forbes*, 12 November, <https://www.forbes.com/sites/eriksherman/2016/11/12/what-a-trump-administration-might-mean-for-income-inequality/#60423cfd3a78> (accessed 23 February 2017).

Showalter, Elaine (1987), *The Female Malady: Women, Madness and English Culture 1830–1980*, London: Virago.

Singer, Ben (2001), *Melodrama and Modernity*, New York: Columbia University Press.

Sinnerbrink, Robert (2012), '*Stimmung:* exploring the aesthetics of mood', *Screen*, 53:2, 148–63.

Sinnerbrink, Robert (2014), 'Anatomy of *Melancholia*', *Angelaki: Journal of the Theoretical Humanities*, 19:4, 111–26.

Skeggs, Beverley (1997), *Formations of Class and Gender: Becoming Respectable*, London: SAGE Publications.

Skeggs, Beverley (2009), 'The moral economy of person production: the class relations of self performance on "reality" television', *Sociological Review*, 57:4, 626–44.

Smaill, Belinda (2013), 'Sofia Coppola: reading the director', *Feminist Media Studies*, 13:1, 148–62.

Smyth, J. E. (2004), 'The three ages of imperial cinema from the death of Gordon to *The Return of the King*', in Janet Brennan Croft (ed.), *Tolkien on Film: Essays on Peter Jackson's The Lord of the Rings*, Altadena: Mythopoeic Press, pp. 3–25.

Sobchack, Vivian (2004), *Carnal Thoughts: Embodiment and Moving Image Culture*, Berkeley: University of California Press.

Springer, Kimberly (2007), 'Divas, evil black bitches, and bitter black women: African American women in postfeminist and post-Civil-Rights popular culture', in Yvonne Tasker and Diane Negra (eds), *Interrogating Postfeminism: Gender and the Politics of Popular Culture*, Durham: Duke University Press, pp. 249–77.

Staiger, Janet (2003), 'Authorship approaches', in David A. Gerstner and Janet Staiger (eds), *Authorship and Film*, New York: Routledge, pp. 27–61.

Steinberg, Brian (2016), 'Charlotte Rampling says "racist" Oscars remark was misinterpreted', *Variety*, 22 January, <http://variety.com/2016/film/news/charlotte-rampling-oscars-racist-1201686690/> (accessed 22 February 2017).

Stillman, Sarah (2007), '"The missing white girl syndrome": disappeared women and media activism', *Gender & Development*, 15:3, 491–502.

Sullivan, Shannon (2006), *Revealing Whiteness: The Unconscious Habits of Racial Privilege*, Bloomington: Indiana University Press.

Tasker, Yvonne (2010), 'Vision and visibility: women filmmakers, contemporary authorship and feminist film studies', in Vicki Callahan (ed.), *Reclaiming the Archive: Feminism and Film History*, Detroit: Wayne State University Press, pp. 213–31.

Tasker, Yvonne and Diane Negra (eds) (2007), *Interrogating Postfeminism: Gender and the Politics of Popular Culture*, Durham: Duke University Press.

Taylor, Anthea (2011), *Single Women in Popular Culture: The Limits of Postfeminism*, New York: Palgrave Macmillan.

Turner, Graeme (2004), *Understanding Celebrity*, London: SAGE Publications.

Tyler, Imogen (2013), *Revolting Subjects: Social Abjection and Resistance in Neoliberal Britain*, London: Zed Books.

Urry, John and Jonas Larsen (2011), *The Tourist Gaze 3.0*, London: SAGE Publications.

Vermeulen, Timotheus (2014), *Scenes from the Suburbs: Suburban Space in US Film and Television*, Edinburgh: Edinburgh University Press.

Walker, Amy (2015), 'Interrogating the relationship of postfeminism and neoliberalism in *Orange is the New Black*', unpublished MA dissertation, University of Huddersfield.

Warner, Marina (1985), *Monuments and Maidens: The Allegory of the Female Form*, Berkeley: University of California Press.

Wearing, Sadie (2007), 'Subjects of rejuvenation: aging in postfeminist culture', in Yvonne Tasker and Diane Negra (eds), *Interrogating Postfeminism: Gender and the Politics of Popular Culture*, Durham: Duke University Press, pp. 277–311.

Weaver, Hilary (2017), 'Meryl Streep's powerful anti-Trump Golden Globes speech: read the whole thing here', *Vanity Fair*, 8 January, https://www.vanityfair.com/hollywood/2017/01/meryl-streep-donald-trump-golden-globes-speech (accessed 23 February 2017).

Weber, Max [1946] (2006), 'The sociology of charismatic authority', in P. David Marshall (ed.), *The Celebrity Culture Reader*, London: Routledge, pp. 55–60.

Wedding, Danny and Ryan M. Niemiec (2014), *Movies and Mental Illness: Using Films to Understand Psychopathology*, Boston: Hogrefe Publishing.

Weidhase, Nathalie (2015), '"Beyoncé Feminism" and the contestation of the black female body', *Celebrity Studies*, 6:1, 128–31.

Wheatley, Catherine (2006), 'The masochistic fantasy made flesh: Michael Haneke's *La Pianiste* as melodrama', *Studies in French Cinema*, 6:2, 117–27.

Whitney, Sarah E. (2016), *Splattered Ink: Postfeminist Gothic Fiction and Gendered Violence*, Urbana: University of Illinois Press.

Williams, Linda (1991), 'Film bodies: gender, genre and excess', *Film Quarterly*, 44:4, 2–13.

Wilson, Julie A. (2018), *Neoliberalism*, New York: Routledge.

Winters, Joseph R. (2016), *Hope Draped in Black: Race, Melancholy, and the Agony of Progress*, Durham: Duke University Press.

Woodworth, Amy (2008), 'A feminist theorisation of Sofia Coppola's postfeminist trilogy', in Marcelline Block (ed.), *Situating the Feminist Gaze and Spectatorship in Postwar Cinema*, Newcastle: Cambridge Scholars Publishing, pp. 138–68.

Woolf, Virginia (1929), *A Room of One's Own*, New York: Harcourt.

Wyatt, Jean (2005), 'Jouissance and desire in Michael Haneke's *The Piano Teacher*', *American Imago*, 62:4, 453–82.

Yancy, George (2012), *Look, A White!* Philadelphia: Temple University Press.

Young, Iris Marion (2005), *On Female Body Experience: 'Throwing Like a Girl' and Other Essays*, Oxford: Oxford University Press.

Yunuen Lewis, Caitlin (2011), 'Cool postfeminism: the stardom of Sofia Coppola', in Su Holmes and Diane Negra (eds), *In the Limelight and Under the Microscope: Forms and Functions of Female Celebrity*, New York: Continuum, pp. 174–99.

Filmography

2 Broke Girls, TV, CBS: 2011–17
13 Going on 30, film, directed by Gary Winick. USA: Columbia Pictures, 2004
The Age of Innocence, film, directed by Martin Scorsese. USA: Columbia Pictures, 1993
Alice in Wonderland, film, directed by Tim Burton. USA: Walt Disney Studios Motion Pictures, 2010
Alice through the Looking Glass, film, directed by James Bobin. USA: Walt Disney Studios Motion Pictures, 2016
All about Eve, film, directed by Joseph L. Mankiewicz. USA: 20th Century Fox, 1950
Ally McBeal, TV, Fox: 1997–2002
American Beauty, film, directed by Sam Mendes. USA: DreamWorks Pictures, 1999
American Hustle, film, directed by David O. Russell. USA: Columbia Pictures, 2013
Annie Hall, film, directed by Woody Allen. USA: United Artists, 1977
Antichrist, film, directed by Lars von Trier. Denmark/France/Germany/Italy/Poland/Sweden: Nordisk Film Distribution, 2009
A Streetcar Named Desire, film, directed by Elia Kazan. USA: Warner Bros, 1951
August: Osage County, film, directed by John Wells. USA: The Weinstein Company, 2013
Bad Moms, film, directed by Jon Lucas and Scott Moore. USA: STX Entertainment, 2016
Batman, film, directed by Tim Burton. USA: Warner Bros, 1989
Batman Returns, film, directed by Tim Burton. USA: Warner Bros, 1992
The Bells of St Mary's, film, directed by Leo McCarey. USA: RKO Radio Pictures, 1945
Bend it Like Beckham, film, directed by Gurinder Chadha. United Kingdom/Germany: Red Bus Film Distribution, 2002
The Best Exotic Marigold Hotel, film, directed by John Madden. United Kingdom: Fox Searchlight Pictures, 2011
Big Little Lies, TV, HBO: 2017
Birdman, film, directed by Alejandro G. Iñárritu. United States: Fox Searchlight Pictures, 2014
Black Swan, film, directed by Darren Aronofsky. United States: Fox Searchlight Pictures, 2010
The Bling Ring, film, directed by Sofia Coppola. United States/United Kingdom/Germany/France/Japan: A24, 2013
Blue Jasmine, film, directed by Woody Allen. United States: Sony Pictures Classics, 2013
Boyhood, film, directed by Richard Linklater. USA: IFC Films/Universal Pictures, 2014

The Brave, film, directed by Johnny Depp. United States: Majestic Films International, 1997
Breakfast at Tiffany's, film, directed by Blake Edwards. United States: Paramount Pictures, 1961
Bridget Jones's Diary, film, directed by Sharon Maguire. United Kingdom/United States/France: Miramax Films/Universal Pictures, 2001
Brokeback Mountain, film, directed by Ang Lee. United States: Focus Features, 2005
Bye Bye Birdie, film, directed by George Sidney. United States: Columbia Pictures, 1963
Carol, film, directed by Todd Haynes. United Kingdom/United States: Studio Canal/The Weinstein Company, 2015
Carrie, film, directed by Brian de Palma. United States: United Artists, 1976
The Carrie Diaries, TV, The CW: 2013–14
Certified Copy, film, directed by Abbas Kiarostami. France/Iran: MK2 Diffusion, 2010
Charlie and the Chocolate Factory, film, directed by Tim Burton. United States/United Kingdom: Warner Bros, 2005
The Cider House Rules, film, directed by Lasse Hallström. United States: Miramax Films, 1999
Cinderella, film, directed by Kenneth Branagh. United States: Walt Disney Studios Motion Pictures, 2015
Closer, film, directed by Mike Nichols. United States: Columbia Pictures, 2004
The Company Men, film, directed by John Wells. United States: The Weinstein Company, 2010
Deceived, film, directed by Damian Harris. United States: Buena Vista Pictures, 1991
Drag Me to Hell, film, directed by Sam Raimi. United States: Universal Pictures, 2009
Dynasty, TV, ABC: 1981–9
Eat Pray Love, film, directed by Ryan Murphy. United States: Columbia Pictures, 2010
Edward Scissorhands, film, directed by Tim Burton. United States: 20th Century Fox, 1990
Ed Wood, film, directed by Tim Burton. USA: Buena Vista Pictures, 1994
Fences, film, directed by Denzel Washington. United States: Paramount Pictures, 2016
Flashdance, film, directed by Adrian Lyne. United States: Paramount Pictures, 1983
Funny Games, film, directed by Michael Haneke. Austria: Concorde-Castle/Rock/Turner, 1997
Game of Thrones, TV, HBO: 2011–
Garden State, film, directed by Zach Braff. United States: Fox Searchlight Pictures/Miramax Films, 2004
The Girl on the Train, film, directed by Tate Taylor. United States: Universal Pictures, 2016
Girls, TV, HBO: 2012–
Gone Girl, film, directed by David Fincher. United States: 20th Century Fox, 2014
The Great Escape, film, directed by John Sturges. USA: United Artists, 1963
Harry Potter and the Philosopher's Stone, film, directed by Chris Columbus. United Kingdom/United States: Warner Bros, 2001
Hidden Figures, film, directed by Theodore Melfi. United States: 20th Century Fox, 2016
The Holiday, film, directed by Nancy Meyers. United States: Columbia Pictures/Universal Pictures, 2006
Holy Smoke! film, directed by Jane Campion. Australia: Miramax Films, 1999
The Hours, film, directed by Stephen Daldry. United Kingdom/United States: Paramount Pictures/Miramax Films, 2002
Househusbands of Hollywood, TV, Fox Reality Channel: 2009
Jane the Virgin, TV, The CW: 2014–
La Dolce Vita, film, directed by Federico Fellini. Italy/France: Cineriz/Pathé Consortium Cinéma, 1960

La La Land, film, directed by Damien Chazelle. United States: Summit Entertainment, 2016

The Last Temptation of Christ, film, directed by Martin Scorsese. United States: Universal Pictures/Cineplex Odeon Films, 1988

The Legend of Bagger Vance, film, directed by Robert Redford. United States: DreamWorks Pictures/20th Century Fox, 2000

Léon: The Professional, film, directed by Luc Besson. France: Gaumont/Buena Vista International, 1994

Letters to Juliet, film, directed by Gary Winick. United States/Italy: Summit Entertainment, 2010

Little Britain, TV, BBC: 2003–7

Little Children, film, directed by Todd Field. United States: New Line Cinema, 2006

Little Women, film, directed by Gillian Armstrong. United States: Columbia Pictures, 1994

The Lone Ranger, film, directed by Gore Verbinski. United States: Walt Disney Studios Motion Pictures, 2013

The Lord of the Rings: The Fellowship of the Ring, film, directed by Peter Jackson. New Zealand/United States: New Line Cinema, 2001

The Lord of the Rings: The Two Towers, film, directed by Peter Jackson. New Zealand/United States: New Line Cinema, 2002

The Lord of the Rings: The Return of the King, film, directed by Peter Jackson. New Zealand/United States: 2003

Lost in Translation, film, directed by Sofia Coppola. United States: Focus Features, 2003

Loving, film, directed by Jeff Nichols. United Kingdom/United States: Focus Features/Insiders, 2016

Maid in Manhattan, film, directed by Wayne Wang. United States: Columbia Pictures, 2002

Marie Antoinette, film, directed by Sofia Coppola. United States/France/Japan: Columbia Pictures, 2006

Marnie, film, directed by Alfred Hitchcock. United States: Universal Pictures, 1964

Melancholia, film, directed by Lars von Trier. Denmark/Sweden/France/Germany: Nordisk Film/Les films du losange/Concorde Filmverleih, 2011

The Middle, TV, ABC: 2009–

The Mindy Project, TV, Fox/Hulu: 2012–

Monster, film, directed by Patty Jenkins. United States/Germany: Newmarket Films, 2003

Monster's Ball, film, directed by Marc Forster. United States: Lions Gate Films, 2001

Moonlight, film, directed by Barry Jenkins. United States: A24, 2016

Mr and Mrs Smith, film, directed by Doug Liman. United States: 20th Century Fox, 2005

Mulholland Drive, film, directed by David Lynch. United States: Universal Pictures, 2001

Mustang, film, directed by Deniz Gamze Ergüven. France/Turkey/Germany: Ad Vitam, 2015

Must Love Dogs, film, directed by Gary David Goldberg. United States: Warner Bros, 2005

The Nanny Diaries, film, directed by Shari Springer Berman and Robert Pulcini. United States: The Weinstein Company/Metro-Goldwyn-Mayer/FilmColony, 2007

Nights in Rodanthe, film, directed by George C. Wolfe. United States: Warner Bros, 2008

The Normal Heart, TV, HBO, 2014

Now, Voyager, film, directed by Irving Rapper. United States: Warner Bros, 1942

Orange is the New Black, TV, Netflix: 2013–

The Piano, film, directed by Jane Campion. New Zealand/Australia/France: Bac Films/Miramax Films/ Entertainment Film Distributors, 1993

The Piano Teacher, film, directed by Michael Haneke. France/Germany/Austria: MK2 Diffusion/Concorde Filmverleih/Kino International, 2001

Picnic at Hanging Rock, film, directed by Peter Weir. Australia: British Empire Films/GTO Films/Atlantic Releasing/Janus Films, 1975
The Pirate, film, directed by Vincente Minnelli. United States: Metro-Goldwyn-Mayer, 1948
Pirates of the Caribbean: Curse of the Black Pearl, film, directed by Gore Verbinski. United States: Buena Vista Pictures, 2003
Pirates of the Caribbean: Dead Man's Chest, film, directed by Gore Verbinski. United States: Buena Vista Pictures, 2006
Pirates of the Caribbean: At World's End, film, directed by Gore Verbinski. United States: Buena Vista Pictures, 2007
Pirates of the Caribbean: On Stranger Tides, film, directed by Rob Marshall. United States: Walt Disney Studios Motion Pictures, 2011
Pirates of the Caribbean: Dead Men Tell No Tales, film, directed by Joachim Rønning and Espen Sandberg. United States: Walt Disney Studios Motion Pictures, 2017
Pleasantville, film, directed by Gary Ross. United States: New Line Cinema, 1998
Portrait of a Lady, film, directed by Jane Campion. United Kingdom/United States: Gramercy Pictures, 1996
Pretty Woman, film, directed by Garry Marshall. United States: Buena Vista Pictures, 1990
Pride and Prejudice, film, directed by Joe Wright. France/United Kingdom/United States: Focus Features, 2005
The Princess Diaries, film, directed by Garry Marshall. United States: Buena Vista Pictures, 2001
The Proposal, film, directed by Anne Fletcher. United States: Walt Disney Studios Motion Pictures, 2009
The Real Housewives of Orange County, TV, Bravo: 2006–
The Red Shoes, film, directed by Michael Powell and Emeric Pressburger. United Kingdom: General Film Distributors/Eagle-Lion Films/J. Arthur Rank Film Distributors, 1948
Save the Last Dance, film, directed by Thomas Carter. United States: Paramount Pictures, 2001
Sense and Sensibility, film, directed by Ang Lee. United Kingdom/United States: Columbia Pictures, 1995
Sex and the City, TV, HBO: 1998–2004
Sherlock, 'The Abominable Bride', TV, BBC One: 2016
The Sisterhood of the Traveling Pants, film, directed by Ken Kwapis. United States: Warner Bros, 2005
Sleeping with the Enemy, film, directed by Joseph Ruben. United States: 20th Century Fox, 1991
Somewhere, film, directed by Sofia Coppola. United States: Focus Features, 2010
Splash, film, directed by Ron Howard. United States: Buena Vista Distribution, 1984
Splendour in the Grass, film, directed by Elia Kazan. United States: Warner Bros, 1961
Strangerland, film, directed by Kim Farrant. Australia/Ireland: Alchemy, 2015.
Suffragette, film, directed by Sarah Gavron. United Kingdom: Pathé, 2015
Star Wars Episode I: The Phantom Menace, film, directed by George Lucas. United States: 20th Century Fox, 1999
Star Wars Episode II: Attack of the Clones, film, directed by George Lucas. United States: 20th Century Fox, 2002
Star Wars Episode III: Revenge of the Sith, film, directed by George Lucas. United States: 20th Century Fox, 2005
Stella Dallas, film, directed by King Vidor, United States: United Artists, 1937
Sunset Boulevard, film, directed by Billy Wilder. United States: Paramount Pictures, 1950

A Tale of Love and Darkness, film, directed by Natalie Portman. Israel: Focus World, 2015
Ted, film, directed by Seth MacFarlane. United States: Universal Pictures, 2012
Thelma & Louise, film, directed by Ridley Scott. United States: Metro-Goldwyn-Mayer, 1991
Titanic, film, directed by James Cameron. United States: Paramount Pictures/20th Century Fox, 1997
Twin Peaks, TV, ABC: 1990–1
Under the Tuscan Sun, film, directed by Audrey Wells. United States/Italy: Buena Vista Pictures, 2003
Up in the Air, film, directed by Jason Reitman. United States: Paramount Pictures, 2009
The Vampire Diaries, TV, The CW: 2009–17
The Virgin Suicides, film, directed by Sofia Coppola. United States: Paramount Classics, 1999
Weeds, TV, Showtime: 2005–12
Wendy and Lucy, film, directed by Kelly Reichardt. United States: Oscilloscope Pictures, 2008
What Ever Happened to Baby Jane?, film, directed by Robert Aldrich. United States: Warner Bros, 1962
What Lies Beneath, film, directed by Robert Zemeckis. United States: DreamWorks Pictures/20th Century Fox, 2000
When in Rome, film, directed by Mark Steven Johnson. United States: Walt Disney Studios Motion Pictures, 2010
Where the Heart Is, film, directed by Matt Williams. United States: 20th Century Fox, 2000
The White Ribbon, film, directed by Michael Haneke. Germany/Austria/France/Italy: Filmladen/X Verleih AG, 2009
Winter's Bone, film, directed by Debra Granik. United States: Roadside Attractions, 2010
The Wizard of Oz, film, directed by Victor Fleming. United States: Metro-Goldwyn-Mayer, 1939
The Wrestler, film, directed by Darren Aronofsky. United States: Fox Searchlight Pictures, 2008

Index

CPSIA information can be obtained
at www.ICGtesting.com
Printed in the USA
BVHW061555300620
582685BV00003B/27

9 781474 430302